The Borderline Personality in Analysis

Edited by Nathan Schwartz-Salant and Murray Stein

Chiron Publications ● Wilmette, Illinois

The Chiron Clinical Series

ISBN 0–933029–13–6

Printed in the United States of America

Book design by Elaine M. Hill

Library of Congress Cataloging-in-Publication Data

The Borderline personality in analysis.

(The Chiron clinical series)
Contents: Before the creation: the unconscious couple in borderline states of mind / Nathan Schwartz-Salant—Primary ambivalence toward the self, its nature and treatment / John Beebe—Subject-object differentiation in the analysis of borderline cases / Susanne Kacirek—[etc.]
1. Borderline personality disorder. 2. Psychoanalysis. 3. Psychotherapy. I. Schwartz-Salant, Nathan, 1938– . II. Stein, Murray, 1943– . III. Series.
RC569.5.B67B69 1988   616.89   88-25616
ISBN 0-933029-13-6

Contents

The Chiron Clinical Series
Policy on capitalizing the term "Self"

Jung's understanding of the Self is significantly different from how
this term is often used in other contemporary psychoanalytic literature. The
difference hinges primarily on the understanding of archetypes: The
Jungian conceptualization of the Self sees it as rooted in the transpersonal
dimension. Hence the frequent capitalization of this term. Since the
clinical concern with the Self often relates more narrowly to the sphere of
ego-consciousness, however, it can be more mystifying than edifying
always to allude to the archetypal level in the literature. Consequently the
editors of *Chiron* have chosen to allow authors to exercise an option on
the question of capitalization. They may choose to capitalize Self and
thereby to emphasize its transpersonal, archetypal base; or, they may
choose to employ the lower case, signifying by this that they are discussing
issues that have to do principally with ego-identity and the personal
relation to this central factor of psychic life, which may be less precisely
articulated by reference to the archetypal substratum.

Before the Creation: The Unconscious Couple in Borderline States of Mind*

Nathan Schwartz-Salant

The field of battle is the hearts of people.
Dostoyevski, The Brothers Karamazov

Introduction

In this paper I explore the unconscious dyad that structures the transference-countertransference field in relation to borderline states of mind. Although my experiences with borderline patients are understandable in terms of transference or countertransference projections that repeat early continual traumas (Kahn 1974) and developmental failures, this perspective nevertheless falters. I find that I must also think of my experiences in terms of field dynamics which engage *a*temporal forms, processes my patient and I are part of yet which are larger than us, something more than what we instill in them through

---

* This paper is extracted from Chapter Six of a larger work, *The Borderline Personality: Vision and Healing* (1988b).

Nathan Schwartz-Salant, Ph.D., is a Jungian analyst, trained in Zurich, Switzerland, and in private practice in New York City. He is the author of *Narcissism and Character Transformation, The Borderline Personality: Vision and Healing*, numerous clinical papers, and is co-editor of the Chiron Clinical Series. He is the director of the Foundation for Research in Jungian Psychology.

our projections.[1] For in some mysterious way our interaction constellates, creates, or discovers—no one word will do—some "third thing." Jung's description of the alchemical god Mercurius seems apt:

> The elusive, deceptive, ever-changing content that possesses the patient like a demon now flits about from patient to doctor and, as the third party in the alliance, continues its game . . . (1946, par. 384)

We can say that the archetypal transference is constellated by the reactivation of early introjects in the transference and countertransference, and that this new material projects outward to yield the wondrous imagery of hermaphrodites and combined or double-sided objects that Jung's alchemical research illuminated. But are we simply dealing with a replay of earliest infant-mother interactions when "archetypal" and "personal" designations were of little value (Eigen 1985; 1986, pp. 59ff.), or are there processes and energy fields not reducible to infant or even prenatal life? This is a crucial theoretical crossroad, for therapists who believe that experiences in psychotherapy may replicate early failed or aborted developmental experiences would do well to consider whether this theoretical pursuit alone is adequate to the nature of the psyche and its archetypal or objective dimension. Object relations theory is rooted in an analytical model that reveals introjects, often bewildering and bizarre, of early experience identified (by the therapist) through reflection upon fusion states and projective identification. But this approach is too limiting. To meet the borderline personality effectively requires an imaginal focus precisely upon those areas of experience that are not conveyed by spatial metaphors akin to projection and fusion, with their focus on inside and outside. Indeed, the therapist must begin to think differently—that is, to focus imaginally upon interactive fields.

These fields can be grasped only as a "third presence," often an unconscious dyad, and not as projections that must be integrated. It is not that the object relations model is unimportant; its value is unquestionable. But while necessary it is not sufficient. Both models are required: the projection model concerned with early developmental issues *and* the imaginal model that incorporates the alchemical imagery of the *coniunctio* and its attendant stages.[2] We would do best to adopt a model that is two-sided, one face pointing toward a space-time world and the other toward a unitary world structured by a multiplicity of archetypal processes. The two faces are interwoven: they cannot and should not be split into the separate and opposing categories of personal and archetypal. The unconscious dyad may be seen to stem from both patient and therapist *while also being* part of a larger, interactive field. Once sufficiently *seen* and experienced, the unconscious couple can eventually lead to an experience of union, which is precisely what the borderline person lacks.

In this paper I shall refer to Jung's research into alchemical symbolism, applying his work particularly to borderline states of mind. In previous papers (1986, 1988a) I have developed the thesis that the imagery from the *Rosarium Philosophorum*, the most famous of alchemical texts and the centerpiece of Jung's "Psychology of the Transference" (1946), represents various forms of the interactive field between patient and therapist. In treatment of the borderline personality, the images designated the *coniunctio*, *nigredo*, and *impregnatio* (or The Extraction of the Soul), are at the core of the interactive field. The *coniunctio* designates a field whose main characteristic is the harmony and transcendence of the opposites of fusion and soulless distance (opposites which characterize much of the borderline person's experience); the *nigredo* represents the death of this field quality; and the *impregnatio* its further dissolution into a field characterized by the absence of linking between patient and therapist, a state that essentially excludes the possibility of empathy (see Schwartz-Salant, 1988a). The remarkable series of images in the *Rosarium* allows us to place the *nigredo* and *impregnatio* within a larger, goal-oriented context. In this manner we may think of the alchemist's goal, the *lapis*, as an interactive field of union stable even amidst the persecutory anxieties of abandonment.

Discovering the Borderline Patient's Unconscious Dyad: Projections and Field Dynamics

"Ed" was an exceptionally intelligent and multitalented 38-year-old man. He entered treatment for several manifest reasons: in a career where his intellectual and creative gifts were only marginally employed, he was generally plagued by a lack of purpose and commitment to any goal. Others were getting along in life, and he was not. A major theme in his life was intense concern about moral behavior. He was obsessed by the actions (past and present) of others toward him, actions he often found immoral, as well as by his own behavior, of which he was a keen critic. He could spend hours alone engrossed in questions about why someone treated him as they did, or why he had been emotionally paralyzed, unable to be forthright, during some interaction with another person whose malevolence was now quite evident to him.

At the outset of our work Ed seemed to be suffering from a narcissistic character disorder. An idealized transference mixed in with the
controlling dynamics of his grandiose-exhibitionistic self was present, so that I felt compelled to have answers to his questions. My
responses were usually well received, but I had an uncomfortable sense
that he was trying very hard to be open to me and was being polite.
Rather than unraveling into idealized and grandiose-exhibitionistic
strands in the transference, his narcissistic character formation soon
revealed itself as a defense against some far deeper and more chaotic
part of his personality.

The following reflections on my work with Ed indicate a complex
interactive field (which to one degree or another is always present in
the treatment of the borderline patient), one that was exceptionally
difficult to apprehend. In fact, the compulsion to act out a pattern of
unrelatedness—by talking without much reflection—at times nearly
nullified my observing ego, and his as well. In these periods the entire
interaction between us and all my attempts to bring coherence or
consciousness to the session achieved only role reversals and often
pain. I felt my own pressure to "get it right," and often I could not keep
quiet. Instead, I attempted interpretations which scant reflection would
have shown me were shallow. At these times I was not disposed to
self-reflection, however, and proceeded with my commentary, all the
while feeling dull-witted and hoping that what I had to say would be
received and accepted. Since the patient was intent upon being truthful,
even at the cost of consensus, this never happened. He had suffered too
many years of being tortured by frustrated and unrealized mental and
creative gifts as well as earlier failed analytical experiences to allow this
one to fail as well.

Often I felt that Ed was the truth-seeker, whereas I was the liar, just
barely hanging on to survive. Survive what? That is not easy to describe,
but I can say that soon after our work began and the strength of his
narcissistic transferences diminished, our unconscious psyches meshed
in such a way that a searing and tormenting energy field was established that all but knocked out my capacities to think and reflect. Each
time he arrived, after a brief period of optimism that some good connection and work might follow, I felt emotionally and physically limp,
and it became for me the most difficult act simply to stay embodied and
be with him. Instead, I usually felt obliged to talk, and thus to *act* rather
than *be*. Often I could not tolerate the absence of meaningful contact
between us, and not infrequently I felt frightened of this man; at times I
even felt that he might strike me. But my usual affliction was to believe

that he was wedded to the truth while I was a fraud. This stance was not much challenged by Ed's own torment about being the subject of his own lies, especially the denial and distrust of his own perceptions.

For more than a year our sessions were comprised of only sparse relatedness, together with multiple desperate attempts to create a sense of connection. During this period I think my work with Ed could best be characterized as that of survival, demonstrating that I could maintain myself amidst his attacks. Every word I used, each tone of expression I chose, came under scrutiny. Yet during this process, Ed also began to show a growing alliance with me. One day he spoke of some reading he was doing and, to my surprise, asked about the nature of our unconscious couple. I believe this represented a crucial shift in his psyche toward more cooperation in the therapy; in ensuing sessions I was able to reflect imaginatively upon what might be structuring our interactive field and come up with something that made sense to both of us: that a couple desirous of non-union was our major obstacle. This state of non-union (the *Rosarium impregnatio*, or "The Extraction of the Soul") is described by Jung as a loss of the soul, similar in impact to a schizophrenic dissociation (1946, par. 476). Our *soul-less* interaction manifested in ways that catapulted us into totally different universes, or so it felt. At such times I believed that we were relating well to one another, yet we were not communicating at all. This would dawn on me as my interpretations became strained, and upon reflection it became clear that at the outset of some such venture at understanding I had not been connected to him and had been speaking to avoid the pain of emptiness, despair, and a sense of impotence. So profound was the level of dissociative intention, in fact, that we might as well each have been talking to different people.

The *Rosarium*, commenting upon *impregnatio*, offers the following recipe to heal this state: "Take the brain . . . and grind it in most sharp vinegar, or in children's urine until it is obscured, and this being begun again as I have written it, may again be mortified as before. . . . He therefore that maketh the earth black shall come to his purpose and it shall go well with him" (McLean 1980, p. 45). Notably, the *Rosarium* also adds that in searching out this black earth "many men have perished" (ibid).

"Grinding the brain in sharp vinegar" is by no means a poor metaphor for the way I functioned with Ed, and he with me. Many of his nights were spent trying to recover from sessions that knocked out his ability to think and left him totally confused and enraged. The *Rosarium* implies that there is a purpose to the tormented states of mind that afflicted both of us. This purpose is suggested by the creation of the lapis in the form of the hermaphrodite (see picture ten, "The Rebis," discussed in Schwartz-Salant 1988a), a combined male-female object that represents the creation of a fertile and stable interactive field. But this illustration also warns of a great danger—perhaps the death of the therapy, and perhaps the activation of the patient's tendencies towards self-destruction, a possibility that always inheres with the borderline patient when these levels are engaged. While there was some ground for faith that the states to which we were subject had some purpose, it was equally clear that our *nigredo* would not become fruitful in any endeavor dominated by acting out and unconsciousness.

Over the course of many trying sessions that took place within a period of approximately two years, the nature of the problem began to emerge. Our interaction was structured by an unconscious couple whose intense, antagonistic desire was for non-union each out to do in the other through lies and malicious envy. At the same time the two images that comprised this couple were stubbornly and inextricably bound to each other. Thus our interaction was dominated by the characteristic borderline quality of simultaneous drives toward fusion and separation, which together produced great confusion.

As a very young child Ed's experience of his parents resembled the dynamics of this dyad. He recalled feeling persecuted by false implications that they actually *saw* him and had his best interests at heart. Over and over again he was perplexed by their antagonistic behavior toward one another and by the destructive fraudulence and deception they practiced on him. Apparently they functioned as a double-sided object, each half contributing to the persecuting dyad. The young, extremely intelligent, and sensitive child earnestly spoke to them about their behavior, and was repeatedly unhinged by the accumulating awareness of having had no effect at all, except as it boomeranged as his father's rage or his mother's martyrdom.

For his survival, this unconscious dyad had been split off from his otherwise normally functioning personality. Consequently, he developed the typical borderline split between normal-neurotic and psychotic personality—a split that was also a fusion state. James Grotstein writes:

> In approaching a psychoanalytic conception of the borderline I should like to offer the following understanding: What seems to give the borderline personality (and borderline state) its uniqueness in differentiating itself from psychoses on the one hand and neuroses on the other is not so much its midplace on the spectrum but is instead a qualitative difference.

This qualitative difference is characterized, in my opinion, by the presence
of a psychotic personality organization *and* a normal or neurotic personality organization which have undergone a unique interpenetration with
each other so that a new amalgam emerges which can well be stated as
"psychotically neurotic" or "neurotically psychotic." It is as if a collusive
symbiosis exists between these two twin personalities which allows for an
unusual tenacity, stability, and cohesion compared to psychotic states
generally. (1979, p. 150)

When Ed's defensive, idealized transference waned, the psychotic part,
largely conveyed by the unconscious dyad, entered the analytical process and nearly usurped it. This led to what could be called a transference and countertransference psychosis, its intensity more extreme
than I would have liked. Yet unless an analysis contains a transference
psychosis—and to a lesser degree, hopefully, a countertransference
psychosis as well—there is little chance of healing the borderline person. By countertransference psychosis I do not necessarily mean a therapist's decompensation or blatant loss of reality, but rather the emergence of parts of his or her personality that are unintegrated, outside
the organizing power of the self. These "mad parts" can take over the
therapy in subtle ways, and the patient may introject them, acting in
turn quite mad, even to the point of becoming endangered in outer life
situations. I have witnessed how a therapist's "runaway behavior" (for
example, by seductively sharing personal material with a borderline patient) led to dreams in which the patient was in a vehicle being driven
by a madman and then nearly got fired from a job for inappropriate behavior. This sequence was the result of the therapist's denial of his
psychotic aspect—unintegrated and compulsive qualities of his personality—which he was sharing in the hope of creating a "holding
environment."

Material taken from sessions that took place two years after our
work began convey the extent to which we were dominated by the
unconscious dyad. At this time Ed dreamed that he was gently embracing two women, one black, the other white. I understood this to be the
image of a combining state, which I, too, could now carry in projection
because there had been sufficient reparation on my part for previous
analytical errors (such as talking too much and acting rather than being
embodied). I thought he found me more reliable and was no longer
obliged to split me up into good and bad parts to be watched over both
consciously and unconsciously.

This dream was soon followed by one in which he and another
man associated with me were flying in a plane very close to the ground

to get a good look at the earth below. At first the other man was guiding the vehicle, but then he taught Ed to guide it himself. This seemed to make it clear that the analysis was now based on mutual cooperation. Indicative of the potential of our interactive field is the emergent image of a fruitful coital couple. In the dream the plane is a container hovering near the earth; it has both spirit and the capacity for a growing therapeutic alliance. Such understanding had been sorely lacking during the prior two years; Ed had suffered as a consequence and had taken great pains to make me understand that *I* was *the* cause of his great distress.

Soon after this dream I was surprised to find him once again in a state of extreme agitation and doubt about me as a therapist and about the analysis itself. Yet this should have been no cause for surprise. My desire to see our process on the right track, free of Ed's searing criticisms, "drove him crazy." I had to ask myself why I would drive him crazy, whether I wanted to do such a thing to him. To use his phrase, which I found unpleasantly apt, "Why was I (again) operating in *bad faith*?" But, before I could arrive at an answer, a row occurred that left both of us doubting the possibility of continuing analysis.

Let me be more specific about the session in question. Ed arrived punctually, and even before sitting down asked me something about a previous remark. Though it had not been expressed in anger, I experienced his question as an attack, becoming instantly very defensive. My response was far stronger than usual, and I lost sight of my own defensiveness as I felt my body literally fill with an agitation that was disintegrating in its affect. My insides were under a global attack. I was anxious, shaking inwardly, and at the same time trying to act as if everything was okay. In effect, I was denying the state of non-union both between us and within myself. Clearly, I was behaving in a borderline fashion. I had previously experienced this with him, though not so intensely, and always as a reaction to a specific issue whose seriousness and prominence had gradually increased during the course of therapy: the accusation of operating in bad faith.

I shall sketch out this theme since the session I am describing cannot be understood without a clear understanding of its evolution. In this particular instance the illusion that a viable and helpful connection existed between Ed and myself was a part of the underlying dynamic, the fact that in significant ways I did not want emotional contact with him. That is, awareness of my desire to *not have* any form of union with Ed was slow in coming; in retrospect I am both chagrined and astonished at the ingenuity of the tactics I employed to avoid this discovery.

Certainly, a subjective countertransference was present, but I believe that much more was at stake—namely a field-quality, inherent in the process that engaged us, of which non-union was the main ingredient.

One unconscious strategy for avoiding real contact with Ed was to stay filled with a surfeit of anxiety and fear (the malignant energy field evoked by our mutual presence) and thereby allow him to take the lead in understanding any material the therapeutic process engaged. At my worst I presented Ed with an extremely toxic double-bind by denying the madness between us and electing to see in him (and by implication myself) those qualities carried by the strength and adeptness of the normal-neurotic self. In fact, I lagged behind, dulled and unable to think clearly. Worse yet, I was in an imaginative and creative void, a leaden state combining heavy Saturnian authority and the compulsion to "know." In contrast, Ed seemed bright, sharp, and intelligent. As if his possession of these qualities meant that they were unavailable to others—more specifically, me—I surrendered to the sense of having lost all acuity, all creative energy. And while I would have capably employed these countertransferential reactions syntonically in another case to unearth the facts of the "other side" and its excess of chaos, its root of despair and helplessness, here I did not. Nor could I recognize that Ed needed me to think *with* him, even if not *for* him. While it was unconscious at the time, I later came to realize that there was a *choice* involved in this profound countertransference whose course Leon Grinberg has described as follows:

> From a structural point of view, one may say that what is projected by means of the psychotic mechanism of projective identification operates within the object as a parasitic superego, which omnipotently induces the analyst's ego to act or feel what the patient in his fantasy wants him to feel or act. I think that this, to some degree, bears comparison with the dynamics of hypnosis as described by Freud. According to Freud, the hypnotizer places himself in the position of the ego ideal, and hypnotic submissiveness is of a masochistic nature. Freud further holds that in the hypnotic relation a sort of paralysis appears as a result of the influence of the omnipotent individual upon an impotent and helpless being. I believe the same applies to the processes I am discussing in that the analyst, being unaware of what happened, may later rationalize his action, as the hypnotized person does after executing the hypnotic command. By means of the mechanisms of obsessive control, the inducing subject continues to control what he projected onto the induced object. The subject's omnipotent fantasies thus acquire some consistency, as they seem confirmed by the object's response. (1977, p. 128–129)

In time, I began to shake free of the hypnotic hold on me and recognize the state of non-union for what it was. This emerging awareness combined with Ed's own concerted efforts to contain me saved the analysis.

I said I "chose" non-union because I have no doubt that a choice was involved, though I was unaware of it at the time. But this means that immorality was involved, lies about understanding, about contact, about being in the same universe. I must emphasize the aptness of Ed's essentially moral complaint of bad faith; the recognition of its truth was shocking. This conflictual discovery was becoming manifest at a time when my self-image was of a person who deeply wanted union, indeed, who held it in the highest regard.

Against this background I finally got hold of the therapy. It was abundantly clear that transferential elements were involved and that my behavior was a representation of Ed's own interaction with his mother and father, more particularly, with the parental couple that their psyches evoked: a couple in intense, antagonistic disunion, each out through malicious envy to do in the other. My own bad faith and lies were a carbon copy of his family experience. The state of being overwhelmed and barely able to hold onto my thoughts replicated how he felt when they continually denied his perceptions. Also, his parents represented deceitful behavior, of which he was capable, acting out with his friends and acquaintances the very lack of truthfulness he found so distressing in others. But I, too, was driven to behave in immoral ways; and while I can lay claim to this compulsion as a countertransferential acting out, which it certainly was—and especially as the resistance to experiencing despair—something else was involved: we were both participants in a process that was not merely a repetition of past histories but a creation in its own right.

In my therapeutic work with Ed I was often thrust into a masochistic stance. In part this was a matter of choice, based upon my belief that the borderline person *sees* what the therapist does not wish to be seen. Acknowledging Ed's perceptions (for example, that I had *chosen* to act in ways injurious to him) obliged me to recognize unconscious shadow aspects of my personality that I had allowed to guide my behavior and helped him to gain faith in the correctness of his perceptions. I could easily have passed off his complaint as a paranoid distortion with some measure of truth. This perception would have comforted me, but undermined Ed.

But I also wish to note that there were times, though perhaps too few of them, when I reacted to Ed in ways that were not masochistic. For instance, I expressed how much I hated the way he was treating me, especially my choice of words and behavior, which he mercilessly scrutinized as careless and incompetent. This expression of hatred was possible—without assaulting him—when I could feel how painful and frightening his attacks, though premised upon truth, were to the small child within me. I was standing up for this child when I talked about my hatred, not attacking him. Indeed, this kind of direct response was a relief to Ed, for it showed that I was real and perhaps even trustworthy, despite the fact that a good deal of what occurred between us was dominated by an intense drive to disrupt contact.

The clinical material that relates to this patient depicts some of the most difficult aspects I have encountered in treatment of the borderline person. It is impossible, I believe, to sort out clearly what is personally transferential and countertransferential from the archetypal field dynamics that are so richly constellated at these levels of treatment. What is certain, however, is that the therapist treating the borderline patient must get firm hold of the experience of non-union and be capable as well of permitting its existence and of respecting it as a state to be survived which is meaningful beyond what can be grasped in immediate experience. Successful therapy depends to a large measure upon faith and the capacity to repair acting-out defenses against the pain of non-union and the despair it engenders.

In my dealings with Ed we seemed to engage a transference couple that desired non-union and was so split off that sometimes neither of us had any idea at all what the other was saying. Some other active thing put us into separate universes. Was he responsible? Was I? Was he out to defeat me, or to see if I could be tricked by his duplicity? For example, would I obligingly act as if things were going well just as he often did as a child when he had to split off his real perceptions and try to believe that his parents were doing the best they could? And was our interaction doomed for its destructive nature, or as the *Rosarium* suggests, was it a process through which somehow a new self was being built? So often our analytical endeavor seemed possessed by some demonic, tricksterlike force that toyed with me as if I was an infant. That is how it felt! How is one to understand this phenomenon? Can it be reduced merely to the component of envy; that is, *my* envy attacking our connection due to "misunderstanding" him? Or, alternatively, my acting out his introject of parental envy? Such interpretations have value, and certainly other equally "valid" interpretations could also be given. But standing alone they would prompt us to miss the essential fact that something of a significantly different nature and scale was operating, an archetypal process much larger than the two of us.

A subsequent session revealed further aspects of our unconscious process. Ed began with a question: "What is your relationship to my inner couple?" It sounded as though the plight of his wasted life was encapsulated in this question, and I acted as if there was no time to lose, feeling pressed to "get it right." My response was a lecture: "The inner couple is also an image of the relationship of your consciousness to the unconscious. If the couple is in disharmony, you will be in disharmony as well." To this he bristled, as usual, with the insistence that I was being as impersonal as a textbook. And of course he was right. There were other intellectualized attempts to answer his question during this session, all spun out of my haste and refusal to take the time to sort out what he was saying, to truly understand. My behavior erroneously allowed me to believe that I was connected to him. We also exchanged roles: at times I felt the need to slow down and be utterly precise, while he galloped along, moving too quickly for me to understand him in a full, grounded way. Then suddenly he would return to the question: "What is your relationship to my inner couple?"

The fact that I was feeling a bit worn down helped me to orient myself back toward what was happening between us. I allowed myself to become more centered, more fully embodied, and far less in control. Only when I finally succeeded in getting back to my own feelings was I able to recognize that I had been frightened of being physically harmed; my fantasy was that I had better get the right answers or he would hit me.

Then I began to realize that I had been experiencing and re-enacting Ed's early life with his parents, for when he failed to create harmony between his parents, he was in fact in great danger of being hit. That is, he experienced their disharmony and antagonism as dangerous both to the family unit and to himself and he had to set it right lest he be attacked by them. His solution was, in effect, to get his mother and father to behave differently both toward one another and toward him. Thus it appears that I had been acting out an introject of his child-self as it compulsively attempted to create union. In this particular case the urgent demand was that I create harmony between us by answering the question about his inner couple. And the compulsion to do so overrode the underlying awareness that a basic lack of connection—a prevailing non-union—was the dominant factor in our relationship.

I expressed these thoughts to Ed and it proved somewhat effective in leading us to a deeper understanding. He suggested the possibility that he was attacking me for acting in disunion with myself, adding that I could be seen as representing both his own couple in disunion *and* his child-self frantically attempting to change the situation. Or, I could be seen as incorporating the potential to evoke the disharmony he found so devastating. Whenever I did evoke disharmony by being out of harmony with myself, Ed became very nasty and had the urge to hit me. My constellation of the verbally abusive negative inner couple (his parental images in their state of disunion) severely affected him.

There was a definite improvement when we became able to objectify the interactive field in terms of a couple engaged in battle while paradoxically desiring no contact at all, as well as in terms of this same couple persecuting a small child; there was some containment of these disturbing patterns of behavior. In turn, perhaps this containment allowed the therapy to continue and even reach the point where our interactive field transformed into a unified field and a working alliance. At that point the significance of transference and countertransference dynamics diminished, and Ed began to make substantial changes in his life. In the *Rosarium, impregnatio* is followed by a regenerative state depicted by falling dew. The soul-less couple, washed and revitalized by the dew, is eventually brought back to life as the Rebis, a hermaphrodite. I believe the hermaphrodite represents the creation of a linking structure, akin to what Jung calls the transcendent function and Winnicott calls transitional space. As a result of our linkage, the therapy gained a playful and explorative quality that had previously been absent. In an important sense Ed's individuation process began anew at this juncture, and the significant life changes that he was able to make further contributed to his healing.

The following example illustrates how the unconscious dyad not only structures the interactive field, but also one's mind-body experiences. As well, it reveals that apprehending the unconscious dyad in its form of non-union can lead to a field of union.

"Jane," a 35-year-old woman, began a session by telling the following dream:

Dream: *In an ancient stone atrium I was doing an erotic dance with an eighteen-year-old boy. He knew more than I ever will.*

I sensed that she wanted me to be excited about the dream, and I felt awkward about having absolutely no response at all. Then my mind wandered to the previous day's session, which dealt with Jane's fears that I would be angry with her because she was emotionally distant. I felt disembodied and disconnected from the dream, and it would have been dismissive to sidestep my thoughts about yesterday's session. So I attempted to link these seemingly separate elements by saying, "Since the dance with the boy and the stone atrium seem to be such positive symbols, perhaps you had the dream to affirm how vital it is to stay on the track of what happened yesterday and to encourage you not to withdraw out of fears of my anger."[3] To this Jane replied, "You'll have to help me; I don't know where to go from here."

Suddenly I felt dull and flaccid, as if all sense of structure, all alertness, had momentarily vanished from my body. Mentally I was engaged and expectant, waiting for something to arise either from her or from me. But I could not readily contain my feelings and almost immediately began to recount yesterday's experience, recalling how frightened she was. With this Jane's countenance changed abruptly and she bitterly reproached herself: "I never do it right. You're cold, angry with me. I can feel it." I had difficulty at that moment sorting out "me" from what felt like a "them" that could have been her parents.

It was clear that something important was going on, and I realized that this patient might be using the session to repeat some family pattern. I followed her to a parental scene. "Where are you with them now?" I asked. "I'm at the dinner table; she is to my left, he to my right. I'm terrified, constantly alert, scanning for danger. I have to be, I have to make sure everything is okay. She's a bit drunk and stuffing herself with food; he is passive, simply waiting. But I know he will explode at any moment. I have to prevent this somehow but I don't know how. I try to humor them; it barely works. I know his anger will eventually come out, he'll explode. Then she'll withdraw and be a martyr, terrifying everyone with her martyrdom. He'll then be frightened, and her martyrdom will turn to anger against me."

With this information, I could entertain the following possibility. When I initially heard Jane's dream, my near-silence stemmed from the fact that my mental processes replicated her silent father's dulled unconscious, and my awkward and flaccid body feelings resembled those of her drunk mother; I was somewhat intimidated by this patient's capacity to put me into such uncomfortable states. I did not feel any recognizable anger, but then again, it was difficult to allow myself even minor feelings of irritation in working with her, since I feared they might set off a paranoid reaction that could lead to a delusional transference certain to doom the analytical work. Thus this aspect of our interaction was a mixture of mutual neurotic and psychotic parts. I had split off the rage I was feeling and as a consequence did not adequately embrace the nature of the couple I had introjected; that is, I avoided the anger embedded in the dulled state, mimicking the martyr in the process by absorbing the anger. In retrospect, I recognize that I could have interpreted this state as an anticipated response Jane might naturally have held, but her paranoid, scanning field was too intense to have hazarded such an interpretation.

Generally, my mind and body seemed to represent her inner, parental couple. Just as they were split and warring so too my mental and somatic selves could be split. When I was well connected, the patient was fine. She was able to keep me centered by telling stories and giving me things to ask about. At such times Jane created a unified inner couple in me that did not terrorize her. But the endeavor always had a sense of incompleteness to it, a foreboding of what might happen next. In "fixing" me Jane only temporarily set aside the battle that would certainly come. For just as her parents would fight in spite of her best efforts to entertain them, so my two natures would eventually fall out of harmony. On one level they already had, for the unity Jane achieved was accomplished only through our mutual splitting—she from fear, and me from the tension and anxiety that was always close by.

Given my moments of disunity, any sense that I did not know what to say or do, or that I felt a bit muddled, would immediately change the session. Jane believed that I was angry with her, as if I was the embodiment of her father at the dinner table. "What's wrong?" she would ask, and feeling that she could not fix me, would become very frightened and complain that she "never does it right."

When I became aware of how my own unconscious was influenced and structured by her internal parental couple, several advantages accrued. First, the patient participated in a corrective emotional experience, in the sense that she experienced me as her parental couple but could see that I did not retaliate; I also required less "fixing" than they did, especially as I grew conscious of not acting out the splitting process and losing sight of the opposites involved. Jane could now free up psychic energy hitherto in the service of the incessant scanning process that had remorselessly energized her internal negative parental couple. And second, by maintaining my own mind-body union while experiencing her disunion, I provided Jane with the new possibility of introjecting a more harmonious dyad.

In the sessions that followed, there was a sense of connection, of working well together. Jane said that it "felt good, but what about the other stuff?" She meant, of course, the disunion we had experienced previously and her fears of my rage. I realized that she was scanning me, for I actually felt its pressure, as if her *vision* exerted force. When I asked for corroboration Jane affirmed my feeling. Encouraged to express what she saw, she reported that I was defensive. I had to look hard to accept her finding, and asked how she recognized my defensiveness. Jane responded by saying, "Maybe you're worried about something." I was aware of an inner tightness and the sense that I was holding back feelings. She wondered aloud if these feelings were sexual, saying, "that's usually the root of things." Here was something new and important, for Jane had dared to *see into* me imaginally and, even more, to express her feelings about me.

The borderline person tends to concretize imaginal perceptions inwardly; for example, at the beginning of a session he or she might perceive the therapist as tired and withdrawn but say nothing about it. After some contact is made in the session the patient, provoked by an inner attack, will comment on being "too much of a burden for you, or for anyone." Their vision, which I regard as a psychic organ or structure that they refuse to acknowledge, and hence communicate through, turns demonic and against them.

Jane dared to share what she had seen; in turn, I could respond, indicating where her perceptions were accurate and also pointing out areas outside her perceptual lens. Thus her imaginal perception was tested, and she was able to depart from the inner certainty that what she saw was *the* truth. On other occasions Jane split off what she saw by relegating it a part of her own madness. What one *sees* is often very disturbing. In fact, a person's imaginal perception is usually denied early in life because what is perceived (for example, a parent's hatred) is too searing to absorb. Many borderline persons begin to integrate split-off psychotic parts once they dare to permit themselves to see that they were hated. Being able to share one's imaginal perceptions is extremely important, though rarely available to the borderline person. Instead, as dreams often reveal, the imagination usually gets stuck in matter. The dreamer attempts to jump over a stream and gets only halfway, or tries to enter a room only to encounter a lead-sealed door. There are endless variants of such themes, in which the linkage between two states is severely hindered.

We continued to explore Jane's scanning process, noting everything she *saw*. She began to experience the positive virtues of *sight* and came to enjoy the fact that it might be a relational, rather than merely defensive, tool, one that could operate like a kind of psychic early warning radar. She also experienced how my *seeing* myself through her *sight* had the effect of enlivening our interaction. This, in turn, we experienced as something autonomous coming to life between us: a sense of union, with a characteristic rhythm that both joined and separated us. In the following sessions Jane and I began to grasp aspects of her negative inner couple and to experience the release of a positive couple that structured our interactive space.

The *coniunctio* is not only an event but a pattern, and disharmonious aspects of that pattern soon began to emerge. In the session after the union experience something was askew; the positive couple was absent, we were not working well together, and it felt terrible. In an effort to resume our good connection I actually said: "What about us?" No longer scanning passively, with her paranoid defenses Jane immediately picked up what was "off" in my remark. "The *us* feels slimy," she said. "That's how my father was and would deny it. Never in the open. If you had said, 'How about you and me?' it would have been different— clear, honest. The *us* feels terrible." In this way an incestuous couple made its appearance as it does in the *Rosarium* after the *coniunctio* experience (Jung 1946, par. 468). Our *coniunctio* served to bring in more unconscious material, facilitating the kinship quality between us as well as another stage in the continual integration of her *vision*.

Integrating one's imaginal sight—that ability usually split off which has taken up domain in the patient's psychotic part—is often accomplished only after the therapist *sees* this *sight* operating in the patient; in effect, the patient must be spied upon. For example, after working with a man for six months I recognized that while he constantly scanned me, he also idealized me and sacrificed his vision, or attempts at vision, to that idealization. Usually the scanning was a very subtle background phenomenon, barely perceptible unless I made an extra effort to be embodied and in contact emotionally with him. But his idealization induced me to lay back and bask in the self-approving light of what a good therapist I was, rather than reach out to him sufficiently to perceive that he *sees* and what he *sees*.

Once I did manage to focus upon his scanning, I listened as the patient spoke about his fear of women. The world, he claimed, is "a batch of piranhas." I was not included in this indictment, however; I was different, safe. Indeed, how else could he have descended to face his fear? Wondering if the piranhas were real, the patient quickly affirmed their presence and their power to dissolve him. Every other creature could tear him to pieces, that is, fracture his sense of identity. It became clear that idealization kept me safe and allowed the patient to split off his intensely negative inner images. Any attempts to descend into these negative images had an as-if quality that conveyed the falseness of the effort.

The patient volunteered that each time I *saw* him scanning me he felt a physical tension in his chest, stomach, and throat, and the reality of inner persecutory attackers. Without this granted *sight*, however, his defenses remained intact. When I interpreted this idealization, its defensive function temporarily abated, only to be replaced by a masochistic defense. He agreed with everything I said and even added examples to prove my point. Then he let me know how anxious all these reflections made him. It was clear that these strenuous efforts to keep me ideal split him from what he really *saw*—namely, that I often did not *see* him or the intensity of his fear. Over and over he complained of the smooth exterior that hid how he really felt from everyone *except me*, and that I alone knew he was very young and afraid. With this double message he attacked and placated me at the same time. Often he told me I did *not see* him, only to be split from his own perception by insisting that I was different from the rest.

Imaginal sight is much like active imagination, *but here it is essential that the unconscious be constellated through the countertransference.* Only after I became conscious of my splitting tendencies and the somewhat flattened affect that did not engage this patient's psychotic parts could I begin to use this unconscious ability. By submitting to the countertransferential state and becoming embodied, I made room for the imagination to lead to the vision that could perceive his background scanning. At this level of perception the imagination is used as an organ of perception. The imaginal realm need not necessarily appear through visual images; feeling and the kinesthetic sense are also natural outlets. Possibly the nature of the imaginal act is determined by individual therapists' strengths, so that some see "visibly," while others see "feelingly." In any event, the process requires that the therapist allow himself or herself to be affected by the patient's material without resorting to the safe margins of interpretation, which would only prove to be a defensive maneuver at best. Here imagination is delivered of the body in confusion and disorder; it arises through faith, rather than through mastery and understanding.

Madness, Religion, and the Self in Borderline States of Mind

The borderline patient has a core of madness that must be uncovered if successful treatment is to be achieved. The patient's true self, or soul, is enmeshed in psychotic mechanisms of splitting and denial. This true self might be represented as a child living in filth, locked up, petrified and watchful from a distance, or frozen in ice. There are countless images to depict it. The following clinical material is drawn from my work with "Amanda," a 48-year-old borderline woman. Her psychotic aspect entered the analysis only after I put an end to her controlling, obsessive reading from a notebook to me under the guise that she otherwise "lost her thoughts." In daily life Amanda functioned quite well, and for the most part her madness intruded into an otherwise normally competent personality only during analytic sessions. A relatively contained and condensed psychotic transference, in which delusional processes are contained by a sense of alliance, is highly desirable in treatment (Grotstein 1979, p. 173).

As a three-year-old Amanda suffered an overwhelming trauma: her father left the family.[4] He never said goodbye to her, ostensibly because the family felt that she would be better off without so explicit a closure. Yet her father had been her only source of love and comfort as well as the only barrier against her mother and grandparents, whom Amanda experienced as cold, aloof, and harsh. Among early memories of her mother Amanda recalled being sent to play outside on a rainy day dressed in new white shoes; she was then scolded for getting them dirty. This memory is a paradigm of her maternal experiences: developmental separation from her mother was undermined by the implicit demand that she stay fused with her mother's narcissism, which demanded that she appear perfect. It was against such a maternal background, and consequently, with minimal internal resources, that Amanda was abandoned by her father, her only love object.

Amanda's confusion, which dominated treatment, proved to be disorienting for both of us.

The abandonment was so traumatic an incident that no analytic work on the relationship with her father occurred for nearly four years. Up until then Amanda never mentioned him. Eventually, she was to refer to him as a "nice person" and say that he "preferred" her mother. Even though he returned to the family fold after a nine-month absence and was present for the next 45 years, there was almost nothing she could find to say about him; her mind went blank.

Gradually, Amanda's abandonment fears became focused in the transference, and session endings became very painful for her. Between sessions Amanda's image of me was often effaced, but occasionally she was able to suffer my *absence* consciously in distinction to splitting and becoming manic. It became possible to begin the reconstruction of what had happened to her inner world when her father left. One memory salvaged was that she "became hysterical and hid under the bed" after she found out that he had left. This was where her memories began and ended, however, and even this recollection felt brittle. (In fact, all of Amanda's recollections had a strange uncertainty to them, a phenomenon I shall return to when discussing the particular logic of the borderline personality, see p. 22.) It seems that upon her father's return nine months later, Amanda believed he was an imposter. Moreover, she created an inner, idealized father who would someday return and love her truly. In the transference, Amanda split me into the imposter and the idealized father, the latter existing only in imaginary conversations with me outside the analytical sessions.

A severe distortion of reality had occurred when this patient's father deserted her. She blanked out her once deeply felt love for him. And having a positive inner world of such meager worth, Amanda could not mourn the loss. Instead, a delusional inner world came into existence, one structured by idealization and its negative, split-off polarity, the imposter father. Neither of these reactions toward her father were felt consciously; indeed life with him went on just as if he never had left. Thus Amanda said that he was "nice," but inwardly her perceptions were dominated by severe distortions: it really was/was not her father who had returned. That is, he was neither her real father nor an imposter.

In the transference I was initially the imposter to whom Amanda had to learn to relate. This took the form of an insistence that I list the rules of patient behavior. "What should they say or do with the therapist?" Amanda would ask. I was depersonalized by her (but not totally—she always maintained a sense of humor, which represented her observing ego, even as she was deadly serious).

When I succeeded in interpreting this splitting, she suffered a loss of the "outside" me, as she put it, and a painful deadness eclipsed her imagination. "Out there you don't love me any more," she would say. This led to a long period of depression and acute abandonment suffering at the close of each session. At these times Amanda's psychotic parts became enlivened, for she could not really be sure that the real me would return.

After further work it became clear that yet another "father" existed—the one who carried the depth of her abandonment experience. This father was identified with money, and the very mention of this theme released almost immediate hysterical flooding. She recalled that her father had left the family home because he had not been able to earn a living that matched the family standard. Amanda's understanding was that her mother and grandparents had kicked him out because of this financial dereliction. In her unconscious, money became the root of all loss. In external choices Amanda did everything she could to "forget" how much money she had. An inheritance she received was traumatic because it forced her to think about money; her only recourse was to hide it in a bank account and forget about it completely. To invest it, or even to draw interest from the principal, was totally beyond her capacities. Money had no other meaning than somehow being linked to loss.

For many months the interpretation of money in its connection to her father was barely effective; and many times the mere mention of money invoked abandonment feelings so overwhelming they disrupted the continuity of emergent memories and insights. Finally, after dealing persistently with this issue in many analytical sessions, Amanda's capacity to deal with money issues gradually improved. With this growing capacity a fog seemed to clear, and the fact that money was unconsciously identified with the father who had deserted her became a more stable psychic reality. We could then recognize three fathers: the imposter father, the idealized father, and the abandoning father—that is, money.

Amanda's splitting in session lessened, but still served to dull her pain, and she remained extremely confused. Mental processes were often blanked out. As she put it, "the head doesn't work." Each thought or memory immediately produced others, so that a multiplicity of centers formed, each competing for her attention and leaving both of us thoroughly confused. Moreover, she rejected all interpretive attempts to sort out what was happening. The experience truly reflected Harold Searles's statement:

> I often have the sense that one or another patient is functioning unconsciously in a multiple-identity fashion when I feel not simply intimidated or overwhelmed . . . but, curiously and more specifically, *outnumbered* by him. (1979, p. 448)

Confusion, splitting, and reality distortion are all part of what we term the borderline personality. Particularly notable is the quality of madness or near-psychotic behavior (rarely is there a total distortion of reality, although the behavioral stance does possess an autonomy that is like a state of demonic possession) that is often stressed in the literature on the borderline personality. But there is a strange kind of order in this "possessed" behavior; we begin to glimpse it in the clinical material as we consider the way in which this patient often rejects interpretations.

Amanda would say something like, "that's not quite it," or "maybe." This response was always frustrating when I had put a great deal of effort into trying to create some coherence for her and myself as well. As a result of her denial I would often become irritated. At times this reaction was quite strong, and it was often clear that projective identification was involved, which led me to attempt to examine her anger with me for "disappearing outside of the sessions." Such interpretation was somewhat effective, but this enterprise hardly reached Amanda's psychotic core.

It should be noted that when given conditional answers, though irritated, I did not feel my interpretations totally negated. In fact, Amanda was often at her best at these moments, and her mode of rejection rarely revealed a strong intent to deny me. If my interpretations were far off the mark she became confused. Then "other thoughts" fragmented her attention, leaving both of us in a confused muddle that may have obscured some anger toward me. But when my interpretations were relatively sound, they illicited in her a reaction that revealed a level of depth usually unseen. If, regarding an interpretation, I asked the question: "Does that seem right?" Amanda would reply, "Not exactly." If I asked, "Is it wrong, off the mark?" she would answer, "No, not completely." At these moments it seemed that she was *using* my interpretation to get close to something. But what? Apparently Amanda found value in the very interpretations she negated; what I said was treated as neither true, nor false. Thus she suspended choice, but not for defensive purposes. Deep within her a process was at work that could only express itself in the suspension of choice. I discovered that if I "hovered" in the suspension without trying to fill in the interpretation she would remember a detail from the past, or a new insight. But each statement had to be balanced by a second statement that revealed the confusion or incompleteness of the first. There was no possibility of saying, "This is right," but only, "It is neither right nor wrong."

The French psychoanalyst André Green, whose thinking has enhanced my grasp of this clinical material, has described the borderline person's "logic" as follows:

> According to the reality principle, the psychic apparatus has to decide whether the object is or is not there: 'Yes' or 'No.' According to the pleasure principle, and as negation does not exist in the primary process of the unconscious, there is only 'Yes.' Winnicott has described the status of the transitional object, which combines the 'Yes' and the 'No', as the transitional is- and is-not-the-breast. One can find precursors of Winnicott's observations in Freud's description of the cotton reel game and in his description of the fetish. But I think that there is one more way of dealing with this crucial issue of deciding whether the object is or is not, and that is illustrated by the judgment of the borderline patient. There is a fourth

possible answer: *Neither 'Yes' nor 'No.'* This *is* an alternate choice to the refusal of choice. The transitional object is a *positive refusal*; it is either a 'Yes' or a 'No.' The symptoms of the borderline, standing for transitional objects, offer a *negative refusal of choice*: Neither 'Yes' nor 'No.' One could express the same relation in experiential terms by asking the question: 'Is the object dead (lost) or alive (found)?' or 'Am I dead or alive?'—to which he may answer: *'Neither Yes nor No.'* (1977, p. 41)

When in acute distress, the borderline patient can never be certain that the therapist is truly present in the flesh-and-blood sense. One could also say the patient is uncertain if the therapist as a functioning self is alive or dead. This state of uncertainty always exists in the patient's unconscious and manifests itself in bewildering ways when splitting defenses or emotional flooding fail temporarily to dispel abandonment anxiety, and confusion ensues. Hence the patient can never answer the question: *Is the therapist alive or dead?* since it appears meaningless and confusing. Moreover, if asked: *Is the therapist both alive and dead?* the patient would also be confused, for this would imply that the therapist was a transitional object, that is, something both created and found.

The last thing the patient experiences in such a state of confusion is the creativity of transitional space. Indeed, the possibility of "play" is usually absent for the borderline patient. The therapist, who tends to be so embroiled in countertransference reactions that the foremost desire is simply to survive each encounter, often feels either depressed and dull or manic, and, like the borderline patient, often *acts* to fill space rather than allowing the *absence* or the suspension of experience (Green 1977, p. 41). Deadness, the absence of experience, is a difficult state to bear and requires faith that if one delays action and simply waits, the object will not be destructive. Indeed, at crucial moments in the analytical process, the therapist's supreme act of faith in relation to the borderline person is to trust that this patient will not "kill" him or her. To be rendered ineffectual and mindless would be one form of killing.

In the material I have been describing, it was not a matter of my interpretations getting closer to the target, or of my needing to augment and deepen them. The effort required was to take account of Amanda's sense of paradox, which was often inherent in her response and sharply contrasted with her usual confused and split-up state of mind. For fleeting moments I would be privy to a depth in her normally hidden by splitting defenses and an infantile ego that "just wanted to feel good." The patient's answers carried within them an awareness that my interpretations were only partially satisfactory, for she regarded them as "not fully correct" *and/or* "not fully wrong." That was the more rational dimension of her reply. On a deeper and more subtle level, however, it was not a question of "whether X is right or wrong" but rather that "X is neither *totally* right nor *totally* wrong."

The subtleties of madness are often perceived only through our own feelings and states of confusion. In the case under discussion more overt forms of madness were uncovered in time. Some of them were not very subtle, and uncovering them merely required an empathic observer, sensitive to the patient's shame. For example, the patient eventually revealed a considerable paranoid process, including fears that her money would be stolen by the bank, and that her checks were just paper with which someone could trick her. Amanda was also persecuted at times by fear that her grandchildren would be stolen from her while she accompanied them to school. But the patient's more subtle forms of madness, in which confusion and reality distortion coexisted as part of a *neither-Yes-nor-No* logic, were more difficult to decipher, *usually because I wished that these states did not exist in her.*

There are a number of reasons for a therapist's tendency toward countertransferential reactions of confusion and irritation. One is not being encouraged to add or subtract something from what one said, although that wish may be implicit in the patient's communication. But more important is the sense of simultaneously getting close to and being far away from grasping something that can only be known as a totality and not as the sum of its parts. Generally, the borderline person hates partial interpretations, and the therapist often feels persecuted for not being perfect and may even complain about it (sometimes aloud to the patient!). Often the therapist's best efforts are diminished by the patient's qualifications or outright anger and rejection.

As Amanda's splitting began to heal further through the experiencing of her abandonment anxieties, confusion diminished and her imagination slowly began to function. Gradually she could begin to "find me" outside our sessions; I was becoming more of a "real" object and less the "idealized father." The analytic hour became a lively place, even though the world outside, in which she functioned well but took little interest, remained a place of deadness. All of her interest was concentrated on returning to the analytical space. A positive self-image was finally resurrected out of the madness in which it had been kept neither alive nor dead, but in limbo.

Amanda's external object relations also became more realistic. Her husband, who for years had carried the idealized projection and had betrayed his wife through affairs with other women, was gradually seen more realistically. Previously his inner deadness had persecuted her, but once she came to know and respect her own angry feelings, she railed at his lack of relatedness. Gradually, and without necessarily liking it, Amanda began to accept him as he was. There was also substantial improvement in Amanda's relationship with her mother; this came about as the result of learning to recognize when she was angry with her mother. At first she grasped this knowledge only with analytic help and often days after the fact. But gradually the interval between incident and anger decreased until finally her inner response coincided with the outer provocation. Amanda confronted her mother more and more assertively and actually forged a better relationship with her. The gradual emergence of a functioning self was epitomized by a greatly diminished proneness to splitting, growth of the imagination, and a willingness to find value and meaning in the pain of abandonment anxieties.

The new split between the affectively dead external world and the lively analytic world represented not only a good/bad dichotomy but also an entrance into the Kleinian depressive position. Our process prior to this took place largely within the paranoid-schizoid realm where splitting was multiple and fragmenting; as the process moved to the level of the depressive position, Amanda's hatred of me as the transference father was displaced onto the dull, outer world, and her love of me as the transference image of the once-loved father was more fully experienced in the analytic work. This splitting, however, was more manageable than formerly and interpretation more effective. What she was facing was the split between love and hate, and, with great trepidation, she began to express her hatred to me. Its first appearance took the form of a jocular remark: "Out there I hate you." In time she began to integrate the affect in my presence.

This new-found courage had a positive effect on the continuing recovery of her imagination, which had been especially vulnerable to splitting between love and hate. Amanda communicated to me an imaginative process more complex than the flow of fantasy that had circulated around me as the idealized father. This important distinction registers the difference Jung underscored in his alchemical studies between what alchemists called true and fantastic imagination (Jung 1953, par. 360). The borderline person often experiences either an imaginative lacuna or else a torrential flow of imagery and affect in countless passive fantasies that *void the experience of feelings*. The false imagination functions to split one from feeling, furthering mind-body splitting and somatic complaints. But true imagination, according to the alchemical metaphor, is far more realistic; it engages feelings and nurtures the growth of consciousness and the awareness of the suffering of one's soul.

There is one other issue worth mentioning in relation to this case. About a year before Amanda's abandonment anxieties and imagination became the focus of treatment, she dreamed of a small girl who was frozen in ice: the ice began to thaw and the child started to come to life. This dream was itself a critical juncture in our work, and it was ushered in by a strange occurrence. At the close of one session the patient suddenly turned around and spoke to me in French, which she had never done before. In the next session she asked me about "subpersonalities," realizing that "another person" had spoken French to me. It turned out that this personality carried her sexuality; she gave this person a name, and for the first time an erotic feeling existed between us. I believe that the "subpersonality" in her dream material marked the first appearance of a self structure, whose emergence had a synthesizing effect that overcame dissociation. Previously, this personality had been split off into a frozen, schizoid state.

The loving and erotic quality remained for several months, then vanished with the re-emergence of Amanda's abandonment anxiety and depression. It would appear that for her self to become embodied and a part of life as felt in space and time this patient had to experience acute feelings of abandonment. Such schizoid elements are always present in the borderline personality, and although they need not necessarily dominate behavior with their pull toward withdrawal, their integration is essential if a sense of self is to emerge.

In sum, the borderline personality's emerging self uses interpretation in a bewildering fashion. When an interpretation is accepted, he or she will often return to the next session with material that seems to deny it. The therapist may feel confused or angry at this point and will often *act* through intervention or withdrawal. "Acting," as André Green says, is "the true model of the mind. Acting is not limited to actions; fantasies, dreams, words take the function of action. Acting fills space and does not tolerate the suspension of experience" (1977, p. 41). The therapist might believe the patient has denied what was said, but this perception actually serves to block out his or her own emerging state of confusion and incapacity to tolerate *absence*. That is, we feel attacked by the patient because of our limited capacity for self-experience, let alone the capacity to experience the patient as absent. So we flee to the safety of feeling hurt, rejected, or angry.

It is worth looking at the discrete parts of this process. If a therapist in this state of mind says something like, "but last time we arrived
at X" (X referring to some understanding that now seems to be denied
by the patient), the patient might say, "What have I said to deny that?"
Now the therapist may feel angry as at a total distortion of reality. Yet
the patient actually *did* say Y, which the therapist *took* to negate X; an
assumption of agreement was made to dispel confusion and avoid the
suspension of experience. And at the point where the patient says,
"What have I said to deny what we did last time?" the sense of confusion
often disappears, leaving the therapist with the feeling of having acted
badly.

At this point it seems that the patient was only reflecting further,
setting aside what had transpired. In fact, the patient was trying to use
the previous interpretation *by temporarily denying it*, which the therapist took as a total attack on the work of the last session, a "negative
therapeutic reaction." The therapist's narcissism is provoked, since
he or she wants interpretations to be definitive, not mere stepping
stones to deeper levels; what must be understood is that the patient is
attempting to disengage from the therapist's narcissism. To do this is
terribly risky, for it means showing more of the true self and daring to
abandon the therapist (that is, the therapist's narcissistic needs that
could prevent the patient from finding that self).

The negative logic of the borderline patient so aptly described by
Green can also be understood conceptually through the *via negativa* of
the 15th-century cleric and mystic, Nicholas of Cusa, a metaphysical
system that provides a way to perceive both the nature and the goal of
the borderline person's use of negation as a path to self-emergence. In
this system any positive statement stands in opposition to another that
demonstrates its finitude or incompleteness; thus, each statement yields
another, ad infinitum. God, the unknowable object of this attempt,
remains unsplit, a *coincidentia oppositorum*. Hence the God-state, in
which opposites are unified and painful and deceitful splitting may at
last be overcome, represents the unconscious goal of the borderline
person. Reaching the goal, however, demands a journey through the
territory of madness, a domain in which the inner life suffers fragmentation and confusion; in other words, the complete antithesis to unity or
the harmony of opposites. Moreover, madness itself seems to guard
against intrusion into a deeper domain. This is because madness is a
quality of the self that has somehow survived and, however weakly, is
manifested in the paradoxical questioning that is the crux of the
peculiar logic the borderline person employs.

Moreover, with the borderline person, a therapist can err in the attempt to *know* the meaning of a patient's communication by affirming what *is*; for example, "The anxious feelings I am having with this person inform me that he may be dominated by abandonment anxieties." This is what Frederick Copleston (1985), commenting upon Nicholas's logic, describes as the level of the senses, which simply affirm. Or the therapist may try to gain knowledge about the patient by deciding what is or is not; for example, "She is in a manic state, but this may not be the core issue; instead, it may be a defense against her abandonment depression." This form of reasoning is what Copleston refers to, again after Nicholas, as the level where "there is both affirmation and denial." What is required is to face the madness and to succeed in existing *without* knowing. In this way, one approaches the unknowable.

In Nicholas's thought, sense-perception corresponds to what Green has called primary process thinking, and discursive reasoning (*ratio*) corresponds to the reality principle. The borderline person's logic, which follows the model of *neither "Yes" nor "No,"* corresponds in Nicholas's system to the *intellectus*.

> Whereas sense-perception affirms and reason affirms and denies, intellect denies the oppositions of reason. Reason affirms X and denies Y, but intellect denies X and Y both disjunctively and together; it apprehends God as the *coincidentia oppositorum*. This apprehension or intuition cannot, however, be properly stated in language, which is the instrument of reason rather than intellect. *In its activity as intellect the mind uses language to suggest meaning rather than to state it* . . . (Copleston 1985, p. 237, italics mine)

One cannot ever *understand* another's madness, but one can know that one does not know. Any understanding that translates madness into a discursive process (such as sequences of causes and failed developmental stages) fails to grasp the nature of madness and also fails to provide a symbolic sense of containment for borderline people. Such reductive thinking turns their madness into a *thing* to be ordered, instead of allowing it to be as vital and alive and characteristic as their more readily acceptable qualities. This method achieves some understanding, but not of the phenomenology itself, which is beyond the province of rational knowing.

The only useful *knowing* is negative logic, since the person's madness has a capacity to distort and destroy perceptions and their memory traces such that seemingly benign interactions, or once-inspired interpretations that were introjected, turn into persecutory objects. But it should be clear that this is not the result of splitting off abandonment anxieties, since those are neither the cause nor not the cause of the madness. We need to inhabit the suspended state of not knowing, without negating the *attempt* to know. This kind of waiting can provide a deeper *experience* of a person's psychotic parts, which gain in familiarity, even if it is not possible to become truly comfortable with the feelings of oddness and terror, absence and mindlessness, they are apt to provoke.

Madness: Personal or Impersonal?

Is the madness one experiences in another person personal or impersonal? Certainly, it can feel like a soulless thing that terrifies subject and object by its very absence of form and clear affect and by the void of experiences that is part of it. For madness is imbued with *absence* or *blankness* rather than the affirmative presence of any thing. In analysis the madness one begins to see seems like an alien other that has nothing to do with *the patient with whom one wishes to be*. It is difficult to accept the mad aspects of a patient; to avoid these we grasp at all kinds of fleeting projective-identification dynamics and interpretations that even include the therapist's fear of being abandoned.. But these choices are all defensive strategies to fill a void, an absence of experience, a core where thought and experience do not exist.

It is easy to think of madness as matter to be organized. "He is fleeing from an abandonment anxiety and fears that I, too, will abandon him in the process." This may be true, but it is also defensive, a way of avoiding the absence and blankness that can characterize madness. Yet the patient, assaulted by "well-intentioned" interpretations, quickly flees into extreme states of mind-body splitting and the intrusion goes unnoticed. Indeed, the patient is as happy as the therapist to have something to hold on to—the patient's *anxiety* is after all a thing to be ordered and understood. It becomes a substitute for madness, reducing it to an impersonal *thing*.

But how can madness be personal? Can I, or need I, love my patient's madness? The image of St. Theresa drinking the pus of her sick patients seems relevant in its excess. How can such madness, which often succeeds in turning both people into automatons, be part of one's humanity? A saintly attitude toward it, the "wounded healer," or a doctor who wears the mantle of the suffering patient, will not be experienced as embracing and containing. Instead such a stance becomes a third thing between therapist and patient, a *notion* of healing the soul.

Yet what if one succeeds in apprehending the phenomena of a hu-

man being's madness? A state of mind that the patient has been terrified of revealing, madness exists as a no-man's land, a place where
meaning, imagery, and all relational potential are destroyed, leaving little but somaticizations and severe mind-body splitting. When one manages to comprehend madness as an aspect of the patient, gradually experiencing the patient and the patient's madness in a personal, human
way, a shift can occur. It is as if the deeper one gets into the alien nature of madness, the less adequate are the human container and the
personal grasp one has to embrace it. Instead, our hold on this phenomenon wants to expand, as if our previous, personal orientation was
too small to contain it. There is a feeling that madness needs a larger
vessel, and as the sense of expansion develops, an impersonal feeling
comes to preside. The patient's madness again seems like an autonomous machine or diety, some separate force that runs both patient and
therapist. Sometimes this feeling becomes acute, strays too far from human contact. Then it is time to return again to the smaller personal
frame, even though it soon feels too confined and requires expansion.

Thus one's perception of madness oscillates between the polarities
personal/impersonal, or personal/archetypal. I cannot say that I relate to
the patient's madness in a personal way, but neither can I say that I
relate to it in an impersonal way. Yet if I say that the relationship is both
personal *and* impersonal I have abstracted my experience in an intellectual way that destroys it; I resist defining the strange and even awesome way in which personal and impersonal qualities are coupled—a
coupling which becomes manifest only when the phenomenology of
madness *as part of the patient* is deeply engaged. What I can say with
certainty, however, is that the patient's madness is *neither personal nor
impersonal.*

This distinction between the personal level and an impersonal
transcendent level is also revealed in the mystic's answer to the question: Is the God you experienced personal or impersonal? The mystic
may respond that the God experienced was intensely personal. But
once said, this seems wrong, and the mystic speaks of God as sublimely
Other, and of having partaken of an experience that belongs to a realm
beyond all human habitation, a realm intensely impersonal. Thus it
would not do to say that the God experienced was both personal and
impersonal; that would bind and falsify the experience. The only possibility is to say that the mystic's soul reached toward a God *neither personal nor impersonal.*

Here the mystic speaks in a paradox that embraces all experience.
The borderline person's *neither Yes nor No* rarely has the fluidity of

paradox but instead is a caricature of it. The mystic's paradox is seamless, while the borderline person's is rent, leaving one empty and
confused rather than whole.

The borderline person's *neither Yes nor No* seems to cancel out
whatever has been achieved. When a session approaches clarity and
confusion wanes, but the next session begins with an attack, the patient
is guarding against the therapist's tendency *not* to see in an experiential
and paradoxical way. What the patient would wish to say to the therapist—if the therapist had not eliminated the possibility through precipi-
tous talk or action—is that the insights of the last session were neither
right nor wrong. By beginning with an attack the patient is simply
expressing an inability to grasp the paradoxical nature of the analytical
experience. If the therapist suspends action and allows for a period
of not knowing and confusion, *then* the person is often capable of expressing the subtle sense that it was neither complete nor incomplete.

The soul of the borderline person would seem to be communicating in the manner that Nicholas of Cusa envisioned God's mystery. It is
as if the patient were saying, "You cannot fully know me; I am beyond
any rational comprehension. You can only know that you do not know.
If the knowing you possess is authentic and hard won, I will allow you
to get closer but only if you remember always that you do not know.
Your need to know and your arrogance are the greater threat to me, as
is your being anything less than your best as you try to understand me."
As one approaches the soul, one traverses the territory of madness.
Jacques Lacan has written: "Not only can man's being not be understood
without madness, it would not be man's being if it did not bear madness within itself as the limit of his freedom" (1977, p. 215). Without
having delved into madness one can never understand any human
being.

While perhaps obvious, it is crucial to underscore that the borderline person's madness is in part the result of extreme pain, confusion,
and bewilderment in the face of overwhelming emotions that lack the
discrimination of feeling. To a degree madness is created—though it
also exists a priori like the chaos of myth and alchemy—by denial,
splitting, projective identification, and identification with archetypal
images. Madness defends against the pain of being hated, scapegoated,
and attacked by parental guilt and envy for any individuation effort,
serving to dull that pain. The soul, as it exits the territory of madness
(when, for example, it is *seen* and *dares to be seen*), is always attended
by the pain that the healing of splitting brings.

The borderline person often acts mad because the pain is so deep and the risk of contact *so* great that all avenues are full of roadblocks, detours, and warning signs. When the borderline sector is approached the danger light goes on. The patient is testing, for example, with the "attacking" question. The *coniunctio*, with its capacity to end splitting, always touches upon the tolerable pain endemic to it; this pain and its attendant madness is at the core of the borderline personality. The patient goes on alert to ascertain whether or not the therapist realizes and is capable of handling the depth of pain and sensitivity. If the therapist is perceived *not* to know, then a detour must be taken until the risk seems diminished. These detours engage madness and lead to the "nothingness" that is the state of suspension—*waiting*—and watching to see if *this time* the pain will be apprehended and understood.

Borderline and Religious Experiences

Is there a relationship between the thought processes of the borderline person and the genuine experiences of the *numinosum*[5] of mystics or Nicholas of Cusa's *via negativa*? In mystical experiences a union is known with the divinity as a *complexio oppositorum*. The soul's immersion and subsequent separation from God is a reality, a union which lives on *in the soul of the mystic*. But for our patients *loss of union* is the critical issue. Whatever experiences of union may have existed during the first months of life or been partially achieved in later developmental stages, the borderline person could not sufficiently own or incarnate them. This essential process was severely impeded.

Often, the borderline person may serve as a link to the *numinosum* for other people, for example, in the role of a psychic, or as a therapist. In such a capacity the *numinosum* may be alive and remarkably healing. But it is not incarnated *for the borderline person*, for whom when alone the *numinosum* disappears; no longer the central core it suggests, it constitutes instead a reminder of painful absence and abandonment that can barely be tolerated. Somaticizations and mind-body splits blank out the capacity to differentiate feelings and experience conflicting opposites; a bewildering simultaneity of contradictory feeling-states occurs.

A link between borderline states of mind and the *numinosum* is not farfetched. The manifestation of borderline states of mind within religious experience is well known. For instance, St. John of the Cross suffered from a terrible sense of emptiness and depression. In "The Dark Night" his mind was often blank and his thoughts fractured; he lived in despair, feeling abandoned by God and by people. Ostracized by his community and even imprisoned, he suffered profound diffi-culties that caused him severe pain. Yet he could be calm, even serene, in the belief that all of his suffering brought greater purification through which to receive God (Williams 1980, pp. 159–179).

His life choices provoke one to think about John in terms of the borderline personality. The workings of a "psychotic twin" are evident in his mental blankness. The persecutory anxieties he suffered are manifest in the external responses he elicited; borderline persons generally project their madness onto the environment. His acute sense of abandonment is characteristic of the borderline person as are his feelings of emptiness and his proclivity to seek out pain. Moreover, John's vision of suffering as a way to God suggests both good/bad split-ting and manic and omnipotent defenses—all borderline dynamics—to counter the opposing state of worthlessness. John may have been a borderline personality, but his influence upon spirituality and his un-derstanding of the complex states of mind he encountered during med-itation has made him an invaluable source of wisdom.

But one need not examine borderline logic and its relationship to various mystical systems of thought to recognize the link between borderline phenomenology and religious pursuit. Consider *The Diag-nostic and Statistical Manual of the American Psychiatric Association, Third Edition* (DMS III), which offers the following eight diagnostic criteria for the borderline personality disorder:

(1) Impulsivity or unpredictability in at least two areas that are potentially self-damaging, e.g., spending, sex, gambling, sub-stance use, shoplifting, overeating, physically self-damaging acts.

(2) A marked pattern of unstable and intense interpersonal rela-tionships, e.g., marked shifts of attitude, idealization, devalua-tion, manipulation (constantly using others for one's own ends).

(3) Inappropriate, intense anger or lack of control of anger, e.g., frequent displays of temper, constant anger.

(4) Identity disturbance manifested by uncertainty about several issues relating to identity, such as self-image, gender identity, long-term goals or career choice, friendship patterns, values, and loyalties, e.g., "Who am I?", "I feel like I am my sister when I am good."

(5) Affective instability: Marked shifts from normal mood to de-pression, irritability or anxiety, usually lasting a few hours and

only rarely more than a few days, with a return to normal mood.

(6) Intolerance of being alone, e.g., frantic efforts to avoid being alone, depressed when alone.

(7) Physically self-damaging acts, e.g., suicidal gestures, self-mutilation, recurrent accidents or physical fights.

(8) Chronic feelings of emptiness or boredom.

But these same criteria are a profile of the Old Testament Creator Yahweh, who certainly possessed at least five of them! He was impulsive and unpredictable in ways that were self-damaging. His relations with His people, Israel, were unstable and marked by idealization and devaluation. His anger was intense and often out of control, and He could behave ruthlessly, with a total disregard for His chosen people; He destroyed His own creation with a flood. His identity is diffuse and needed constant mirroring. His moods often changed capriciously.

Diagnostically speaking, Yahweh is a borderline personality. This is very instructive. If a borderline personality, He is also the supreme Light, source of the *numinosum*. In the Old Testament Yahweh's personality includes not only numinosity, creativity, and wisdom beyond any mortal frame, but *also* borderline characteristics. Perhaps we should ask if it is possible for a human being to touch the *numinosum* without also being borderline. Is the borderline characteristic of one who has suffered so much traumatic loss of the *numinosum* that the self's structure has been rent—split between a borderline pathology and a numinous Other (Beebe 1988)? In the figure of Yahweh the Light and the Dark are united, albeit in an often bewildering mixture; that combination of the positive *numinosum* and borderline characteristics is the mark of the creative genius of the Old Testament. This must be remembered amidst the essentially moral effort to separate Light and Dark qualities, as Jung does in his analysis of Job (1952). But paradox abounds, for unless one can separate out the Dark aspect of God, the Light is not incarnate (Jung 1942).

The truth of this becomes apparent as one learns to *see* the dead or blank self of the borderline personality and survive persecutory attacks and the suspension of mental processes that its "neither/nor" or negative logic induces. To reach and uncover the chronic states of abandonment so often in the foreground of treatment is an absolutely essential aspect of work with the borderline person, especially because these states of mind cover deeper layers of blankness and mind-destroying fury. If sufficiently embraced the *torment of abandonment may be seen as a rite of passage for an incarnating self.* Abandonment issues alone cannot explain the borderline condition, and to focus upon them at the expense of deeper levels of the *numinosum* and its incarnation results at best in firming up repression and creates a form of reality functioning that will, however, not facilitate embodiment of the self as a center in contact with the *numinosum.*

Treatment Issues: A Model of the Borderline Psyche

As a way of summarizing my thoughts on the treatment of borderline states I would like to develop a model, drawn in part from Bion's concept of a normal and a psychotic part of the personality, from Jung's alchemical researches, and from my own clinical experience of the importance in healing of both the negative and positive aspects of the *numinosum* as well as the discovery of an unconscious dyad. The psychotic part of a person contains the image of a child, who represents the true self, or soul. This child image often appears in a depleted or helpless state, a *dead self* not unlike Osiris languishing in the Underworld, attacked when he dared to rise up. Another image that presents itself is of a couple who are fused yet in a state of radical disunion. Violently rejecting separation, they are at the same time totally without genuine contact. Based on my clinical work with patients, I have found that the unconscious couple assumes a violent form, each member striving to attack the other; the female part often has a powerful phallus, and the male part is engulfing and mutilating. This couple at times manifests in interpersonal relations and causes confusion or a sadomasochistic interaction. But this interaction is already a defensive operation against experiencing the actual nature of the couple as an internal reality especially hateful toward the soul. The couple, locked in deadly combat, is actually a single double-sided object (Green 1977, p. 40) deeply antagonistic to the child held captive within its territory.

Thus the psychotic element contains the soul as well as an extremely persecutory dyad, a couple born "before the creation" when opposites were not yet separated. The dynamics operating within this dyad are complex and only to be inferred, but Jung's alchemical researches are a good guide. Should one regard the extremely destructive affects manifested by the psychotic part as the result of developmental traumas that have been split off from the normal, functioning ego? Or might these affects instead be the result of union experiences that include but are not simply reducible to historical antecedents? In *Mysterium Coniunctionis* Jung discusses texts that show how union at first creates what is identified in alchemy as the thief or devil, which assumes animal forms such as the rabid dog, snake, basilisk, toad, and raven (Jung 1955, par. 172). Prominent forms of the borderline person's shadow are the renegade, seeking to destroy anything positive or life-giving, and the seductive death drive (which Neumann calls uroboric incest), which lures the soul back into a regressive fusion and plays upon memories of its original experience of the *numinosum*.

It is important to have a dual understanding of these destructive contents. On the one hand they can be grasped as an introjective structure, built out of a continual need to deny through idealization the horror of one's early perceptions. In the process a kind of inner fifth column is created—what Bion represents as the lying *fiend* (Meltzer 1978, pp. 106ff), clearly calling upon the image of the devil, who personifies this destructive function in many religions. But on the other hand, extremely destructive states of mind are created through union, the products of which attempt to destroy the experience and any shred of the *numinosum*. The so-called negative therapeutic reaction is susceptible to containment only when both patient and therapist become conscious of the fact that a union experience, though barely perceptible, has occurred. These experiences, registered in dreams, are also felt as palpable occurrences between two people (Schwartz-Salant 1986, 1988a).

In work with the borderline person union is of special significance; through it the therapist introjects the person's previously split-off, helpless self, which, as I have noted, commonly takes the form of an injured or tormented young child. Union, including its resulting demonic products, can bring to light the patient's constant inner struggle: a battle between life and death fought by God and the Devil. When unconscious this conflict is manifest in sadomasochistic dyads that structure both inner life and external relationships. This sadomasochistic style creates a relatively safe territory for the patient, even though the toll in terms of relational failures and the undermining of creativity and all forms of self-assertion is high.

But when the truly demonic becomes conscious a new stage is set, one in which death through suicide, illness, or accident becomes a serious concern. At this stage the therapist often wonders if the other's splitting devices and unconsciousness might not have been a better state of affairs! But by helping the patient to face the death drive within the context of union—that is, to see its relationship to positive experiences—new self-images and a reason to live may be discovered. In alchemy, the previously dangerous forms (such as the rabid dog and the thief) become protective of the "child," which is the new self. In some mysterious way, the demonic aspects may be necessary to break up structures in the old personality so that a life of the true self can be lived.

Throughout this process the therapist's need to be in control poses a real threat, for in this pursuit he or she aligns with the "old king" ruling the normal, competent personality and may severely undermine the healing process by creating more splitting. *One needs the patient's help*; otherwise no collaboration can stand against the powerful forces of death and destruction.

To *see* that the psychotic part is also the link to the *numinosum* in the borderline person is, to my mind, crucial for the healing process. The existence of the archetypal level of healing through the *numinosum* can often be inferred within their *Neither Yes nor No* logic. But once their madness is more fully uncovered and mutually acknowledged, then the *numinosum* may be even more directly encountered as what Grotstein (1979) calls the "Background Object,"[6] a transcendent Self that is the soul's true home. The *numinosum* is often the last thing one expects to find amidst the confusion, splitting, and denial that can dominate treatment. But it is there, not created (through interpersonal relations), but rather as an *increatum* (an a priori state) and birthright. When the *numinosum* incarnates healing is near at hand.

But the forces of death or destruction must never be underestimated. The devil works at this stage as a trickster, luring the therapist into thinking all is well and splitting yet again from the other's madness. When the *numinosum* becomes part of the (normal-neurotic) functioning personality, often through the patient's imaginal sight, then we enter a phase in which the balance shifts toward life and against death.

The linking of the normal-neurotic and the psychotic part is a crucial treatment issue; the importance of imaginal sight has been underscored in this regard. Another point my clinical examples make clear is the therapist's need to remain vigilant and avoid splitting the other into "functioning" and "psychotic" parts; the borderline person's own splitting and denial can be so strong that the "normal" part will be favored. The parts must be seen as fragments of a whole.

There is yet another important aspect of work with the unconscious dyad. Discovering its existence and entering the imaginal process it engenders can lead to the transformation of the interactive field so that play and the transcendent function emerge. This transformed space is crucial because it allows for the possibility of precisely that linkage between the normal and psychotic personality that cannot be achieved through interpretation (Grotstein 1979, p. 175).

The borderline person lacks a transcendent function. This is not to say that a link between conscious and unconscious does not exist; in fact, a channel might freely bring the unconscious to consciousness. Rather, as André Green and others have emphasized (*see* Meissner 1984, pp. 55ff.), these individuals do not manifest transitional phenomena:

> Borderline patients are characterized by a failure to create functional byproducts of potential space; instead of manifesting transitional phenomena, they create symptoms to fulfill the function of transitional phenomena. By this I do not mean to say that borderline patients are unable to create transitional objects or phenomena. To say such a thing would be to ignore the fact that many artists are borderline personalities. In fact it can only be said that from the point of view of the psychic apparatus of such individuals, transitional objects or phenomena have no functional value, as they do for others. (Green 1977, p. 38)

What the borderline person lacks is a functional relationship between conscious and unconscious through which consciousness exerts an influence upon the unconscious. Thus he or she has little capacity to play with the unconscious, to affect it consciously and vice versa. Instead, the unconscious pronounces itself with very concrete associations to dreams which rarely lead to other associations, or with a random flood of ideas, or in polarized fashion with a total incapacity for free association and imagination. The borderline person may be a psychic or a creative personality of great gifts, yet he or she is a "receiver" for this information, rarely interacting with it in a meaningful way. Borderline persons can often use their psychic gifts to help others, but can do little for themselves. Subject to the unconscious, they feel totally helpless in the face of its contents. This is why creation of a transcendent function is especially crucial for the therapy of the borderline individual.

I suggest the model of a psychotic space inhabited by a parental couple still a single object, the negative hermaphrodite, wherein the soul is terribly afflicted by the renegade forces of death. Imaginal work with the unconscious dyad allows a transcendent function to emerge, linking the normal-neurotic and the psychotic parts of the individual. Throughout, vision is severely curtailed unless there is due recognition of the *numinosum*, that uncreated element that often fills the background or pollutes the normal personality, yet must be seen as the borderline person's true birthright and an essential source of healing.

Endnotes

1. The following statement by Claude Lévi-Strauss describes an approach to psychic material that precisely mirrors Jung's model, and, indeed, my own:

Many psychoanalysts would refuse to admit that the psychic constellations which reappear in the patient's conscious could constitute a myth. These represent, they say, real events which it is sometimes possible to date. . . . We do not question these facts. But we should ask ourselves whether the therapeutic value of the cure depends on the actual characterization of remembered situations, or whether the traumatizing power of these situations stems from the fact that at the moment they appear, the subject experiences them immediately as living myth. . . . The traumatizing power of any situation cannot result from its intrinsic features but must, rather, result from the capacity of certain events . . . to induce an emotional crystalization which is moulded by pre-existing structure . . . these structural laws are truly a-temporal. (1967, p. 197f.)

2. André Green's discussion of what he calls "tertiary processes" is pertinent here. He defines these processes as

not materialized but made of conjunctive and disjunctive mechanisms in order to act as a go-between of primary and secondary process. It is the most efficient mode of establishing a flexible mental equilibrium and the richest tool for creativity, safe-guarding against the nuisance of splitting, whose excess leads to psychic death. Yet splitting is essential in providing a way out of confusion. Such is the fate of human bondage, that it has to serve two contrary masters—separation and reunion—one or the other, or both. (1977, p. 41–42)

Green's "tertiary processes" link "conjunctive and disjunctive mechanisms," or, in our terms, the separating and conjoining aspects of the *coniunctio.* We also recognize the need for interpretation, which always involves some degree of splitting.

3. This clumsy interpretive attempt was useless to the patient and essentially stated to relieve my own discomfort.

4. In this discussion I have deliberately not focused upon the patient's maternal experiences, which certainly contributed to her splitting defenses. My impression, however, is that they may have had lesser developmental significance than the abandonment issues with her father.

5. In both positive and negative forms, the *numinosum* poses exceptional difficulties for the borderline patient. The *numinosum* is the root of religious experience. It is characterized by the most sublime as well as demonic qualities and always refers to an agency beyond conscious control. The *numinosum* seizes one, and though we might rely on all sorts of rational devices to weaken its effect, the fact remains that it is situated at the core of humankind's most central experiences. We find the *numinosum* implicitly contained in the psychoanalytic concept of primary process and in the emotional flooding and archaic imagery that dominate it. But this conceptualization fails to recognize the genuine transformative power of the *numinosum.* Jung has said that his entire approach toward healing was based upon the *numinosum* (1975). By this he meant that the ener-gies and structures of the archetypes have a powerful renewing potential, and that to imaginatively engage these "gods" and "goddesses" opens up healing paths which would otherwise rarely become actualized.

6. He writes that this "corresponds to the most archaic organizing internal object which offers background support for the infant's development. My conception of it is as one which is awesome, majestic, unseen, and behind one. It 'rears' us and sends us off into the world. In moments of quiet repose we sit on its lap metaphorically. In psychotic illness and in borderline states it is severely damaged or compromised." (1979, p. 154n)

References

American Psychiatric Association. 1980. *Diagnostic and Statistical Manual of Mental Disorders, Third Edition.* Washington, D.C.: APA.

Beebe, John. 1988. Primary ambivalence toward the self: Its nature in treatment. *The Borderline Personality in Analysis.* Wilmette, Ill.: Chiron Publications.

Copleston, F. 1985. *A History of Philosophy*, vol. 3. New York: Doubleday/Image.
Eigen, M. 1985. Toward Bion's starting point: Between catastrophe and faith. *International Journal of Psycho-Analysis* 66.
──────. 1986. The personal and anonymous 'I'. *Voices*. 21/3&4.
Green, André. 1977. The borderline concept. In *Borderline Personality Disorders*, P. Hartocollis, ed. New York: International Universities Press.
Grinberg, L. 1977. An approach to understanding borderline disorders. In *Borderline Personality Disorders*, P. Hartocollis, ed. New York: International Universities Press.
Grotstein, J. 1979. The psychoanalytic concept of the borderline organization. In *Advances in Psychotherapy of the Borderline Patient*, J. Le Boit and A. Capponi, ed. New York: Jason Aronson.
Jung, C. G. 1942. A psychological approach to the Trinity. In *Collected Works* 11. Princeton, N.J.: Princeton University Press, 1958.
──────. 1946. Psychology of the transference. In *Collected Works* 16. Princeton, N.J.: Princeton University Press, 1954.
──────. 1952. Answer to Job. In *Collected Works* 11. Princeton, N.J.: Princeton University Press, 1958.
──────. 1953. Psychology and alchemy. In *Collected Works* 12. Princeton, N.J.: Princeton University Press, 1968.
──────. 1955. *Mysterium Coniunctionis*. In *Collected Works* 14. Princeton, N.J.: Princeton University Press, 1963.
──────. 1975. *Letters*, vol. 2. Princeton, N.J.: Princeton University Press.
Kahn, M. M. R. 1974. *The Privacy of the Self*. London: Hogarth.
Lacan, J. 1977. *Ecritis*. A Sheridan, trans. New York: Norton.
Levi-Strauss, C. 1967. *Structural Anthropology*. New York: Doubleday.
McLean, A., ed. 1980. *The Rosary of the Philosophers*. Edinburgh: Magnum Opus Hermetic Sourceworks Number 6.
Meissner, W. 1984. *The Borderline Spectrum*. New York: Jason Aronson.
Meltzer, D. 1978. The Clinical Significance of the Work of Bion. In *The Kleinian Development*, Part III. Perthshire, England: Clunie Press.
Searles, H. 1979. Dual—and multiple-identity processes in borderline ego-functioning. In *Borderline Personality Disorders*. P. Hartocollis, ed. New York: International Universities Press.
Schwartz-Salant, N. 1986. On the subtle body concept in clinical practice. *The Body in Analysis*. Wilmette: Chiron Publications.
──────. 1988a. Archetypal foundations of projective identification. *Journal of Analytical Psychology*, 33:39–64.
──────. 1988. *The Borderline Personality: Vision and Healing*. Wilmette, Ill.: Chiron Publications.
Williams, R. 1980. *Christian Spirituality: A Theological History from the New Testament to Luther and St. John of the Cross*. Atlanta: John Knox Press. (British title: *The Wound of Knowledge*.)

Lines and Shadows:
Fictions from the Borderline

Randolph S. Charlton

Theoretical Shadows

There have been thousands of different drawings of the world, many maps made of reality. Each puts the gods, the good, the false and the true in a different place. They cannot each be correct—there are too many counterclaims—yet society after society has sailed to greatness (not simply to the doom they also doomed themselves to) following these false charts, these fictions that have been projected on the planet. And the planet, like the great screen of a drive-in movie, accepts them all, lighted by the illusions of passion, for as long as the passions last. If so, then our lives are made of fictions, beliefs we construct and then dwell in like a beach house in Malibu.

William H. Gass

No one becomes a psychoanalyst without worms gnawing at his soul.

Allen Wheelis

Randolph S. Charlton, M.D., is a member of the C. G. Jung Institute of San Francisco and a fellow of the American Academy of Psychoanalysis. He is a clinical associate professor of psychiatry and behavioral sciences at the Stanford University School of Medicine and maintains a private practice.

I would like to acknowledge a particular debt to Roy Schafer, whose work on the language and attitude of analytic practice has been invaluable. Many of my comments about the relevance of the multiple meaning and function of our psychological stories are reiterations of his wonderful presentations. I also wish to thank Dr. Louise B. Buck for reading over this manuscript and making helpful and supportive suggestions.

I

Come with me down a winding path into the shadows cast by our analytic identity.

It is a joy and a curse to be an analyst. Struggling in an honorable but impossible profession, we face inevitable frustration, limitations on the success of our efforts, and persistent difficulty even communicating how and what we do. The task of self-understanding is a demanding and always painful one, and many choose an easier course. Our analytic community is continually split by differences of opinion on theoretical and technical issues, so that even within a group of relatively like-minded analysts there is endless variation in how a particular clinical situation may be conceived and managed.

Nowhere are the problems of being an analyst greater than in coming to terms with a theory of the borderline person.

All theories of the mind involve world-making. The reality we perceive is the creation of the people we are and the theories we devise: avowed Jungians really do hear Jungian dreams and Freudians Freudian dreams. Truth is an unfaithful companion, a changeling child who alters form depending upon the criteria we use to find him. All of our psychological concepts—conscious/unconscious, ego/id, shadow/persona, neurotic, psychotic, and borderline, the use of spatial descriptions like above and below, superficial and deep, and the concepts of mind and soul themselves—are metaphors. Symbols in their own right, these terms do not refer to things we can touch, feel, or fully understand.

Sometimes, however, we reduce these metaphors of mental life to tangible *things*, some mundane, some fantastical, some secular, some profane. Then, girded for the moment in our conceptualizations, we are relieved of all uncertainty and behave as if we *know*. We profess and exhort, diagnose and treat, all the time assuring ourselves that we understand what we are doing. But what happens to those who believe they hold Psyche in the palm of their hand?

An analyst is not so much a detective searching for the truth, as a child, earnestly playing at finding the proper place for the pieces in a great jigsaw puzzle. Here the best criterion for relevance is not simply truth, but fit (Goodman 1978).

When presented with analytic theory or cogent case material some hear true stories. Our efforts to convey psychological truth, however, involve the creation of a multiplicity of fictions. An analyst's understanding is never exactly the analysand's story. It is our version, one version out of many.

In *The Analytic Attitude*, Roy Schafer (1983) eloquently argues that just as there are multiple understandings an analyst might use in his retelling of an analytic case, so there are multiple realities an analysand might focus upon in order to define, communicate, and shape his inner and outer worlds. The analysand has not just one true history, one life, one experience of analysis, but many; alternate channels of reality, each has its own theme, design, and intent. Similar to the open-ended symbolic approach of C. G. Jung, this view holds that there is no one positivistic reality, but a series of multiple possibilities, some with more truth, more coherence and narrative strength, more emotional and rational appeal, more symbolic potential.

Schafer, following literary critic Frank Kermode (1966), defines the term fiction not pejoratively as a set of untruths, but as

> an organized set of beliefs and a corresponding way of defining facts. A fiction amounts to a structuring principle or a shared vision of reality which can be shown to have some significance and usefulness but which is recognized as an approach to reality, rather than a picture of reality plain and simple. (p. 283)

As the great tales and myths which have survived from antiquity attest, there are many true versions of a story. The process of analysis involves the discovery of such fictions, ever more relevant, with ever better fit: tales multiply told, first by the analysand, who may believe he is telling the only truth, and later by the analyst, who offers views of the analysand's narratives from different levels and perspectives. Eventually, as consciousness and unconsciousness mingle together, new stories are born within the unique frame of interaction we call analysis, and tales are told by analysand and analyst together. The analyst for his part expends his efforts listening, wondering, questioning, being effected and affected, offering himself as an actor in the analytic play. He works to be aware of elements left out of story lines, hears contradictions not apparent, points out how one story hides or discredits another. He is aware that there is not one true fiction, but many, swirling within the depths, waiting to be discovered. In concert the analytic duo reconstruct the stories written by the analysand, making more of them than was made before.

II

Via the process of analysis we help explore the subjective reality of an analysand's fictions. But as analysts we also create fictions among and for ourselves, not to share with the analysand, but to structure, inform, and direct our own thoughts and actions. Existing on a level once removed from the actual analysis, these are the fictions of psychological theory or metapsychology.

The fiction of the borderline personality is one such metalevel abstraction.

Let me say the obvious: No human being is a borderline. Can a person *be* a line? A two-dimensional string? I think not. The idea of a borderline *person*, I believe, belongs not to the patients, but to the analysts.

When thinking of the so-called borderline patient, why do we not speak of a man without a country, a woman without a mother, a child without a family? As metaphors of internal experience these approximate the narratives conveyed by patients themselves in the analytic process. Although I suppose it possible, I have never heard an analysand spontaneously either in dream or association present himself, his sense of identity, his personality, or his reality as a borderline. A victim, an orphan, a seer, a prisoner, an outcast, a runaway; one torn between opposing choices, on the horns of a dilemma, split into pieces; a refugee, a nobody, an outsider: all of these are commonplace identities in patient narratives, but not the borderline.

Can an analyst tolerate a multiplicity of fictions about the patient with a borderline personality? One who falls across psychological boundaries all unawares, arriving on the other side with a crash? A Humpty Dumpty, who once broken cannot easily get back together again? One with no line of transit, no entrance or exit visa, no special relationship to the inner border guards? One who leaves pieces of his broken insides behind and recrosses internal borderlines as a glued-together shell?

Moving away from a literal viewpoint, to *be* a borderline might imply a personality that does not belong to any claimed territory; that functions as a divider, separating this from that; that is frozen in time and direction and cannot move; that does not exist in the world of three, or four, dimensions. Perhaps these metaphors will fit our jigsaw puzzle?

Analysands themselves do however present the *image* of the borderline when dealing with aspects of movement and resistance: in dreams of passing over borders, in images of a Berlin Wall which entraps and divides, in thoughts of moving from one place to another, in the desire for initiation, and the wish to become a different person. It is here that issues of the borderline are alive, woven into the matrix of stories analysands live out. When it tells us, not of a borderline *person*, but of compartments, demarcators and terminators, shades of color divided one from the other, foreign places and strange occurrences, the imaginal metaphor of the borderline belongs to the analysand.

III

The enormous increase in attention paid to the borderline personality, which reportedly makes up two to four percent of the general population in America, but may account for as much as twenty percent of those in psychological treatment (Gunderson 1986), is the product of optimism. For years thoughtful commentary had been directed toward those patients neither psychotic nor neurotic who did poorly in analysis, developed "malignant" regression, and experienced transient psychotic episodes as well as significant turmoil in interpersonal relationships (see Deustch 1942, Winnicot 1953, Knight 1953, Frosch 1960, Balint 1968, Guntrip 1969); but the mainstream of analysts paid only marginal attention. It took the infant-child observations and developmental theories of Margaret Mahler (1970, 1972, 1979), the structural descriptions and therapeutic strategies proposed by Otto Kernberg (1967, 1975, 1976, 1984, 1987), the growing interest in the psychology of the self (Kohut 1971, 1977), and a more general acceptance of ego psychology and object-relations theory to open a floodgate of interest in areas formerly on the borderline of analytic attention.

Rebounding from previous pessimism, the ensuing therapeutic zeal has clouded the great difficulties that attend exploring the borderline territories. In the present-day atmosphere it is uncomfortable for a therapist to acknowledge confusion, and the term borderline has become an epithet closely associated with shame. Frustrated therapists contemptuously exclaim, "Oh, that patient's impossible! He's borderline." Indeed, analysands have come to fear that they will be considered borderline. Some even co-opt the diagnosis, "I'm a mess. I feel like I'm coming apart. I must be borderline!" Would that we could discard this label, but I think it unlikely at this point. Perhaps even throwing away the diagnosis (something I routinely find myself doing after analysis begins) does not solve the dilemma, since the connection between shame and the borderline designation arises precisely because we are dealing with lives permeated with such feeling.

Approaching the borderline we often lose our analytic attitude, fall into intense emotion, become lost, bend or break the therapeutic structure, inadvertently resort to unconscious, unwise, and disorganized measures, and all too often feel ashamed ourselves when we fail in our attempts to understand and help.

The borderline, no longer a small, disreputable no man's land on a side street of analytic interest, has become a most popular spot for the psychological theorist to sojourn. It has been variously described as: a wastebasket diagnosis for patients who are neither neurotic nor psychotic (Knight 1953), a transient regressive state (Zetzel 1971), a stably unstable personality organization (Kernberg 1967), a medical-psychiatric disorder based upon discreetly definable symptoms (A.P.A., D.S.M. III), an analyzable cryptopsychosis (Kohut 1984), a developmental disorder involving the layered, complex sequelae of the failure to manage the rapprochement subphase of childhood separation-individuation (Mahler 1970), a structural disorder involving pathologically split rewarding and withdrawing object relations (Masterson and Rinsley 1975), a drive-related disorder of pathological aggression (Kernberg 1975), the result of a developmental defect involving the inability to function in a self-soothing manner (Buie and Adler 1982), a biopsychosocial disorder with probable organic and genetic components (Gunderson 1986), a condition afflicting patients whose psychoticlike core can best be apperceived via the analyst's emotional resonance (Searles 1978), a disorder involving individuals with split neurotic and psychotic identities (Grotstein 1982), part of the "widening scope" of disorders treatable by liberal psychoanalysis (Stone 1954), an illness amenable to couch psychoanalysis (Boyer 1982, Giovacchini 1979), an unanalyzable disorder of an irreversibly splintered self (Kohut 1971, Goldberg 1980).

Except for Machtiger's contribution (1984), which discusses how Jungian psychology "legitimizes" the borderline personality style, this bevy of observations, descriptions, and conclusions is based upon an admixture of psychiatry, psychoanalysis, ego psychology, and object relations. Volumes on how to find the borderland, what the countryside looks like, where the major attractions are, and what the mores and customs are often contradict each other. Discovering a single atlas reassures one that at least someone understands the complicated geography and architecture of the place. But examine the diaries of several travelers, and assurance is replaced with curiousity and question. If you are foolhardy, diligent, or driven enough to read on, wondrous confusion is just around the corner.

Clinical Lines

Borders between juxtaposition for exploration and juxtaposition for evasion are shadowy. No. There are no borders. Exploration and evasion fill the same room. M. Robert Gardner

It is a capital mistake to theorize in advance of the facts. Sherlock Holmes

What facts? Anonymous

I

How do analysts, each from a unique background and particular life experience, possessing individual talents and weaknesses, and of differing psychological attitude and type, understand the inner world of another person, whose life in and out of analysis is stormy and at times confusing, and whose experience, both past and present, is revealed over time in different and contradictory ways?

Here intersubjectivity, vicarious introspection, or if you will, empathy, is a risky but necessary business. The analytic process begins with empathy because without it there is no connection, no movement; but analysis based upon empathic immersion alone is like a stringless kite on a blustery day. Empathy is a changeable wind, unruly, fickle; like intuition and imagination it can reveal the possible and miss the inevitable. Empathy also takes its toll on the analyst. This is especially true with the borderline patient, where affective states fluctuate rapidly, where emotions are primarily used as communicative-motive agents, and where for a great period of time the emotional range is restricted to painfully traumatized and/or defensively restrained and/or righteously enraged affect images. Thrown into the miasma of his own feelings of impotent helplessness, pouting self-pity, shameful inadequacy, fear of physical injury, annihilating anxiety, bottomless emptiness, formless depression, and vengeful outrage, the analyst learns first-hand what the borderline knows well, having experienced a lifetime of such painful emotions. Without some form of anchor outside the empathic process, there is no connection to the ground; an analyst can fly off on the winds of emotion and become lost in the clouds. Oscillation between related immersion in the other and a differentiated, distanced position is necessary. In addition to a knowledge of human nature, the unconscious, and the process of analysis, the analyst needs a genius for the obvious and a pragmatic awareness of contradiction and nonsense.

II

Some time ago, directly after having had her tubes tied so she would "never have to be a mother," a twenty-six-year-old woman came to my office. Blonde, attractive, her face marred by anxious tightness, green eyes searching out the corners of the room, she sat down quickly, pulled her coat tight around her, and began without preamble or introduction: "I'm mixed up. I don't know what matters to me any more. I'm afraid I'm coming apart and I don't know what to do."

Three sentences. Five *I*'s. Two *I don't know*'s. One *me*. The very beginning is always an important part of any story. *What is she trying to say?* Images—mixed up, matter, coming apart. Emotions—afraid. Actions—coming, do. Passive Verbs—am, know. *What do you see?* Mixed-up matters coming apart? *What do you hear?* I am because I am mixed up? I'm coming, I do, I don't? *What do you know?* Nothing? Fear?

Words spilling out breathlessly, hands writhing, she rushed on to tell of a recent falling-out with her best, and in many ways only, woman friend. Devastated by the abandonment, she had become intensely frightened and lonely, hiding in her apartment, not going to work, spending her days watching television and eating cookies. Her sad, pleading tone made it clear she was desperately hungry for a relationship, some kind of response; yet she left no room for another, no space for a response.

For many weeks it was impossible to keep up with her emotionally pressured monologue on a rational basis, and I found myself responding to intimations of unconscious content. A kaleidoscopic mélange of images moved through my mind: red wine spilling from a jaggedly broken crystal goblet, a thorny rose, a wounded and cornered animal. When she tearfully characterized her mother as "not wanting to open her legs to let me be born," I imagined an infant trapped, alone, underground in the dark.

She was hopeless, complained that life was meaningless, and told of friends and family who had forgotten her. Since leaving home she had always lived alone. Lost, isolated, devastated, her associations were guided by the intensity of her emotion. Forgetting what she said almost as soon as it passed her lips, she was overwhelmed by a myriad of daily betrayals, remembered hurts, pressured dreams, and frantic pleas for help. She was an innocent victim, a mistreated and misunderstood child severely wounded by uncaring parents, fickle friends, and chauvinistic men. I did not debate the validity of such a tale, and soon realized that she drew my sympathy, left me wanting to offer not analysis but help, as one would a little girl who had fallen and hurt herself.

She presented the following initial dream:

Dream: *I am dressed in strange clothes. I realize that the outer layer is covered with dirt and grease and I strip it off only to find*

*another layer similarly soiled. I remove this to a third soiled layer
and take that off. I find my naked body covered with small black
spots which, on close inspection, are bugs. I begin to pick them off
one by one, and as I remove each they either pop or are replaced
by a spot of red blood, like a blister.*

What a story! Aren't you captivated? Magic, burlesque, danger,
blood. All the timeless makings of a Grimm tale. Three layers of magical, grimy clothes no less. Why three?

She had no direct associations and, as was often the case, had so
very much to get out during the hour that she rushed on to other
things. She often used the analytic process to evacuate painful inner
content and at times her dreams were like the bugs, disgusting things to
be picked off and squashed or thrown away (see Grinberg 1987). Her
dream posed themes central to all borderlines: a person alone with a
difficult, almost unmanageable task; the existence of a multilayered,
false self none too easy to remove; excessive dirt and shame; an invasion or infection; a deeply wounded instinctual body; the portrayal of
an innocent; and the experience of bloody suffering upon confrontation
with the problem. In the course of her analysis we would discover a
multitude of "bugs": anorexia, binge eating, shameful (to her) sexual impulses, abuse of laxatives, the enraged beating of a pet, doors
slammed so hard they break, intractable lower back pain, self-destructive actions, including an eventual suicide attempt, and memories and
fantasies of a childhood not fit for a dog.

As the analytic process took hold she reported another dream:

Dream: *I was somewhere and my parents called me. They sounded
upset. It felt like a situation you might see on T.V. There was a man
there with me and I wanted to explain it to him so that he could
understand the feelings in his body. I kept trying to do it so Mother
would not find out as I would then get into trouble.*

People have entered her inner world, but her dream-parents, pale
shadows vaguely upset instead of wrathful as we would later encounter
them, are as yet experienced only at a distance. One man is "there" and
she wants him to understand *her* feelings in *his* body. There is the
fear/desire of merging self and other, a veiled sexual reference under
the gaze of the Terrible Oedipal Mother. As the hour went on she
related an incident in which a man had promised to call but never did.
She told of waiting up all night, and her anger mounted until she glared
at me and shouted at the top of her lungs, "I hate you, Randy! [Like

other relationship-starved individuals was she straining immediately to know me well enough for first names?] I'd like to take a knife and slice your damn chairs, your fucking couch! Watch them bleed and suffer and not move an inch to help as they cry out in pain. No guilt, just satisfaction." Suddenly, I was pushed into feeling what it was like for her to be in her family, what it was like to be inside her psyche. I knew first-hand the wounded child and the enraged parent, the enraged child and the wounded parent. These were simultaneously her versions of people and relationships from the past and inner aspects of her present psychic reality, for the moment become *our* psychic reality. In the silence that followed her outburst, I had my first taste of understanding *her* feelings in *my* body. My autonomic nervous system responded and my skin grew cold, my testicles drew up, and my stomach turned sour.

As young children, borderline individuals learn that dependency, trust, and revelation of self bring disappointment and pain. This woman's tortured, angry outburst was a tentative step toward allowing me into her innermost world. I avoided genetic or symbolic interpretation of this and other early encounters, realizing that most anything I said would be misheard, either as a demand that she stop her attacks, as the defense that I was an innocent party, or as punishment for her rebellious outrage. When she saw that I did not die or retaliate, she apologized profusely and reverted to her loquacious suffering. As Kernberg (1987) has noted of the borderline transference, conviction and relevance must come from the present and interpretation of the past is most useful when the dynamics of present relationships are in hand. I believe this is likewise true for constructive or archetypal interpretation of dream and symbol.

As intermittent forays toward dropping her ego defenses proved tolerable and elements of trust and dependency began to coalesce, there soon came a stage when she could not differentiate herself from me or the multitude of images and feelings which sprang helter-skelter out of her. For a long time I *was* the wonderful, the horrible, or the wounded; or the indifferent self, parent, child, dog, or god; and she was inseparably joined with me through her experience of the opposing pole of any particular complex. In the grasp of this regressive delusional transference she was not capable of interpreting anything symbolically, but like a pre-abstract child took everything literally, even (or maybe particularly) unconscious perceptions. Conscious awareness of metaphor, fiction, and multiple levels of psychic reality did not exist for her. We were now living her fictions fully and everything was seen through the eyes of her divided and split-off complexes. Her inner child did not know her inner parent, the obedient child was ignorant of the rebellious one, left did not recognize right, and top and bottom did not meet in the middle. As her introductory comment suggested, mixed-up matters had truly come apart.

For a time we lived like Coyote of the old Indian tales, not knowing one end of ourselves from the other. Like a battle-fatigued war veteran she began to reexperience, and reenact, terrible primal injuries. In dreams men would hit, bite, and pinch her, tie her up and leave her, lock her in a closet for days, chase her threateningly, and abuse her sexually. Here she was the victim. These experiences soon entered into the consulting room as she either "did" them to me or felt that I was "doing" them to her. I felt battered, beaten, abused, defeated, and demoralized. I was the victim to her torturer. My very sense of adequacy, of identity, of self was constantly and thoroughly threatened.

It was helpful for me to know that these images, actions, and feelings were part unremembered memories, part a child's imaginative response to overwhelming stimulation and unbearable abandonment, and part an attempt to reach toward assertiveness and individuation. Silently, and sometimes out loud, I wondered about various combinations of painful childhood experience, primitive fantasy, and psychological defense. I commented on her vicious, destructive attacks, wondering if she had experienced something like them, wondering about a desire for revenge. I looked and hoped (I had to carry Hope for both of us) for the breaking through of a compensatory masculinity to balance her alienation from men and her one-sided, severely wounded, hyperfeminine ego. I feared the good-enough, strong and firm mother was dead and it took my own analysis to keep that part of myself alive and protected from insidious assault. Dreams of murder, torture, and death burst from her underworld as drawn-and-quartered dream animals cried out and died. What tenuous wholes there were within came apart, and the building blocks of her core were scattered into her dreams and our analytic relationship.

We had begun, and as often happens in this kind of case, before very long I was wondering how we would ever finish.

III

The psyche is always composed of multiple identifications and we express our crowded internal world in the variety of confused, contradictory, and compromised actions and stories we live. Carl Jung understood something of our many-headed personality, composed of multiple seats of initiative and vulnerable to dissociation. For him, consciousness was not the unquestioned master of the psychic house, but one resident among many, holding power only temporarily. Unconscious complexes often co-opt the ego, forming nonobjective, emotion-filled seats of control. Jung believed such complexes coalesce into personalities. Made up of personal identifications, emerging aspects of self, and archetypal impersonal characters, our inner lives are crowded with action, movement, and conflict. Behind it all Jung saw an inner pattern, a developing organization, a striving toward individuality, a supraordinate self. Like a Shakespeare overseeing the dreams of a midsummer's night, or a Tolstoi moving and being moved by the patterned *Totentanz* between Vronsky, Anna, and Mother Russia, an inner self offers the possibility of integration of multiple identities each with disparate aims, affects, and thoughts.

In Jungian terms the borderline personality is unique not in the vertically split nature of his identity, for this is seen as commonplace, but in a psyche splintered into multiple components and dominated by bipolar affect-images of a victim-aggressor complex which attacks the relationship between a weak ego and the self. Neumann (1964) believed that it is the mother who initially functions "as" the child's self. The obverse of this is that aspects of the first experience of the child's inner self are introjected, or rather reflected, from the relationship with the mother. Like sensitive tuning forks the child vibrates to the mother's tones/tunes and the mother vibrates in turn to the child. To paraphrase Winnicot, there is no child without an other. If the child experiences inordinate victimization in the early parental relationship, dread of the self becomes a source of terrible anxiety and destruction. In rational developmental terms: if children learn that abandonment, contempt, and physical distress follow being noticed, successful achievement of age-appropriate skills, and genuine interpersonal confrontation and struggle, they will withdraw, hide their most real selves, take in elements of the frightening world around them, and act toward themselves (and eventually toward others) in the way in which they were treated.

IV

There are other types of regressive movement across borderlines, some not themselves traumatic. Although the dynamics here resemble those we have been discussing, there are important differences.

Fred Pine (1985) describes the forerunner of this condition in borderline children who exhibit "shifting levels of organization" in the face of growing anxiety. As their dysphoria reaches severe levels, they flee from it by regressing to earlier, more primitive modes of functioning, leaving behind age-appropriate behavior and ego organization to voice peculiar ideas, act strangely, withdraw emotionally, and finally cease to communicate altogether. While this regression appears externally to be similiar to other borderline conditions, it is substantially different in that it does not produce anxiety. It is ego-syntonic and serves the *successful* defensive function of avoiding a disturbing reality. This defense is internally adaptive, but in terms of initiation into new levels of a freer and more complex psychic reality, it is at the very least a barrier to growth and maturation, and at worst a catastrophe.

When these people reach adulthood they continue to manifest multiple personality organizations, the most developed patterns being vulnerable to dissolution in the face of anxiety.

For example, a professional man, who though often depressed usually functioned quite well in his work, would at times become "lost in a daydream world." He would withdraw from his colleagues, friends, and family, stare blankly into the distance, talk to himself, become irritable, and behave in an unrelated manner that frightened those around him. His ability to think clearly and function adequately was severely impaired during these times.

In his daydreams he lived in a private fantasy where worlds were brought to the edge of collapse but in the blink of an eye he could magically rescue them.

Fleeing into these daydreams particularly when feelings of anger or destructiveness approached, he ran from his terror of the effects of conflict and disagreement, of aggression and rage, into a world where people were destroyed but easily resurrected, where his strange guttural phrases were beautiful poetry and telepathy and telekinesis were everyday occurrences.

Different from the woman with the dream of the three layers of clothes, whose coming apart was accompanied by enormous apprehension and dysphoria, for this man regression did not accompany emotional pain, but relieved it! His regressed, primitive retreat into one compartment of the unconscious provided him with a haven from fears and anxieties his more developed personality organization recognized, but was unable to manage. Experience of one chamber of his inner world was defensively substituted for a fuller, yet terrifying confrontation with the totality of his psychic reality.

This process resembles the classic neurotic use of regression as a defense from oedipal anxieties, and in part this was occurring, but the situation was more complex in that his personality was not primarily structured around triadic oedipal wishes and fears, but around the same type of victim-aggressor dyads which are common within the borderline personality.

In the therapy of such adults, and to a large extent for all border-line individuals, it is not enough to be empathically holding, or to amplify unconscious images contained within fantasy and dream. Emotional support and synthetic interpretation may allow for maintenance of the higher level of personality functioning, but will not alone affect defensive use of the more primitive organization still called into play in times of anxiety.

Analysis requires careful observation of the *shifts* in the use of fantasy and the accompanying ego-self status. Pointing this out, bringing the analysand back to the moment of the shift within the analytic hour, the analyst helps the patient work toward explication of the nature of the provoking stimuli, the defensive gain in regression, and eventually the historical genesis of its use (see Pine 1985, pp. 212–13). Here the initital movement of analysis involves forsaking protective, but dead, regressive fantasy.

In the case at hand the patient was able to use confrontation and interpretation of his fears to begin the task of relinquishing his protective daydreams. Becoming aware of his own internal conflict, he recognized that when faced with anger and frustration he continually disavowed his own feelings by giving up the highest level of psychic function, where he could perceive imminent conflict, and moving to a more primitive level of organization where perceptual abilities and cognitive function were limited and magical fantasy ruled omnipotent. As therapy progressed there was a therapeutic return of anxiety; he felt himself getting "worse," and wanted to quit.

In his search for understanding and relief he became interested in Jungian psychology. The time previously spent daydreaming he spent reading Jung's *Collected Works*. Intelligent and genuinely interested, he went to seminars and public lectures, absorbing ideas, terminology, and techniques. Finding the notion of personification of his inner world particularly fascinating, he discovered his "shadow," a voluble, physically indomitable anti-hero, a beguiling "anima," an infirm, crazy old lady, and a puckish gnomelike child. These personalities gave him latitude to discuss for the first time many of his hidden and feared impulses, feelings, and needs, and for several months he made significant progress.

Something, however, remained amiss, for what began with a spark of life and a sense of spontaneity quickly became dry and dead. The sense of emotional excitement evaporated, and I found myself becoming sleepy, as I had previously during his repeatedly presented daydreams. While he talked of the complexities of alchemical transformation, of *coniunctio* and *nigredo*, of *participation mystique*, the transcendent function, and numinosity, nothing was happening.

Finally I asked him if he might have replaced one set of daydreams with another. He was incensed. "How could a Jungian analyst say such a thing? I'm doing just what Jung did!" he exclaimed, arriving in the hours that followed with volumes of Jung in hand to show me passages confirming the reality of his interests.

My sleepiness disappeared. Certainly not because he was reading Jung to me, but because he was angry! He maintained his emotion, blasting me up one side and down the other at length, able finally to do what had once been forbidden to him. He began to write a new story of himself, one in which he could fight, disagree with me, know more about Jung than I did, and still survive, even flourish.

After a time he left his literal incorporation of Jung's vision behind to find one of his own, realizing that in part he had been repeating the defensive regression using Jung's concepts, but missing something of Jung's creativity and soul-wrenching turmoil. He came to see that the center of Jung's method was not simply the description and labeling of specific figures of the unconscious, but the quest for one's own story, which to be a living reality must spring spontaneously *from within*.

I have found it not uncommon for analysands, particularly those with borderline conflicts, to use personification of unconscious figures not primarily to confront the inner world, but to deny and distance it. By giving dream figures names, by calling them "someone else," as this patient came to say, they may fail to come to grips with the idea: This is *me* and I am responsible. They may retreat from the painful uncertainty involved in the birth of one's own mythology, splitting off unpleasant, frightening aspects of the self.

In this case the use of personification was helpful as a middle stage in which the patient could begin to work with the notion that aspects of his personality went beyond his usual vision. In order to fully come to terms with his psychic reality he had to discard the arcane terminology and the metaphors of Carl Jung to find his own words and concepts.

Like this man, borderline individuals have a disordered relationship to initiation. The process of giving up a known reality to accept the challenge of a new, larger, more developed, more sophisticated world is constantly thwarted and the symbolic ordeal of the vision quest eternally rejected. In the most common borderline situation (experienced by the woman analysand) this involves anxiety-ridden, regressive collapse into a primitive, terrifying fusion with a dismissive hateful other. There is no chance of initiation into a wider circle as the world is repeatedly experienced in terms of the sadomasochistic warfare in which, as the immortal Pogo once said, "We have met the enemy and they are us." In a second type of borderline situation (that encountered by the professional man) there is no anxiety associated with regressive collapse; instead the desperate retreat to a reassuring and soothing set of fictions voids the possibility of forward movement. In both cases there is no shortage of unconscious imagery; in fact, sound and fury abound. The problem is not the loss of unconscious potential, but the single-minded, clinging defensiveness of a beleaguered ego.

Theoretical Lines

> *We know that the first step towards attaining intellectual mastery of our environment is to discover generalizations, rules and laws which bring order into chaos. In doing this we simplify the world of phenomena; but we cannot avoid falsifying it, especially if we are dealing with processes of development and change.* Freud
>
> *There is a theory which states that if ever anyone discovers exactly what the Universe is for and why it is here, it will instantly disappear and be replaced by something even more bizarre and inexplicable.*
>
> *There is another which states that this has already happened.* Douglas Adams

I

Analysts like Kernberg (1967, 1975, 1976, 1984), Masterson (1976), and Adler (1985) have described principles thought to unite all borderline personalities. Each has put forward a point of view giving special emphasis to one or another element of unconscious dynamics or treatment strategy. Kernberg's influential ego psychology–object relations theory differs from others in its broad approach. Rather than a limited personality disorder, he sees a stable and specific organizational malfunction of the personality that involves identity diffusion, the use of primitive defenses, and difficulties in reality testing. Thus severe narcissistic, masochistic, and self-destructive character disorders are grouped together under the rubric of borderline-personality organization.

Acknowledging that the borderland is an amorphous and diffuse territory, Grinker et al. (1968), Pine (1985), Gunderson (1984) and others have tried to divide it into smaller municipalities, each with its own related but individual dynamics and common experience. Meissner (1984) separates the borderline territory along hysterical and schizoid continuums registering the degree of emotional expressivity and defensive style of the person. He suggests that eight categories are necessary to define the breadth of the borderline spectrum:

> (1) instinctual defects of excessive (pathological) aggression, (2) failures in the maturity of the ego's defensive functions, (3) defects in the ego's organization and integrating functions, (4) a variety of failures of the normal developmental process, (5) the type of narcissistic defects described by self psychology, (6) faulty object relations, (7) a false self organization, and (8) aspects of identity diffusion. (p. 35)

Other analysts, including Winnicott (1975), Searles (1978), Kohut (1971, 1977, 1980), Boyer (1982), Giovacchini (1979), Modell (1968), Khan (1978), Green (1977), Little (1966), and Gedo (1979), less concerned with the creation of a descriptive nosology, have put their energy toward describing a particular kind of internal world and the analyst's experience of entering into it.

In their summary of ego psychology Gertrude and Rubin Blanck (1979) suggest that the use of such a categorization as the borderline is "felicitously chosen," as these patients reveal a variegated pattern of ego functioning in that elements of adequate or high function are adjacent to primitive and inadequate function, requiring not a diagnostic category, but a therapeutic approach to variable organizational malfunctions of the ego.

In spite of many differences, common elements exist across these views. They all utilize observations and formulations of the interrelationship between an infant-child and his earliest caretaking environment, drawing conclusions about the first internalization process, the formation of a sense of self, and the consequences of a damaged, split, or conflicted identity.

Implicit in these commentaries is a spectrum of distinction between the structuralized dynamics of the postoedipal neurotic personality, which deals in "whole" objects, developed defensive operations, and intrapsychic conflict between various agencies of a mind that has attained a cohesive and functional stability, and the borderline personality, which deals in preoedipal relationships composed of unintegrated, "split" objects, primitive editions of intrapsychic defenses, and a splintered, vulnerable identity which, lacking the cohesion to offer a place upon which the personality might stand to experience intrapsychic conflict, divides into various self and object complexes.

II

Let me present a complex narrative: a developmental and descriptive fiction, a metapsychological tale that contains several interrelated ways of understanding and organizing reality but is not itself reality. Woven into this narrative are some of the stories I as an analyst use to understand the plight of the borderline analysand.

Adults we call borderline were once severely mistreated children, or at the very least, they experienced themselves that way.

Following failures in the earliest nurturing and mirroring environment, the development of a prospective borderline person's first inner world is defective in quality and internal cohesion. Mother-infant observation (Mahler 1970, 1979, Mahler et al. 1975), analytic treatment of children and interaction with their families (Pine 1985), and reconstruction from the analyses of adults (Stolorow and Lachmann 1983; Dorpat 1982) indicate that significant inconsistencies and deficits in holding, feeding, and loving of the child are present. Physical and emotional unavailability or overinvolvement of confused, needy parents who fail to adequately separate their own needs and those of the infant; abusive physical or sexual cruelty; and, as Masterson and Rinsley (1975) have demonstrated, reward for regressive behavior and abandonment or punishment for developmental strivings are commonly found. Constitutional givens and/or a reactionary response to less-than-adequate conditions and/or extraordinarily poor infant-parent matching lead the level of frustration, anger, and rage in the child to rise toward unmanageable levels and the experience of victim and aggressor is entrenched within the evolving psychic world. Buie and Adler (1982) suggest that the lack of empathic, good-enough parenting leaves a child unable to develop adequate self-caring and soothing abilities. This places a strain on the infant-child, who cannot manage to integrate conflicting interpersonal relationships and the internal state into a smoothly functional whole. Kaleidoscopic movement from almost-annihilated victim to enraged aggressor, from the depths of inferiority to extreme inflation, reflects the tumultuous experience of early object relationships.

As children strive to obtain love from parents experienced as hostile or disinterested, patterns of primitive masochistic self and object interaction become part of the developing identity. In an effort to maintain a connection and manage rising anxiety they learn to be selectively sensitive—not to feelings emerging from within, but to feelings existing around them. Particularly familiar with contempt, depression, deadness, dismissal, anger, and blame, children contend with these by

accepting roles as the object of such feeling. This masochistic orientation protects the parent from facing inner conflict by taking one pole of
it away, thus preserving for the child a connection to a less-conflicted,
partially mollified object. These children do not enjoy suffering *per se*,
but need it as a prerequisite to attain the security of a bond to loved
ones.

In the words of psychoanalyst Albert Lubin:

> Though he complains bitterly of his misery, the masochist tends to mini-
> mize or deny himself the affect of depression. The affect is distilled out of
> the depressive mixture, leaving behind a residue of depressive ideation.
> Depression is infectious; gloom spreads in its wake. But, partly because of
> this dissociation between affect and thought, masochism stirs resentment
> and recrimination, and the masochist is sometimes condemned as a fraud
> who exaggerates his woes. Analysis, however, discloses profound unhap-
> piness.

> The depressive feels the misery inside himself and blames himself for it.
> Using provocative behavior, the masochist manages to cause others to
> bring it on him. This helps him to deny the inner unhappiness. Through
> externalizing it, he can exhibitionistically appeal for help and sympathy,
> righteously express anger toward his persecutors and absolve himself of
> guilt. These safety valves are not available to the depressive. The expres-
> sion of anger in itself is an antidote against depression. (1966)

The borderline personality contains both masochistic and depressive compromises, leading toward a confusion of oscillating psychological states.

The presence of primitive victim and aggressor identifications re-
duces the potential for the emergence of a normal pattern of integration of identity. The forms of unavailability and persecution actually experienced (Kohut, Guntrip, Masterson) and/or fantasized (Kernberg
stresses the combination of infantile fantasy and parental difficulties)
function to attack any glimmer of newly won selfhood and signs of independence, success, or innate talent are soon met with an internal assault. Hope, which may spring eternal for some, becomes a harbinger
of potential vulnerability and is often the first thing to be bludgeoned to
death.

With much energy dispersed in the effort to manage an unmanageable situation, distortions in perception and their conscious acknowledgement arise, leaving the child vulnerable to confusion between interior and exterior, self and other. The sense of time is, as
Hortocollis (1983) illustrates beautifully, so distorted that the past and
future are not coherently linked to the present: there is only an ever-
present, ever-threatening now.

In the best of times the sense of identity is seamless and unfelt, but in this circumstance the unconscious, autonomous unfolding of development becomes separated from the building of the child's identity. The inner world, fraught with danger and conflict in the most vital relationships, becomes more and more confused and distanced from the instinctual maturational pattern (see Modell 1985). Instead of a relatively secure sense of self there is created a fragmented, endangered multiplicity of self-images competing one with the other and with primitive, internalized object-images of rejecting and punishing figures, leaving little room for an emerging *I*.

The father of a prospective borderline person has often abandoned the family entirely or been lost to ambition, alcoholism, or drug abuse. He is usually remembered by the borderline adult in extreme terms; either as frightening, intrusive, and abusive, or as weak, spineless, and lacking a useable, digestible masculinity. His sexuality is perceived as a weapon or as impotently limp, and his nurturing side is spoiled by a combination of weakness, ambition, aggression, and narcissism. It is difficult to unravel the many narratives of him, for he is often coated with memories and feelings displaced from the early mother; sometimes his own conflicts lead him to yield to a primitive mother's pathological compromises (Volkan 1982). However, he can also be independently involved in the child's victimization, either passively, by not relating to the child in an authentic and helpful manner, or actively, via episodes of sexual abuse, beating and battering, and authoritarian attempts at control and domination.

In this world of danger and injury interactions come to involve a painful sensitivity to separation; the child does not grow to experience himself as independently secure in space and time, but fears that aloneness will cause damage or annihilation. This leads toward what Modell (1985) terms a transitional relationship, in which connection to another offers magical protection from the threat of dissolution of the self. However, an internal sense that the other exists as a whole person with both good and bad aspects, and is consistently present over time, is either absent or fragile. Aggression in the service of separation-individuation becomes threatening. Motivation is not mainly pleasure, but freedom from unpleasure. Perceptions leading toward hurt, anger, disappointment, or dissimilarity with an ideal self image are disavowed, and emerging aggressive impulses are suppressed, masochistically turned into provocative behavior and/or turned against the self. The disproportionate level of dependent need for the presence of the other leads to the desire/fear of being swallowed up, and the risk of loss of self appears again: Scylla and Charybdis. This need-fear dilemma has no solution other than to cover it and the real, yet painfully desperate sense of self with a distancing, rigid and false identity (Winnicott 1975), or to continue walking an impossible tightrope between just-enough closeness and just-enough distance.

Self-contempt, self-disgust, self-pity, and self-hatred, the four horse-men of self-destruction, become firmly linked to the body. Just as the formation of the earliest self is primally linked to the physical, the con-tinual autonomous striving toward emergence of a functional, cohesive self is likewise bound to the physical, and the body becomes a gladia-torial arena in which the bloody battle for selfhood will be fought. The experience of victimization often includes attack upon the developing sense of gender identity, and the child responds with a sense of injury and insecurity about gender adequacy. Body image, security with mas-culine and feminine identifications, and eventual erotic preferences, both for activity and fantasy, are influenced. The adolescent and adult masturbation fantasies of these individuals are particularly replete with images of submission, pain, injury, reversal, and revenge (see Stoller 1976).

Defenses called into play to manage the child's intolerable anxiety and painful affect are multiple. At this level of development repression fails, and the multiplicity of good and bad affect-images are kept apart via the splitting of self and object complexes, alternating projection of one pole and identification with the other (Kernberg 1975). The ma-jority of the personality remains involved with dyadic relations, but elements of triadic, oedipal, and other more developed conflicts do emerge. A rigid, punitive conscience coalesces out of primitive moral directives and forms its own set of multiple compromises (Brenner 1982) based primarily upon talion-organized victim-aggressor dyads. As more mature defenses are sporadically discovered by a beleaguered ego and merge into earlier compromises, primitive conflict and a fragile self are confusingly embedded within islands of structuralized conflict.

In later relationships that allow for significant regression, such as work, friendship, marriage, parenthood, or analysis, higher level com-promises come unraveled and both the inner and outer world become places of fascinatingly dangerous magic. Craters appear in the ability to think rationally *and* the ability to think symbolically. The already existing problem appreciating multiple levels of meaning worsens. Unpleasurable emotion no longer acts to spur the person into resolving action, and a disorganizing sense of imminent annihilation reemerges.

Intense bouts of depression fluctuate with states of primitive, presexual masochism. Disconnected emptiness, desperate clinging, tearful pleading, exhibitionistic self-destructiveness and righteous outrage flicker in and out of existence like images on a movie screen.

III

A multilayered, multidimensional transference emerges with the borderline analysand. While a discrete and differentiated transference-constellation may in the later stages of treatment coalesce into a coherent whole, the initial situation is marked by the development of a complex and fluid transference which often reaches delusional proportions wherein the patient no longer distinguishes reality from fantasy. The analyst ceases to be perceived *as if* he were a savior or a terrible demon, and *becomes* such a godlike being. Then, in various mixtures, elements of the narcissistic transference described by Kohut (1977)— mirroring, idealizing, and the alterego—interdigitate with elements of the split pre-oedipal victim-aggressor dyad.

This is often difficult to sort out because of a double oscillation between projection and identification on the one side, and various transference dyads on the other. For example, a borderline man began an hour working hard at associating, yet seemed to be uninvolved in his comments. This superficial, compliant, obedient patient-self (which was tied to a demanding, yet fragile parental other) was something we had seen and discussed many times. As he talked on he came to imagine that I was sitting behind the analytic couch sound asleep. Then he felt himself the innocent, misunderstood victim of my callous and uncaring disinterest. When a few moments later I asked about the suffering tone of voice which had taken over from his initial cheerfulness, he proceeded to "flip" the situation, saying coolly that he didn't care if I was asleep because I never said anything worth listening to anyway. For a brief time he felt expansive, enlarged, big and powerful, not needing anybody. As we tried to understand his response, the transference changed again and he became tentative, began stuttering, and seemed frightened. A small, terrified child was now relating to a monstrously enraged parent. Surrounding all of this, perhaps containing all of it, was the idealized vision of me as a magical being whose proximity provided safety and cohesion for the scattered elements of his identity.

As regression beyond the outer layer of defenses proceeds, connection to the analyst becomes vital to the survival of the more naked self, which is revealed in all its vulnerability. Separation of self and other falls away and the analyst is thrown across several borderlines into the world of preverbal psychology.

Now the rules and frame of the analysis become incorporated into the analyst-patient dyad and take on deep-seated presymbolic meanings; that is, while we require a symbolic vocabulary to speak of such a situation, the borderline analysand experiences only a concrete reality with no multiplicity of meaning, shading, or nuance. Now hatred causes death, desire means consummation, and hunger for another is cannibalism. In this situation both the analyst and the analysand are in the realm where soul murder, annihilation of the sense of identity, destruction of the connection to the self, are no longer simply stories; all are experienced as reality. Encounters around the frame of therapy, which for borderline analysands are ubiquitous and momentous, become occurrences within the physical body of the fused analyst-patient. Heart pains, physical numbness, gut-wrenching cramps, desperate hunger, panic unto death, genital stimulation, and even soothing inner warmth become somatic expressions of fluctuations in the body-as-frame of the analytic relationship.

Errors, some of which are humanly unavoidable, some of which involve underestimating the importance of such frame issues as confidentiality, neutrality, money, time, and the unconscious communication contained in the analyst's behavior and verbal comments, become the vital crucible in which the outcome of the therapeutic endeavor is determined. Times when the analyst misunderstands, misinterprets, or mismanages the structure of the analysis are experienced as abandonment and attack, their meaning filtered through the unconscious of the patient. Exquisitely sensitive to the unconscious meaning in another's behavior, borderline analysands exhibit an intensification of the victim-aggressor relationship when the analyst's efforts include attempts to discharge his own anxieties and impulses into the patient. As the victim-aggressor dyad is an integral aspect of the internal world of the borderline and an inevitable aspect of the unraveling of the borderline's painful psychic experience, it becomes particularly important for the analyst to be attuned to the ways in which his behavior involves elements traumatic to the analysand. It is all too easy at this point for the analyst to become frustrated and defensively dismiss the patient's outrage, violent acting out, or cringing fear as "borderline." As Goodheart (1984) and Parks (1987) have both pointed out, there is often a reality, albeit distorted, behind the analysand's perception of the analyst; it is paramount that the analyst examine his own behavior in the search for a meaningful and relevant fiction behind the analysand's responses.

Often, repeating the original childhood process of traumatic injury and defensive disavowal, the analysand cannot allow himself to know the intensity of his perceptions and feelings about the analyst and then associations will involve images of victimization displaced from analysis onto others, or if of the self and analyst, displaced in time, import, and initiating stimulus.

IV

Many have recognized that the composition of the borderline psyche is very close to that of the narcissist. Modell (1985) differentiates the two by noting that the borderline has a basically psychotic structure whereas the narcissist does not. Buie and Adler (1982) believe that therapy of the borderline largely involves recognition and analysis of a major narcissistic sector. Kernberg (1975) includes the narcissist among those with a borderline-personality organization. Kohut stated that the true borderline exhibits an irreversibly divided self, yet in his last work (1984), he presents a case vignette of a "borderline patient" who makes the transition to narcissistic dynamics as steadfast, empathic analysis allows for a stable form of narcissistic transference to develop. Thus for Kohut an analyzable borderline becomes by definition a narcissistic analysand. Clinically, while there is a significant overlap between the two, the centrality of the victim-aggressor dyad is greatest in the borderline and decreasingly influential as patients become more clearly narcissistic.

Borderline and narcissistic patients are inordinately susceptible to shame, borderline individuals more often responding in a sadomasochistic manner, narcissistic patients revealing grandiose and depressive responses. At times the borderline's shame is invisible, hidden behind withdrawal or violent and chaotic actions, yet remains prominent internally. Shame more than most emotions leads to an intensification of conflict, for it tends to feed upon itself; one is ashamed of feeling ashamed (Wurmser 1981). The borderline person often seeks out relationships in which the connection is woundedness—not out of guilt as does the triadically structured masochist, but in part as an attempt to reenact a particularly binding kind of dyadic love relationship. The cycle of shame and masochistic compromise can rarely be broken without the help of an outside person to whom the judging function of the self is bequeathed; in Kohut's terminology there is a need for a valuing selfobject.

Clinical Shadows

A human being hardly ever thinks about other people. He contemplates fantasms which resemble them and which he has decked out for his own purposes. Iris Murdock

Illness is the night-side of life, a more onerous citizenship. Everyone who is born holds dual citizenship, in the kingdom of the well and the kingdom of the sick. Although we prefer to use only the good passport, sooner or later each of us is obliged, at least for a spell, to identify ourselves as citizens of that other place. Susan Sontag

I

A woman college student in analysis presented the following dream:

Dream: *It is Christmas and my mother is holding beautiful ornaments and bright tinsel. Before her is a Christmas tree, but next to it is a terrible, sleeping pteradactyl. Mother blithely goes about decorating the giant prehistoric bird, ignoring the tree, and I am terrified that the monster will awake.*

Throughout her life this woman wrestled with dire conflict, yet from a distance she appeared an organized, gracious, polite, nicely decorated and decorating person. In her innermost experience and within the circle of her intimate relations, however, the terrible prehistoric bird was king.

In earliest childhood her infantile ego had been overwhelmed by the desertion of her father one week before she was born. In an angry depression, her mother had taken her brother with her and then abandoned the infant girl to her grandmother from the time she was six months until she was two years old, at which time the mother returned to take the young child back from a grandmother she had begun to love and trust.

What do you rely on, little girl, when mother and father are gone? Tears, guts, faith? Archetypes? Do mixed-up matters come apart?

I don't know. We don't know.

Our theories fail us. They describe only fantasms: primary process, transitional relationship, separation anxiety, the transcendent function, deintegration, archetypal compensation.

What your experience must have been! Do we have words, images for such a thing?

You were afraid? Lost, terrified, drowning in existence? What could you do? Run, hide? Lose your mind? Reject what you saw? Maybe there was nothing to do. No thing.

Must I learn about nothing, about no thing, in order to help you? Must I go beyond my theory, my training, my developmental stories, and trust that between us we can tolerate horror and persevere to write a new tale? Is such a thought arrogance? If the fires of your torment sear our souls, can I hope a Phoenix will arise from the ashes of your pteradactyl? Must I confront with you a Gorgon and a Minotaur, Grendel and Dracula? Is there meaning in terror and chaos?

You tell me a story worthy of legend! With trembling I hear your tale. You were cast deep into the mythic depths long before most of us even knew they existed.

II

Experiencing her mother's disappearance and lifelong depressive bitterness as her own fault, the growing child formed a defensively hypertrophied, smiling, polite, appropriately decorative identity, creating a protective and problematic entity akin to Winnicott's compliant and false self and Jung's persona. Such formations, be they archetypal or personal, do not exist alone, but like a spider web are always linked to other elements of the personality. In this case the complaint persona was closely bound to idealized images of mother and an oft-hidden, suffering, wounded shadow-self which emerged in symptom and fantasy. At the time of oedipal consolidation, when the decorative identity was most alien to her growing sense of basic values, to the needs and aims of her unique personality, and when themes of sexuality, death, and resurrection were dancing in her head like sugarplums, a martyred, pitiful identity solidified and was expressed through school phobia and (symptomatic and symbolic) trichotillimania.

Most important, her ability to perceive reality was distorted to the point that unconscious perception split off from conscious recognition and her ability to make value judgments and to conceptualize clearly became constricted and distorted. This process of disavowal stands near the center of the chaotic and tortured world of the borderline.

To borrow a line of questioning from Paul Gray (1987) and amend it to fit "widening scope" analysands, as analysts we need to ask: "What was it that made you need to stop knowing about yourself and your perception of the world outside yourself, and how did you manage to stop knowing?"

If this woman had acknowledged the reality of her parent's unavailability, the loss of her grandmother, and her mother's depression, if she had accurately known that a loving relationship was missing from family interaction and that she felt blamed and scapegoated, then her childhood situation would have been even more horrendously hopeless. At one and the same time she was both overstimulated and abandoned to sensory deprivation. Perhaps a partial solution to such a calamity was to say, "I don't know."

Connection to inner reality for her thus involved memories, perceptions, and experiences which were terrifying intrusions of primal trauma, and for many years she lived from her defended, superficial, protective identity. This resulted in inner emptiness, a loss of identity, and a severe and generalized depression. In spite of continual attempts to push the horrible sleeping bird deep into the shadows, it did erupt unconsciously in nightmare, projection, and uncontrolled rage. Fraught with chaos and fearful flights of fear and anger, the full awakening into consciousness of her prehistoric (pre-memory, preverbal, pre-persona) bird seemed the only path to a deep and real connection to her self.

As is often the case when working in this borderland, the sudden and overstimulating release of raw emotion which accompanies analytic engagement destroyed the safety of a stable, if superficial, seat of consciousness by trashing the previous persona adaptation. Her level of functioning in the world deteriorated drastically, sacrificed to regression and the possibility of a new integration.

It is crucial that the analyst not romanticize this type of regression, manifest either as a return to preverbal childhood states, the unfolding of a narcissistic-sadomasochistic transference, or the deeply meaningful emergence of symbolic potential. A struggle with the question of which patients will benefit and maintain themselves in the face of such a powerful onslaught, and which will require supportive psychotherapy, is a responsibility which cannot be forsaken. Malignant regression does exist. Like an engineer lowering fuel rods into a atomic pile, the analyst must keep a watchful eye on the temperature of the reaction lest there be a catastrophic meltdown.

This particular analysand was determined and courageous, able to maintain the glimmer of a connection to her self through the analytic relationship, and most important had an ego resilient enough to survive and wrestle with the enormous tension contained within projections of and identifications with a monster's primitive flying rage and a victim's gaping wounds. While her collective adaptation suffered during the prolonged and stormy breakdown of her persona-bound identity, she did, with support and hard work, maintain human connections, intellectual and artistic interests, and the distant goal of finding a meaningful career for herself.

Suicidal images and impulses were rampant, arriving with the establishment of a dependent and chaotic transference relationship. They were an unavoidable part of the unraveling of her defenses and the nonverbal remembering of her childhood hopelessness. Suicidal pressure increased in deepening spirals if my relationship to her was disturbed by separation or by any failure to keep the analytic relationship clearly and safely defined.

Most important (because more subtle, substantially hidden within the whorls of my own identity), suicidal crises were also precipitated by failures in my ability to understand how my actions or comments might themselves be victimizing her.

For example, several times when she described her boyfriend, fearing he was flirtatiously interested in other women, I made comments which, although I never used the words and was not consciously aware of what I was doing, leaned toward a view of her perceptions as paranoid distortions. Becoming *unconsciously* distrustful of me while simultaneously losing the *conscious* perception of her boyfriend's unfaithful attitude, she quickly came to believe I was correct. Briefly reassured, her depressive-masochistic oscillation abated, she appeared more stable and optimistic, and she acted as if everything was going to be all right: her boyfriend was trustworthy because I, the analyst, had said so.

At such times, when the surface of her life was calm, when she had been sailing along smoothly, when we seemed to be working well and our course was clear, I could not understand the deep plunges into suicidal depression, the desperate destruction of every eyelash, the portentous dreams of death which burst from the depths like a harpooned whale.

I was lost in uncharted waters, unaware of the unconscious meaning of my comments. I did not see *my* part in the interaction clearly as we focused on *her*, dissecting the meaning of her suicidal fantasies, doing productive work on the dual meanings of death and resurrection contained in the pulling out of her eyelashes (today the ugly me dies, to be reborn tomorrow as a beautiful, acceptable me), and learning that the dreams of death were photographs of the dying of her inner self. Yet we did recognize that she had been "killed" *before* the suicidal imagery emerged and were able to back up and search for the killer.

It was not easy to recognize that I was Ahab. Yet finally I did see that in my efforts to understand, to know, I had acted with subtle arrogance, unconsciously proclaiming my perceptions valid, decreeing that I could see and she could not.

Metaphorically speaking, I told (albeit unconsciously) an abandoned infant, a child blaming herself for the collapse of the world, a little girl torturing herself so that a black queen might ask the magic mirror who was the fairest in the land and hear her own name, that her family was just fine and it didn't matter that her father had abandoned her, it didn't matter that her mother was furiously depressed, it didn't matter that her beloved and desired brother physically and emotionally abused her—because these perceptions were not real, just crazy distortions. I did not mean to do this; I did not even know I had done it, but in her world unconscious meaning counted for more than good intention.

She began to hate herself, and vibrating to her experience of my unconscious intent, she became actively suicidal. Healthy aggression was shifted away from her boyfriend, reactionary anger away from me, and an unhealthy, murderous rage fell like radioactive rain silently, fatally onto herself. She began dying in terms of a connection to her deeper self. Her legitimate perceptions were sacrificed in order to maintain the connection to me, functioning at that moment in the way Neumann (1964) described the mother, "as" the analysand's self—in this case a defective one. We repeated the process which first led to the splitting of her connection to the self into parts: the basic internal connection experienced as damaged and shameful, the connection to mother "as" self experienced as necessary, but terrifying and ultimately murderous.

A similar process occurred when she accurately, but unconsciously, perceived me as tired, unavailable, depressed, or preoccupied. When her observations were correct and in a misguided attempt to be the perfect analyst, I denied her awareness, the same deadness and suicidal impulse overtook her.

Deeply hidden within her suicidal preoccupations were forbidden rages at me, the devouring mother-bird who had eaten her connection to self but was yet necessary for the existence of any semblence of potentiality. It was not possible to directly examine this rage until the nature of my involvement in her experience was clarified. Attempts to confront her anger before dealing with her perception of me simply reinforced her sense of being shamed and attacked, intensifying the conflict.

It took some time to understand this complex process. As is always the case, the analysand told me what was happening and my job was to hear it; this happened not all at once and not simply or logically. Once I perceived, could let in, and tolerate my part in it, we jointly began to rewrite the script. In order to contend with the situation I had to alter my understanding of her vision of reality and to take seriously the effect of my unconscious upon her. This experience follows Jung's notion that the analyst must change in a significant way in order for the analysand to change.

Finally we were able to direct our analytic attention toward her difficulty perceiving, formulating, and maintaining *her own vision of reality*. Bringing the cause of her deadness and suicidal preoccupation into consciousness, it gradually lost much of its sting.

Full Circle

> *I can only make direct statements, only "tell stories." Whether or not the stories are "true" is not the problem. The only problem is whether what I tell is my fable, my truth.* Jung

I have come again to our starting place along this winding path, having followed some high trails and some low, walked in shadow and in light, forsaken several inviting glades and breathlessly avoided some precipitously steep descents. Along the way I have told only a few stories of the many possible, trying to suggest that all stories function multiply and that as analysts it is our job not to reduce any story to simplistic truths, but to look again and again, to retell simple stories in ever greater complexity.

I have suggested that on one end of the borderline spectrum are individuals with unalterably fractured and chaotic inner worlds whose periods of optimal function are brief and fragile. Inextricably bound to stories in which the strength of the victim-aggressor pair is maximal, they can only see themselves as mistreated, frightened, vengeful, self-hating prisoners. They cannot allow themselves to know what they know, and their inner disorganization is acute and extraordinarily painful; their efforts to bury the torment are nothing short of heroic. Erecting massive defensive barriers to the naked experience of their core, they are unable, or wisely unwilling, to reopen themselves to the area of their initial wounds. Regression when it occurs is abrupt, often chaotic, and always catastrophic. Analysis for these people is not at issue.

At a different level are those whose identity, though splintered, is still capable of coalescing into a functional whole. These people are not only accessible to therapeutic relationship, but actively seek it out. The potential for autonomous development remains alive, buried deep within the unconscious. The level of primitive sadomasochistic impulse stops short of self-destruction and their innermost self is approachable, their defenses mutable. The potential to tell new stories and see old ones in new ways exists. Perseverence, confrontation, and interpretation through the tumult of their regressive transferences can lead toward the formation of a more stable center of identity.

Every analyst is inclined to recognize certain paths more readily than others. Those roads which pass into mythic, cultural, and collective territories glow with an inner light for most who owe a debt to Carl Jung, and the trails that lead to areas of growth and individuation, or at least the potential for it, shine for all. Further, as Roy Schafer (1983, p. 259) has commented, "We know that in the dreams of analysands all journeys are, among other things, trips through transference country."

Where one analyst on the journey might discover sexual and aggressive conflict and compromise, another might see a mother and child merging and separating, drinking of one another, each swallowing and throwing up pieces of the other's self; and still another will find the compensatory symbols of an inner integrating force.

We were all children once, have all been wounded, and have all tried to build walls to protect ourselves from things that go bump in the night. At times we hide from the frightening, terrible, but fascinating gods within, yet nightly (if not more often) we all regress and drop across psychic borders to meet them. If we are fortunate, tolerant, and patient, we may emerge as more than we were before.

We all reside in the borderland. We live out the many stories written in, around, and beyond it, going over and over them. Sometimes the stories have words, can be told and heard, and we learn of our deepest selves. In analysis we help the analysand to see that many of his own stories have been forsaken and forgotten, covered up and hidden; that he has lost not only much of his past, but more importantly, the ability to value, perceive, and *know* the multiplicity, complexity, and richness of his present.

References

Adams, D. 1980. *The restaurant at the end of the universe.* New York: Harmony Books.
Adler, G. 1985. *Borderline psychopathology and its treatment.* New York: Jason Aronson.

Adler, G., and Buie, D. 1982. Definitive treatment of the borderline personality. In Robert Langs, ed., *International Journal of Psychoanalytic Psychotherapy* 9/51–88. New York: Jason Aronson.

American Psychiatric Association—DSMIII. 1980. *Diagnostic and statistical manual of mental disorders, 3rd ed.* Washington, D.C.: A.P.A.

Balint, M. 1968. *The basic fault.* London: Tavistock.

Blanck, G., and Blanck, R. 1979. *Ego psychology II: Psychoanalytic developmental psychology.* New York: Columbia University Press.

Boyer, B. 1982. Analytic experiences in work with regressed patients. In P. Giovacchini and B. Boyer, eds., *Technical factors in the treatment of the severely disturbed patient.* New York: Jason Aronson.

Brenner, C. 1982. *The mind in conflict.* New York: International Universities Press.

Deutsch, H. 1942. Some forms of emotional disturbance and their relationship to schizophrenia. In *Neurosis and character types.* New York: International Universities Press, 1965.

Dorpat, T. 1982. An object-relations perspective on masochism. In P. Giovacchini and B. Boyer, eds., *Technical factors in the treatment of the severely disturbed patient.* New York: Jason Aronson.

Freud, Sigmund 1937. Analysis terminable and interminable. *Standard Edition* 23:216–253. London: Hogarth Press, 1964.

Frosch, J. 1964. The psychotic character: Clinical psychiatric considerations. *Psychoanalytic Quarterly* 38:81–96.

Gardner, M. Robert. 1983. *Self inquiry.* Boston: Little, Brown and Company.

Gass, W. H. 1987. The *Counterlife* by Phillip Roth: A review. *The New York Times Book Review.* 4 Jan. 1987, p. 1.

Gedo, J. 1979. *Beyond interpretation.* New York: International Universities Press.

Giovacchini, P. 1979. *Treatment of primitive mental states.* New York: Jason Aronson.

Goldberg, A., ed. 1978. *The psychology of the self: A casebook.* New York: International Universities Press.

Goodheart, W. 1984. Successful and unsuccessful interventions in Jungian analysis: The construction and destruction of the spellbinding circle. In N. Schwartz-Salant and M. Stein, eds., *Transference/Countertransference.* Wilmette, Ill.: Chiron Publications, 89–117.

Goodman N. 1978. *Ways of worldmaking.* Indianapolis: Hackett Publishing Company.

Gray, Paul. 1987. On the technique of analysis of the superego—an introduction. *The Psychoanalytic Quarterly* 56:130–155.

Green, A. 1977. The borderline concept. In P. Hartocollis, ed., *Borderline personality disorders: The concept, the syndrome, the patient.* New York: International Universities Press.

Grinberg, L. 1987. Dreams and acting out. *Psychoanalytic Quarterly* 41:155–176.

Grinker, R., Werble, B., and Drye, R. 1968. *The borderline syndrome.* New York: International Universities Press.

Grotstein, J. 1982. The analysis of a borderline patient. In P. Giovacchini and B. Boyer, eds., *Technical factors in the treatment of the severely disturbed patient.* New York: Jason Aronson.

Gunderson, J. 1984. *The borderline personality disorder.* Washington, D.C.: American Psychiatric Press.

_____. 1986. Borderline Personality disorder. *Charter Psychiatric Series* 7. Tape of talk given 31 July 1986. Macon, Ga.: Charter Medical Corporation.

Guntrip, H. 1969. *Schizoid phenomena, object relations and the self.* New York: International Universities Press.

Hortocollis, P. 1983. *Time and timelessness.* New York: international Universities Press.

Jung, C. G. 1961. *Memories, dreams reflections.* New York: Random House.

Kermode, F. 1966. *The sense of ending: Studies in the theory of fiction.* London: Oxford University Press.

Kernberg, O. 1967. Borderline personality organization. *Journal of the American Psychoanalytic Association* 15:641–685.

————. 1975. *Borderline conditions and pathological narcissism.* New York: Jason Aronson.

————. 1976. *Object-relations theory and clinical psychoanalysis.* New York: Jason Aronson.

————. 1984. *Severe personality disorders: Psychotherapeutic strategies.* New Haven: Yale University Press.

————. 1987. An ego psychology-object relations theory approach to the transference. *Psychoanalytic Quarterly* 41:197–221.

Khan, M. 1978. Secret as potential space. In S. Grolnick and L. Barkin, eds., *Between reality and fantasy.* New York: Jason Aronson.

Knight, R. 1953. Borderline states. In R. Knight and C. Friedman, eds., *Psychoanalytic psychiatry and psychology.* New York: International Universities Press, 1954.

Kohut, H. 1971. *The analysis of the self.* New York: International Universities Press.

————. 1977. *The restoration of the self.* New York: International Universities Press.

————. 1984. *How does analysis cure?* Chicago: University of Chicago Press.

Little, M. 1966. Transference in the borderline states. *International Journal of Psychoanalysis* 47:476–485.

Lubin, A. 1966. Discussion of Bernhard Berliner's paper, Psychodynamics of the depressive character. *The Psychoanalytic Forum* 1/3:254–256.

Machtiger, H. G. 1984. Reflections on the transference/countertransference process with borderline patients. In N. Schwartz-Salant and M. Stein, eds., *Transference/Countertransference.* Wilmette, Ill.: Chiron Publications, 119–145.

Mahler, M. S. 1970. A study of the separation-individuation process and its possible application to the borderline phenomena in the psychoanalytic situation. *Psychoanalytic Study of the Child* 26:403–424.

————. 1972. On the first three subphases of the separation-individuation process. *International Journal of Psychoanalysis* 53:333–338.

————. 1979. Separation-Individuation. *The Selected Papers of Margaret S. Mahler, M.D.* New York: Jason Aronson.

Mahler, M. S., Pine, F., and Bergman, A. 1975. *The psychological birth of the human infant.* New York: Basic Books.

Masterson, J. 1976. *Psychotherapy of the borderline adult.* New York: Brunner/Mazel.

Masterson, J., and Rinsley, D. B. 1975. The borderline syndrome: The role of the mother in the genesis and psychic structure of the borderline personality. *International Journal of Psychoanalysis* 56:163–177.

Meissner, W. W., 1984. *The borderline spectrum: Differential diagnosis and developmental issues.* New York: Jason Aronson.

Modell, A. 1968. *Object love and reality: An introduction to a psychoanalytic theory of object relations.* New York: International Universities Press.

————. 1985. *Psychoanalysis in a new context.* New York: International Universities Press.

Murdoch, Iris. 1969. *Bruno's dream.* New York: Viking Press.

Neumann, E. 1959. *Art and the Creative Unconscious.* Princeton, N.J.: Princeton University Press.

————. 1964. *On the origins and history of consciousness.* London: Routledge & Kegan Paul.

Parks, S. 1987. Experiments in appropriating a new way of listening. *Journal of Analytical Psychology* 32/2:93–116.

Pine, F. 1985. *Developmental theory and clinical process.* New Haven: Yale University Press.

Schafer, R. 1983. *The analytic attitude.* New York: Basic Books.

Searles, H. 1978. Psychoanalytic therapy with the borderline adult: Some principles concerning technique. In J. Masterson, ed., *New perspectives on psychotherapy of the borderline adult.* New York: Brunner/Mazel.

Sontag, Susan. 1978. *Illness as metaphor.* New York: Farrar, Straus and Giroux.

Stoller, R. 1976. Sexual excitement. *Archives of General Psychiatry* 33:899–909.

Stolorow, R., and Lachmann, F. 1983. *Psychoanalysis of developmental arrests: Theory and treatment.* New York: International Universities Press.

Stone, L. 1954. The widening scope of indications for psychoanalysis. *Journal of the American Psychoanalytic Association* 2:567–594.

Volkan, V. 1982. A young woman's inability to say no to needy people and her identification with the frustrator in the analytic situation. In P. Giovacchini and B. Boyer, eds., *Technical factors in the treatment of the severely disturbed patient.* New York: Jason Aronson.

Wheelis, Alan. 1987. *The doctor of desire.* New York: Norton.

Winnicott, D. W. 1953. Transitional objects and transitional phenomena. *International Journal of Psycho-Analysis* 34:89–97.

_____. 1975. *Through pediatrics to psycho-analysis.* New York: Basic Books.

Wurmser, L. 1981. *The mask of shame.* Baltimore: Johns Hopkins University Press.

Zetzel, E. R. 1971. A developmental approach to the borderline patient. *American Journal of Psychiatry.* 127:867–871.

Subject-Object Differentiation in the Analysis of Borderline Cases: The Great Mother, the Self, and Others

Susanne Kacirek

Translated by Ronald Jalbert

I know this effect very well from my practice; it is the therapeutic effect par excellence, for which I labor with my students and my patients, and it consists in the dissolution of the participation mystique . . . the nondifferentiation between subject and object. . . . How did this come about?

Jung, on *The Secret of the Golden Flower*

Introductory Remarks

The borderline personality clearly remains deeply entrenched within an archaic identity, even if it is seen solely from the perspective of major defenses such as splitting, primitive idealization, and projective identification (Kernberg 1967). Attempts by the borderline's ego to escape this archaic identity end in failure. Taking a uniquely Jungian point of view on the concept of the Self and presenting clinical material drawn from analytic experience with three patients, I hope in this article to contribute to the study of subject-object differentiation in the analysis of borderline patients.

Susanne Kacirek received her Ph.D. from the Université de Paris VII, where she has been teaching since 1980. She is currently a training analyst and vice-president of the Société Française de Psychologie Analytique as well as a member of the Collège des Hautes Etudes Psychanalytiques. In private practice as a Jungian analyst in Paris, she is also the author of several articles and essays relating to clinical subjects.

In clinical work, sorting out the psyche from the outer world—a process that Jung designated "the therapeutic effect par excellence" —depends basically upon the creation of a space that allows for inner confrontation.[1] Indeed, before the proper contours of outer reality can be delineated, it is most important that the inner world come to be. Undoubtedly, in order to distinguish between inner and outer realities, one has to know how to relate, that is to say, one has to know how to designate the "place of the other," or to recognize what is "other" than oneself.

When caught within a nondifferentiated state where subject and object are fused, one has fallen under the domination of the Great Mother.[2] Put differently, the archetype of the Great Mother is here understood as the organizing principle that maintains participation mystique, in contrast to the Self that, according to Jung, makes differentiation possible. It is thus important to focus particularly upon the roles the Self and Great Mother archetypes play in giving birth to the individuation process in the analysis of the borderline personality. My goal is not to retrace the interplay of archetypes in the individual's history as would a developmental view. Rather, my intention is to understand how, in the course of analysis, the particular therapeutic moment is constellated that permits the borderline patient to take a decisive step toward subject-object differentiation. A confrontation with the Shadow in the framework of the transference-countertransference relationship is an indispensable catalyst for this moment.

For me, the category of the Shadow has a broader meaning than the usual Jungian understanding since it includes the Freudian contribution on the subject. Thus what I have to say about the treatment of the borderline personality is incidentally relevant to the "borderline" situation of psychoanalysis itself, where sophisticated systems of splitting prevent mutual cross-fertilization between analytic schools.

Participation Mystique and its Dissolution

In his "Commentary on 'The Secret of the Golden Flower,'" which incidentally hardly mentions any clinical issues, Jung refers to the Self in order to account for the dissolution of participation mystique. The Self designates the "way"—that is to say, the method—according to which subject-object differentiation can take place. What matters is that the unconscious be "recognized as a co-determining factor along with consciousness." Because the Self is also "a natural and spontaneous phenomenon," it helps to constellate the polarity between consciousness and the unconscious.[3] Paradoxically, the Self further presents itself as the result of this very same differentiation; it is the "hypothetical point," the "center of gravity of the whole personality" (*Gesamtpersön-lichkeit*), and because of this makes possible both inner psychic space and the true insight so difficult for the borderline personality.

We might ask ourselves what motivated Jung to be so positive about the role the Self plays in the dissolution of participation mystique. There are three reasons for Jung's optimism, the first theoretical, the second clinical, and the last personal. Each of these will be analyzed in order to determine its validity.

1. Jung followed up on the necessary implications of his own theory of libido, which he formulated in 1912. Indeed, according to Jung's monistic theory, libido arises from an energetic wherein inner and outer are fused with each other in the same subjective context of endopsychic perception (Kacirek 1980). Hence the outer world, as a reality distinct from psychic reality, has yet to be constituted. One could say that Jung's monistic energetic relies upon interpretation to differentiate the inner world from the outer. Jung uses interpretation masterfully, to the point of making a method out of it, when he distinguishes between the subjective and objective planes in the interpretation of dreams. Stated more clearly, the Jungian concept of libido quite naturally accounts for participation mystique. The problem for Jung is then to spell out how differentiation from it is possible. Thus the Self, which is supposed to differentiate the inner from the outer, becomes a theoretical necessity. Jung would have had to invent the concept of the Self had it not revealed its archetypal dynamics to him.

The Freudian understanding of libido, in contrast to Jung's, sacrifices primary narcissism.[4] The existence of the outer world, of "otherness," of what is real, is posited as primary, and the narcissistic turning in upon oneself occurs only later (Freud 1914). The whole Freudian theory of drives presupposes such a confrontation between the psyche and outer reality. Freud's seduction theory, even though partially abandoned in 1897, is an illustration of that point (Laplanche 1984). Jungian libidinal monism, which articulates so well the experience of participation mystique, has the further advantage of allowing for therapeutic work at the most regressed levels of the psyche. It might even be said that the Jungian clinical approach more than any other allows for the reparation of fundamental narcissistic wounds by making it possible for the analyst to accompany the subject in a lived symbolic immersion within the Mother-World.

2. If Jung claims that the Self works at dissolving participation mys-

tique, it is because he believes he has discerned its effects within his clinical work. In "The Relation between the Ego and the Unconscious" (1928) he recalls "with the utmost astonishment" how the dissolution of a transference came about after the spontaneous development of a "transpersonal control-point" in the patient's psyche. The transpersonal control-point becomes a "virtual goal": It finds symbolic expression here "in a form which can only be described as an image of God" and which leads to the "withdrawal of projections."

Two qualifying remarks can be made here. First, this image of God, which is related to the representation of a Nature Spirit, undeniably belongs as much to the Great Mother as to the Self. Second, Jung says nothing about the complexity of what actually happened to allow the patient to withdraw projections and live life in a more ordinary fashion, with more realistic object relations. At any rate, nothing in Jung's text tells us if the activity of the archetype, which is visible in dreams, was the only factor allowing for the differentiation of the inner world from the outer, or if this activity was occasioned by other psychic agencies as well.

Consequently, it is appropriate for us to seek out in our clinical work what it is that contributes, at times imperceptibly, to the release of archetypal energy, and also determines the interplay of forces that brings about the "therapeutic effect par excellence." At the same time, one has to be careful not to succumb too easily to the fascination of the image and its numinosity. I do agree that the *numinosum* is an important healing factor; however, contrary to what first impressions might lead us to believe, it is not the only one. The process of transformation can also be put into motion by the transference or by the analysis of drives.

3. Jung invokes personal experience to state in his commentary on "The Secret of the Golden Flower" that the Self brings about the dissolution of participation mystique. Whatever difficulties may be presented by projecting personal experience into a theoretical framework—to a degree unavoidable in psychoanalysis—there is no reason to dismiss the inner confrontation from which that projection emanates by invoking rigid ideological criteria, as a Freudian perspective tends to do. Of course, we may think, on the one hand—as does Satinover (1985) —that Jung refers to the Self as a defence against deep psychic suffering; just as we may say, on the other hand, that he seems to have paid dearly enough for the right to talk about it. One can ascertain, claims Jung, "the hypothetical point between conscious and unconscious. This new center might be called the Self. If the transposition is successful, it

does away with the participation mystique and results in a personality that suffers only in the lower storeys, as it were, but storeys singularly detached from pain, as well as from joyous happenings" (Jung 1931).

At this point, it is important to emphasize Jung's understanding of the dissolution of the participation mystique. As a result of this dissolution, a superior personality is born, which corresponds to the creation of a subtle body that ensures the cohesiveness of different moments of "detached consciousness." Jung places the emphasis exclusively on detachment from the world (*Weltentrücktheit*), but he does not ask how such a personality's relationships to the world and others are to be structured. "The man who has attained . . . fuller consciousness [that] removes him further from his original, purely animal *participation mystique* with the herd . . . is solitary" (Jung 1928).

The painful "lower storeys" of such a personality, however, retain the mark of their unconscious ties to the Mother World. Before objecting to this way of thinking of the subject-object differentiation, we might best examine what clinical experience with the borderline personality has to tell us.

The Vicissitudes of the Drives in the Borderline Personality

In order to determine characteristic vicissitudes of the drives in the borderline personality, and also to account for the kinds of regression that follow them, I have chosen to follow the "psychogenetic hypothesis" proposed by Jean Bergeret (1984), a French psychoanalyst who has recently written an impressive book on borderline states.[5] Bergeret's reflections (which follow a classical Freudian approach) presuppose that the borderline has suffered an initial trauma, an affective shock brought on by excessively intense drives at a time when the ego was not yet mature enough to face this onslaught. This "traumatic moment" is supposed to have taken place before the oedipal period. Thus, the borderline ego would not have been able to acquire a neurotic structure, nor would it have suffered, at the moment of trauma, real limitations of such intensity and precociousness as to structure it along psychotic lines.

A major consequence of this disorganizing trauma is the immediate decathexis of drives and a narcissistic withdrawal so massive as to fixate the subject's libidinal development at regressed narcissistic levels, fostering a kind of early pseudo-latency that will extend beyond adolescence.

The borderline subject subsequently denies the surge of the oedipal complex and withdraws to pregenital stages of development, particularly to early fixations relating to the omnipotence associated with anal mastery. The borderline's regression to the anal stage has this particular trait: It acts as a "safety locking pin" that limits the ego's collapse in the direction of a psychotic structure that would, in turn, entail a state of regression "beyond narcissism." For want of a real psychic structure—whether of a neurotic or a psychotic sort—the borderline's ego simply adjusts to the situation by remaining neither too rigid nor too lax. However, it irremediably and anxiously clings to the object by forming an attachment best characterized as anaclitic and by no means oedipal.

Because the Oedipus complex has never really been constellated in the regressed borderline personality, at least the following three elements of the borderline psychic structure need to be considered:

1. The claim to narcissistic omnipotence, which consists of a strong tendency to idealize, and which actually compensates for pronounced deficiencies at the level of primary narcissism.

2. An anaclitic attachment to the object, which again is affected by the borderline's inclination to idealize.

3. A pregenital drive level, coupled to a superego reduced to its sadistic dimensions. This pregenital drive structure attempts to hide behind splitting and projective identification in the hope of preserving both the object and the ideal. Splitting and projective identification will, for a long time, affect the quality of the transference-countertransference work in the analysis of a borderline personality.

The Self Under the Domination of the Great Mother

We now come back to a specifically Jungian view when we ask: What happens at this stage of the borderline's analytic regression? It is clear that Jung did not deal thoroughly with all of the implications of this question. Careful clinical observation shows that the borderline personality fails to differentiate the Self from the Great Mother archetype. From a practical standpoint, and particularly in the analysis of the borderline personality, I hold this lack of differentiation to be the crucial problem. As long as the Great Mother dominates and readily dons the images of the Self, the Self's own dynamism remains paralyzed. Furthermore, the Great Mother archetype prevents the constellation of the ego-Self axis, resulting in such distortion of the capacity for insight that it fails to relate to the transcendent function so necessary to its development.[6]

All experiences of the inner world are then put in jeopardy or distorted. The outcome can be a "black" unconsciousness (as will be seen in the case of Philippe), or a subject perpetually on the fringe of a psychic process, which is experienced as a treadmill leading nowhere (as shown in the case of Alexandra).[7] Or, again, we witness the proliferation of "great" archetypal images. This latter consequence should not prevent us from seeing how the patient continues to stagnate (illustrated by the case of Elsa) within an archaic identity in which visions and synchronistic phenomena substitute for real insight. We are caught in a vicious circle: To the extent that the Self is held prisoner by the Great Mother, the latter infiltrates the subject's defective personal identity. This personal identity is defective precisely because the ego-Self axis has not and cannot be constituted within the cohesiveness of its own inner psychic space. It cannot become a place of psychic confrontation and an agent for the integration of unconscious contents.

This Great Mother-Self archetypal constellation corresponds to the anxiety associated with object-loss. This is the kind of anxiety that is experienced in the anaclitic relationship and for which the Great Mother-Self constellation compensates more or less successfully. An unbearable lack brought on by the loss of the object calls the Great Mother archetype to the forefront. Consequently, the subject's narcissistic nucleus remains fused to the Great Mother, whom the ego invests by proxy with infantile omnipotence. Thus, the idealization of the object feeds on the fact that the Great Mother contains the Self, and keeps the subject's own narcissistic potential captive. We touch here upon a key problem in the analysis of the borderline: Psychic development can take place only by relying upon narcissism, but the latter is "contaminated" by the Great Mother's domination. The choice, then, is between deflation, which could degenerate into a feeling of complete nonexistence, and inflation, fed by a grandiose Self. A further difficulty is that the state of participation mystique in the very regressed borderline personality demands a nearly "absolute" projection of the Great Mother archetype upon the personal mother. This quasi-absolute projection, therefore, makes object relations unanalyzable and generally induces the subject to deny object relations altogether. The transference relationship meets up with the same obstacle. The possibility of establishing an analytic relationship with a borderline personality depends foremost on the release of the Self from the clutches of the Great Mother. The possibility of pursuing an individuation process outside oedipal "norms"—which are, in my opinion, never fully retrievable and perhaps not even "necessary"—is also contingent upon the release of the Self.

Three clinical examples are presented to discern those particular moments when the grip of participation mystique first loosens up and releases the Self's own dynamism. For those clinical moments to occur, several analyzable elements need to coincide, namely: the activation of the transference-countertransference field, including that of the drives; and elaboration of the trauma-fantasy; and the archetypal movement itself.

Alexandra

Dream: *After walking along endless aqueducts dried up centuries ago, I [Alexandra] finally find the road that takes me to a Guru Great Mother who is seated by a riverside, surrounded by a court of young maidens who venerate her with offerings of flowers. When I draw near, I am rejected, humiliated. I alone have no flower.*

Alexandra presents as a deeply depressed borderline personality. For her, the Self is entirely possessed by the Great Mother to whom the ego can only vow unconditional, idealizing adoration. In return for its devotion, the ego receives a feeling of deep unworthiness and threats of annihilation. Side by side with the idealized object, a Death Mother is constellated; it is said of this Death Mother in a dream that death would surely come to the child, were the child to touch her.

Alexandra's ego is maintained by a deadly and paradoxical pact that the Mother-Self archetypal object be kept intact at any cost, including the sacrifice of everything vital within her, a sacrifice that implies, above all else, the decathexis of instinctual life. She consents to this sacrifice in order to protect the Virgin Mother, whom she showers with projections of omnipotence, from the intrusion of sexual contaminants. Pre-genital potential is entirely dominated by an archaic Mother Animus who possesses Alexandra's ego in a masochistic and anally constrictive way.

Before entering analysis, Alexandra had gone so far as to sacrifice to the Virgin Mother not only her sexual life but especially her own reproductive organs. This sacrifice was consummated by means of indirect but explicitly self-mutilating behavior. Alexandra suffered repeatedly several early childhood traumas that reverberated in the relationship with her mother. These traumas were brought on by the successive absence, illness, and death of both father and grandfather, so that she was left without any supportive masculine figure. There was not even the possibility of activating the oedipal conflict. Alexandra's relation to the outside world is deeply imbued with an anaclitic and illusory dependency upon the Mother object whom she necessarily finds disappointing. The Great Mother prevents her from conferring an identity on herself by impeding her relationship with the Self. Alexandra oscillates between solitary and bitter withdrawal, on the one hand, and, on the other, excessive giving in desperate attempts to establish emotional rapport—rather with an institution or a collective (for instance, she regularly donates blood, even bone marrow) than with individuals.

She tended to recreate a similar dependency in the transference relationship with the analyst, while basically remaining outside the analytic process. I should add that I found little opportunity with her to use my countertransference therapeutically. I became, indeed, this Great Mother, or a sort of analytical institution, who withholds an identity from Alexandra and whom she feels too unworthy to approach.

One of Alexandra's dreams described the analysis as a celebration of the mysteries of Isis—another Virgin Mother. In her associations, Isis is essentially the Great Goddess and guardian of prostitutes, another reason Alexandra is utterly unable to take part in the celebration. This association suggests why an activation of drives is unthinkable: It would only reinforce her masochistic behavior and the obsessional constraints that rule her everyday life.

In another dream, Alexandra's vagina is painfully stuffed with a ball (in French, *pelote*) of string ("it serves to tie up"). It seems that the anaclitic bond definitely prevents any access to sexual pleasure she might have in a relationship with another human being.[8] The anaclitic bond provides her with the only exposure to wholeness she is capable of having in the form of closed auto-eroticism (*pelote* evokes the verb form *peloter,* which means "to pet, to caress").

The seemingly impossible nature of this analysis worried me a great deal. I saw no way Alexandra could be rescued from this Great Mother who had so invaded the Self that the analytic process could hardly begin.

Movement began to occur when Alexandra's mother became terminally ill. Alexandra told me this dream: Her mother, lying on her sickbed and connected on all sides to tubes as if at the center of a spider's web, tells her, "Don't forget to bring me a Christmas present."

Upon hearing this, I experienced an intense emotional reaction. Before making any real attempt to interpret the dream, I told myself: "Here it goes! She is going to take the Christ Child along with her to death!" But then Alexandra confessed: "I did not get a present for her since I thought she would die before Christmas."

It would seem that the conjunction of her avowal of this death wish—which was the last stronghold of resistance against the final destruction of her personality—and of my own personal revulsion at her dream for the first time allowed for a feeling connection in the transference; indeed, in our mutual complicity to snatch the Child-Self from the Death Mother, we discreetly acknowledged to each other the impression that a feeling had passed between us.

The old woman died but several months later. Alexandra devotedly attended to her, but henceforth, in the analytic hour, she could admit her ambivalence toward her. The night her mother died, Alexandra dreamed that she herself had given birth to a child. "The child must be breast-fed," Alexandra told me; her left breast gave abundant milk. That same night, she also dreamed of a joyous wedding in a black community.

The imaginary compensatory aspect of the dream, which "compensates" for object loss by a birth that overcomes death, is obvious. But in this case, it would have been a therapeutic error to accept this reductive understanding. Alexandra commented: "This means that my mother had to die in order that I could be born. Truthfully, I should no longer be alive." In order to escape this denial of her right to live, Alexandra must come to appreciate the symbolic dimension of the dream and accept the "offering" coming from the unconscious. The identification of the ego with the Good Mother, who still remains for Alexandra a Virgin Mother, makes this *Umstellung* (transposition) happen. This "transposition," which Jung mentions in his "Commentary on 'The Secret of the Golden Flower,'" situates a person's center of gravity midway between consciousness and the unconscious, "and results in the suspension (*Aufhebung*) of the *participation mystique*." In Alexandra's case it allows, for the first time, for an ego-Self dialogue that is significantly and authentically her own, one that relates to feelings and matters of the heart. This dialogue will, no doubt, still take place under the auspices of the Great Mother. Nonetheless, death has undermined the Great Mother's omnipotence by revealing the fundamental, brutal reality of "otherness" and by allowing for the irruption of the outer world through radical discontinuity.

Released at the same time are possibilities for the ego to identify with various images and the spontaneous activity of the Self. These allow Alexandra, in the first instance, to experience a narcissistic recovery and to recoup a sense of Self. From this time on, Alexandra, instead of always remaining on the sidelines, became involved in the analytic process. It was at last possible to differentiate the reality of the personal

mother from the projection of the Great Mother archetype, and therefore to work in earnest on object relations.

Dream: *A monstrous brownish-green snake comes down a moun-
tain. Someone says: It's the end of the world.*

Alexandra had had this dream shortly after the birth dream. As a matter
of fact, that the Snake should in some way attack the newborn is fair
game: All it does is confirm the archetypal nature of the Child and the
constellation of the hero motif. A process is set in motion. But if the
dream of the "black wedding" from the previous evening—however
contaminated it may have been by the Shadow—tended to a union of
opposites and, in this way, protected the newborn from destructive
drives, the "monster" of the following morning was immeasurably more
explosive. Through the image of the "end of the world," Alexandra
recalled and relived the only vision—a traumatic one—she had of
her parent's bed: Her childhood memory is of herself as a young girl,
feeling overwhelmed as she is squeezed between her parents' bodies
during extremely anxiety-provoking air raids.

Indeed, it was the brutal awareness of finitude that released the
totalitarian grip within which the Uroboros of primordial incest held
Alexandra. Only after this awareness could the Uroboros become the
Mercurial snake in potency.

What about this snake? "Sexuality," replied Alexandra, her only
association to that image. Only since the Great Mother released her
hold and allowed Alexandra to reclaim for herself an inner narcissistic
space was Alexandra able to experience her own body. And only then
was she able to realize how poorly defined the boundaries of her body
were. The release of her pent-up impulses highlighted her fantasies of
omnipotence, particularly that of wanting to be in many places at one
time. This woman, who during her whole life had drained herself of
blood by giving "transfusions," began to have fantasies of these liminal,
Shadowless beings, the living dead or vampires.

More recent developments in Alexandra's analysis lead me to believe, however, that Jung's idea of the birth of a "superior" personality,
which is released from participation mystique while still continuing to
suffer at "lower storeys," is not simply a metaphor with no clinical bearing on the borderline personality case. Indeed, it seems that, if the
dynamism of the Self is properly engaged, the ego is able to regain dig-
nity, a new center of gravity, and a feeling of identity that will influence
the analysand's relationships with the world and with others. However,
the entire potential of pregenital libido, even if attended to closely, re-

fuses to be integrated into the *Gesamtpersonlichkeit*, and, insofar as it cannot enter the oedipal, continuously slides down a regressive slope in the direction of the Great Mother, eluding the individuation process.

Philippe

> . . . *the primordial* participation mystique *with things is abolished. Consciousness . . . dissolves in contemplative vision . . . as the Chinese text says beautifully.*
>
> Jung

For Philippe, death is a state he almost always experiences through long periods of severe depression, depersonalization, and numbing emptiness that make him feel "that no day ever has a beginning." In the second session, he told me of a dream in which he had to speak from a "black hole," a feat that is to him obviously impossible. Philippe, a physicist, patiently explained to me, in a rare lyrical vein, that matter is so heavy and so dense in this cosmic hole as to absorb all light. He was convinced that there was no way out of this "black hole."

He shook with anxiety as he then told me of an old dream: A calf, with which he manifestly identifies, is skinned alive. The only safe haven in real life, as in his dreams, is his aged parents' tiny apartment, which he refuses to leave since the dream warns him that everything outside has come to an end, everything is silent and dead. The boundaries of the living are thus clearly demarcated and consist of the womb-like space of the narcissistic family triad.

Philippe considers himself unworthy to relate to women. He experienced his first severe anxiety attack—the source of his depression—after writing a young girl a love letter that remained unanswered. To overcome his hatred and disappointment, he then undertook a quest for mystical experience.

An erotic transference toward me, whom he saw as an angel, gave Philippe an intense, long-unknown feeling of being alive. Above and beyond this idealization of me in the transference, a somewhat unusual fantasy came to me: that I could not use the toilet while Philippe was in the waiting room. I became conscious of what this countertransference reaction had to say about the state of Philippe's unconscious infantile desires; my impression was confirmed by a strange scene that took place around this same toilet question, a scene in which Philippe ostensibly tried to involve me. After that incident, my attention was drawn to something disquieting in Philippe's attitude which barely showed through his exquisite politeness and his retiring, silent discretion:

Something suspicious and provocatively seductive lurked behind his fa-
cade. After a session dealing with his feelings of unworthiness and fears
of annihilation, feelings induced in the past by others, Philippe came
unusually close to me as he was about to pay for the session. And with
light in his eyes, he asked, "So, as far as you are concerned, I am not all
that bad—I have the right to exist?"

The following night, Philippe had a dream: In the middle of a
zoo, there is a castle that Philippe enters by way of a very small opening. He flies. The hall he finds inside the castle is made of huge, cubic
rough-hewn stones. On one of the walls, Philippe sees the soul of a
wicked person pasted like a sticker or a grayish communion wafer. The
"wicked" soul suffers, for it cannot, or will not, enter Paradise. Paradise
is imaged as a small black hole that opens into nothingness. Philippe
flies toward the sticker-communion wafer, and unsticks it from the wall
in view of helping it. The little circle flutters away and transforms itself
into a bulky, evil man. He is evil because he has broken the law that
forbids sexual intercourse between humans and nonhumans. He
broke that law—a law that Philippe admits is bad—when he raped the
ostrich-woman. This rape was a horrible crime. "I pity this ostrich-
woman—she suffers, yes—I think she has a soul," added Philippe with
infinite gentleness. In French, as in English, *autruche* or "ostrich" and
Autriche or "Austria," my native country, are phonematically quite similar.

It seems to me that intense pregenital seduction[9] needed to be enacted in the transference relationship with the analyst before Philippe,
filled with a fantasy of omnipotence, could activate an embryo of the
Self—of his Self-Desire—in this cold, womblike cathedral with angular
dimensions suggestive of a maternal animus. This grandiose Self-Great
Mother construction has nothing spontaneous about it, and the only alternative to its stony embrace is the black hole: Nothingness. The Self is
indeed the prisoner of the Death Mother.

"Do I have the right to exist?" and, first of all, as a being with desires? Philippe did not yet know that his Shadow would manifest itself
violently and reveal to him the existence of a soul—that of the ostrich-
woman.

The turmoil I perceived in him was, indeed, not innocent: A tendency to experience repeatedly some primitive, traumatic violence
gestated within him.

What was this violence all about? Bergeret (1984) explains it by
claiming that the primal scene was witnessed at too precocious an age,
a point of view I do not find very satisfactory. I am more inclined to

follow J. Laplanche's theoretical position (1984), which stays closer to a strict Freudian line of thought concerning the fundamental, primary seduction to which the infant child is subjected in relation to the breast; this seduction is "traumatic" to the extent that it exceeds the infant's capacity for comprehending the abrupt intrusion of the object, which is charged with unconscious sexual meanings that even the adult fails to grasp. Philippe's painful early history alludes fleetingly to an attempt at incestual seduction on the part of his mother, a seduction that could well have fixated the trauma. However, it seems that, in Philippe's case, the anxiety provoked by the intrusion of the object by way of a violent seduction, on the one hand, made the embryo of healthy narcissism withdraw into the bastion of the immutable Self-Great Mother constellation (even if a fortress can never take the place of its hide for a skinned calf). On the other hand, this anxiety brought on a decathexis of the drives, leaving empty the psychic space the object would otherwise occupy. That emptiness was filled by the negative pole of the combined Self-Great Mother archetype, i.e., the black unconsciousness of a Death Mother.

If I hold to the hypothesis of the original seduction, it is because it emphasizes the existence and effective intervention of the object as coming from outside the subject's psyche; this is not the same as relying solely on the innateness of drives. Reliving the seduction in the analysis (even if only symbolically) through the transference, as Philippe did, opens up a breach in the participation mystique. The experience is symbolic because, while it finds expression at the level of archetypal images, it integrates the reality of a drive. The first and most remarkable effect of this symbolic experience is to restore the Self's dynamism. Coming back to the dream, we have to keep in mind what Jung says in his "Commentary": "When there is no consciousness of the difference between subject and the Object, an unconscious identity prevails . . . . Then . . . animals behave like human beings—human beings are at the same time animals. . . ."

Philippe is not psychotic, but he is indeed borderline.[10] There is a law that differentiates human beings from animals—the prohibition of incest. Because the "fundamental trauma" was never elaborated at the oedipal level, this prohibition is not the symbolic Law of the Father, but a law of hate, contempt, and discrimination emanating from the Mother's negative animus. (This was to prove correct. One day, when the question of his unworthiness was again raised, Philippe pointed out: "I feel unworthy maybe because I resemble my father, and my mother despises my father." He was able to make this observation because the identification process had become possible for him once the Great Mother had withdrawn.)

Since it has not developed an oedipal super-ego, the borderline personality has difficulty integrating itself within a moral order. Now it is up to the Self to point the way to ethical and personal values, most particularly by freeing up the anima or the animus.

To begin with, the archaic law is replaced with the following judgment, a feeling judgment that values: "Yes, she has a soul."

Philippe had to transgress the archaic law, but this symbolic transgression left him feeling deprived, so much did he feel possessed by the Shadow of the "rapist." I offered relief only by insisting on the difference between the reality and the fantasy of violence, assuring him, as it were, that there would be no acting out.

In the next session, he told me at the outset that "for three consecutive mornings, the day has had a beginning." He was eager to tell me a dream he did not understand very well. In the dream, Philippe is in a sleeping bag, perched on a gigantic tree. The tree is dead, leaning to one side, and covered with vermin. Philippe then sees plantations in full bloom below. He is told: "Those are plantations of Colombian coffee. This coffee is prepared directly from the flowers. Contemplation ensures the growth of these plants, their self-generation." After telling me the dream, Philippe added that his mother had, in fact, just found some Colombian coffee that he particularly liked.

This dream inevitably brings to mind the "Secret of the Golden Flower": It is when the Giant Mother Tree that has lifted the ego to the heights of omnipotence in the deathlike unconscious state of participation mystique, when the tree, attacked by vermin on one side, leans toward the earth, it is at that moment that the ego awakens to the conscious states engendered by the Self, which is represented in the dream by the flowers and doves (the French word for Columbia, *Colombie,* is quite close to the word for dove, *colombe*). The dove stands in marked contrast to that unfortunate, flightless bird whose sight remains buried in the sand, the ostrich. The Self is also symbolized by the somber beverage that sees to it that "each morning has its beginning." The coffee trees self-generate by means of *Schauen,* (contemplative vision, self-knowledge by means of self-brooding, says Jung elsewhere). What is fundamentally at stake here is a renewed possibility for insight, a possibility that had up until now been aborted in the womb of the Great Mother.

Indeed, the metaphor of "self-brooding" is still tied to mother; this form of detachment of consciousness by way of the *Schauen* is not pure

Logos. But here the mother mediates by giving access to a conscious identity she "found" for him. This mother is related to the everyday personal mother, not to the Great Mother who obliterates all horizons.

Philippe appeared pleased after telling me his dream. "But I am wary," said he, "of contemplation. It can lead me to withdraw so much that I would no longer meet other people."[11]

Actually, the greatest outcome of the differentiation of the Self from the Great Mother lies in the mutation of the transference relationship. Incidences of projective identification seem considerably reduced (I go into the sessions without fear, if not with pleasure), and the transference encompasses that dimension within which relationships to others become the central arena for Self-Object differentiation.

Elsa

A common preconception would have us go to the deepest layers of the psyche, back to the primordial breast. This is an error; the fundamental fantasy is not there . . . the solution is to be found . . . in the fantasy that is isomorphic to the Oedipal complex: that of the primal scene. I insist on this fantasy of the primal scene to distinguish my position from that of Freud, who expounded his views in the "Wolfman." In that work Freud seeks evidence for his theory of the primal scene, in a polemical attack against Jung. Now what matters about the primal scene is not that it has been witnessed, but precisely the contrary, i.e., that it should have taken place in the absence of the Subject. (Green 1983, p. 239)

The "absence of the Subject": this means suffering exclusion.

How can Elsa enter the oedipal conflict? It is in approximately such terms that I formulated to myself this woman's problem; I arrived at this formulation after years of analysis with her. She originally came to see me in a state of utter disorientation and depression after her husband had left her. Until then, her role of "Queen Mother" (an identification characteristic of a particular type of expansive "borderline" which gave her the appearance of having a warm, outgoing nature) had compensated for her complete dependency, her inability to assert her identity, and the fragmentation of her deeper Self, which last became quite evident early on in the analysis.

In the first phase of her analysis, she embarked upon a grandiose, inflated narcissistic quest for participation mystique with a cosmic Great Mother, which did not preclude the temptation to seek "encounters of a third kind."

In the transference, I appeared to her either as the permissive Great Mother who gratified her narcissistically, or, at those moments when some "containing vessel" was necessary to prevent fragmentation, as the representative of a restrictive moral order derived from the maternal animus, since the symbolic Law of the Father was nowhere to be found. The grand images of the Self that her dreams supplied in abundance did, under the circumstances, on the one hand compensate on an imaginary level for the anxiety of object loss and, on the other function as a defense against the threat of fragmentation. But too systematic an effort at elucidation and reduction would have been harmful at this stage, for she would have understood it as coming from a negative and deadly maternal animus. Moreover, a dream image wherein Else holds on to a large rock in the middle of a fast-rushing torrent, then realizes that the warmth of her body might melt the ice holding the rock together and shatter the rock, suggests the danger of prematurely "unfreezing" certain affects. The imaginary was protective.

But this process dragged on, and the moment to confront her defenses had arrived. For several sessions running, Elsa diverted herself by indulging in pleasurable narcissistic regressions that I could barely stand. Despite uncertainty as to the precise origin of my discomfort, I thought it right to tell her my feelings. I argued that, given her present level of psychological development, it was most important she not regress to the profound fantasy of the primordial breast since it was time she pulled herself away from the Great Mother, however sybaritic the latter might be.

From the controversy came this dream: Young addicts who show signs of withdrawal are in the shadow of Notre Dame cathedral. Elsa looks into the gutter to find a little powder for them. All she sees is a small ball with a hole in it and some sand inside.

I reflected back to her the expression "ball hole" (*trou de balle*), a vulgar French expression to designate the anus. My reply prompted Elsa to speak of a symptom that had become more acute, one she experienced in a rather ambivalent way: anal itching, which she described as being like "an ant's nest in the anus." (Here the fantasy of oral devouring is displaced to anality; in one of her first dreams, the ants had attacked an image of Christ). The narcissistic ideal of the Great Mother-Self unity, which Elsa experienced through regression into states of intense participation mystique, constellated, as Shadow, the infantile willfulness associated with pregenital omnipotence which attempts to relieve the suffering brought on by psychic lack.

But the dream also shows to what extent voluptuous delight in "grand" archetypal images is but "dust in the eyes," or illusion, for a content, narcissistic borderline who is possessed by the Great Mother-

Self dyad. These "grand" images can sometimes deceive us into believing we have a genuine capacity for *Schauen,* leaving us, in fact, with a distortion of "insight."

Elsa then had two dreams, the first of which goes as follows: Elsa holds a child in her arms. The child, who is taken away by an invisible force, disappears into the wall. The Great Mother has magically absorbed the Child-Self.

Her second dream: Elsa is next to her mother. A plain glass pane separates them from the threat of invading cosmic ice. Elsa experiences with extreme anxiety the threat of ultimate fusion with the eternal ice (in French *glace* refers to both "ice" and "mirror").

In the following session, Elsa returned to a period of her childhood, to what she believed was her first memory, one we had already discussed in therapy: When her sister was born, her mother nearly died of a hemorrhage, necessitating that she be away for an extended period of time. Elsa was sent to stay with an uncle who consoled her by indulging her with chocolate. A miscarriage had previously threatened her mother's life; she had been advised then not to have anymore children as another pregnancy might prove fatal.

"I wonder how they managed not to have any more children," said Elsa wistfully. The phone rang then and I took a moment for a very brief exchange. By the time I got back to Elsa, she was in a complete stupor and remained so motionless that I reassured myself that she was still alive by checking to see if she was still "warm." I leaned toward her and voiced my deep concern, but to no avail. Waiting until the end of the session, I just managed to touch her before she finally emerged from this "comatose" state with a confused laugh. She paid for the session and left.

"When the phone rang, I felt abandoned by you. I thought to myself that surely it was a matter of life and death," she explained when she arrived for the next session. I reminded her of the question we had left off on: "How did they [her parents] do it?"

Indeed, this is what was unthinkable: the petrified fantasy of a primal scene in which fantasy collided with reality and endangered her mother's life. It was impossible to constellate the oedipal conflict since if she took her mother's place next to her father, she, like her mother and along with her, would certainly die.

No striking effects upon psychic structure will follow reactivating the symbolic matrix of the oedipal complex. The borderline personality's emergence from participation mystique is only asymptotic.

But this fantasy of a primal scene that Elsa experienced when feeling abandoned led her to take some distance from the Great Mother, to recombine the parental imagos in the context of the drives (even if only at the pregenital level), and, foremost, to restore a creative transcendent function. After that famous session, Elsa had this dream:

> Dream: *I am a substitute teacher in a kindergarten.* [In French, *maternelle* is identical to the feminine adjectival form of "mother." Elsa is twice removed from the *maternelle,* since she is a *substitute* teacher.] *There is a marvelous girl-child under my care.* ["This time," adds Elsa, "the child does not disappear into the wall."] *The child is precocious and determined: "I want to be a designer," says the child. My parents arrive and ask me for toilet paper to go to the bathroom.*

Thus the parent complex supplies the matter[12] that the Child-Self shapes and opens up to a certain symbolism, a feminine Will; the ego functions as coordinator and custodian of these dynamics.

One could say that releasing a self-sufficient Will through creative activity compensates for the loss of the fantasy of omnipotence which the experience of exclusion from the primal scene implies. This takes away none of the value proper to this dynamism, which sets up through the intermediary of the Self a new relation to reality.

Elsa, who now has a say in her reality, henceforth will manage to have the creative dimension of her identity recognized. She allows herself to strive for her own goals and to receive remuneration commensurate with her worth.

Discussion

We have attempted to describe the "analytic events" that must coincide in the analysis of the borderline personality if the Self is to activate, in the individuation process, the organizing dynamics that lead out of participation mystique.

References to exteriority and the experiences of separation, finitude, discontinuity, and lack are very much needed to disentangle the borderline personality from a stagnant archaic identity. As long as the Self is held captive in the Great Mother, wholeness remains marked by a fusion that aims at eliminating conflict and lack so as to paralyze the psychic process.

We believe, along with Jung, that, given the constellation of a positive therapeutic relationship, the activity of the Self will tend to reestablish intrapsychic polarity. The tension of opposites, and along with it the conflict of drives, may then take place within the inner psychic space of confrontation which is the cornerstone of Jungian analysis.

True oedipal/genital drive conflict heightens the process of subject-object differentiation. The borderline personality that has not experienced true genital conflict will, in its "lower storeys" and to varying degrees, remain enmeshed within the Mother World. Relationships with others will then always be strongly accentuated with narcissism. One should keep in mind, of course, that this narcissism can also work in the direction of a possible release. But it is most important to remember that once analysis has been able to release the Self as a potential organizer, the borderline personality may come to value the ability to reimmerse itself within the Great Mother as archetypal womb. Provided only that the modalities of regression remain supple, the archetypal matrix can then offer potential regeneration. The borderline is thus assured of more creative exchanges with the unconscious and with the outer world.

Endnotes

The notes in this paper are mostly the result of the author's reflections on the stimulating comments received at the 1987 Ghost Ranch Conference. She is grateful to the participants of the conference for their lively discussions.

1. The "confrontation with the unconscious" (Jung 1961; Humbert 1988) and the interactive field necessary to it are closely related to what Jung defines as the "transcendent function" (1916). N. Schwartz-Salant rightly observes that "the borderline person lacks [such] a transcendent function. This is not to say that a link between conscious and unconscious does not exist. . . . What the borderline person lacks is a functional relationship between conscious and unconscious through which consciousness exerts an influence upon the unconscious" (1988). One of the ideas this paper attempts to demonstrate is that this "functional" capacity of the subject to confront the unconscious is made possible by freeing the action of the Self archetype.

2. It might be useful to describe certain aspects of the Great Mother as understood in this paper. E. G. Humbert (1981) puts it the following way:

If we are now speaking of the Great Mother, we are referring to an organizing schema that precedes emotion. It seems both to take hold of the psyche from where the psyche is in what arose in the relationship with the actual, real, and historical mother, and to carry the psyche beyond. . . . It is the Great Mother who creates in the psyche the conditions for wholeness, a wholeness that is admittedly projected and that consists in uniqueness, all-being, omnipotence, omniscience, all of the magical thinking of the child . . . The Great Mother is the one who lends her face to this primordial state of the psyche which Jung calls at times "archaic identity" and, at other times, "participation mystique". . . . The world of the Great Mother is that world where my ideas and images are taken for what is real.

As for wholeness, I would add that when it evolves from the Great Mother, it tends to reduce psychic tension. Wholeness that results from the Self, in contrast, generates the dynamics of opposites.

3. Jung follows a similar line of reasoning when he talks of the transcendent function as "the cooperation of conscious judgment with the data supplied by the unconscious," and adds "moreover, it is a natural and spontaneous phenomenon—and it forms a part of the individuation process" (1954).

4. P. L. Assoun (1980) stresses the fact that, in the fundamental Freudian myth of the primal horde, the death of the Father (i.e., the "original father," the "superman," endowed with the sovereign privilege of primary narcissism) also signs the death warrant of narcissism:

" . . . the perfect type of the most complete narcissism conceivable to man is thrown back by Freud into an interrupted and lapsed 'prior time'."

5. It matters little that the study of psychogenetics is not currently in fashion in French psychoanalytic circles. Such a study will nevertheless provide valuable and relevant insights into the subject area of interest to us. It is also true that Jung never studied psychogenetics since he was eager to explore the perspective of finality, which governs the organizing process of psychic transformation. When, on rare occasions, Jung talks of genetics (phylogenetics) as in 1912 in *Symbols of Transformation,* what we read (and here we disagree with Satinover's interpretation of this text) is less a discourse on biological causality than a purely mythical text. The reason for this is that it is only by way of mythical discourse that the subject can, from the perspective of finality, give meaning to its own origins. This contrasts with the Freudian psychogenetic perspective that untiringly seeks the "factual rock" upon which the subject's psychic development is situated relative to tangible reality.

6. The work on complexes hardly seems effective so long as that fundamental separation of the Self from the Great Mother has not taken place. Activating complexes then leads only to repetition-compulsion and fails to constellate the tension of opposites that alone reaches out for the "third thing not given" (*tertium non datur*).

7. One of Alexandra's typical dreams demonstrates this:

The washing machine is running with nothing in it since Alexandra consistently drops the laundry behind it. Furthermore, Alexandra's name can be related to the laundry itself. Thus the process, emptied as it is of its contents, takes place alongside the subject and without it.

8. This ball of string clearly suggests how much that bond itself is cherished when wholeness comes from the Great Mother: The string is wound around its own center. Only by freeing the Self can a new Eros be born. This Eros includes, as part of its development, the ability to accept another's autonomous desire. At the time the patient had this dream, such an Eros was still impossible in the transference relationship with the analyst. The Great Mother drew everything back into herself.

9. In France, Grunberger (1975) has made a convincing analysis of the interaction between the power of pregenital drives and narcissism. This exposition is very useful in understanding the organization of the borderline personality.

10. According to the Lacanian way of thinking, the borderline personality structure is related to that moment when the child is seen as a substitute for the phallus. The child identifies with what it takes to be the mother's unique object of desire. As phallus, the child fills the mother's lack in order to maintain a merger relationship with her. In the child's desire to be the mother's phallus, the father is excluded, although he is implicitly "named" in the phallic symbol (*le signifiant*). He is denied, but not "foreclosed" since, for Lacan, the foreclosure of the father would introduce a psychotic structure.

11. Philippe's case illustrates what N. Schwartz-Salant so effectively emphasizes—that, by reestablishing the heretofore rejected Feminine Principle (the anima), Philippe finds access to the "central quality of the Eye, imaginal sight" (*das Schauen*). The Self—which was previously "dead to relationships" (dead within the Great Mother's wholeness)—can now be open to a possible encounter.

12. In French, *matière* can refer equally to feces and to the creative matter that, as *prima materia,* can be molded and fashioned like putty or clay.

References

Assoun, P. L. 1980. *Freud et Nietzsche.* Presses Universitaires de France.

Bergeret, J. 1984. *La dépression et les états-limites.* Paris: Payot.

Bergeret, J. and Reid, W. et al. 1986. *Narcissisme et états-limites.* Paris: Bordas, for the Presses Universitaires de Montreal, Dunod.

Dor, J. 1985. *Introduction à la lecture de Lacan.* Paris: Denoël.

Freud, S. 1914. On narcissism: An introduction. In *Standard Edition* 14:67–102. New York: Norton.

Green, A. 1977. The borderline concept. In P. Hartocollis, ed., *Borderline personality disorders.* New York: International University Press.

——————. 1983. *Narcissisme de vie, narcissisme de mort.* Paris: Les Editions de Minuit.

Grunberger, B. 1975. *Narcissism.* Paris: Payot.

Guy-Gillet, G. 1986. Le Jeu du soi. In *L'espace intérieur. Cahiers de Psychologie Jungienne,* No. 50.

Humbert, G. E. 1981. Eros et volonté de puissance dans la perspective de la Grande Mère. Conference, Paris: forthcoming.

——————. 1988. *C. J. Jung: The fundamentals of theory and practice.* Wilmette, IL: Chiron Publications.

Jung, C. G. 1912. *Métamorphoses et symboles de la libido.* Translated from the German by L. De Vos. Paris: Editions Montaigne, 1927.

——————. 1916. The transcendent function. In *Collected works* 8. Princeton: Princeton University Press.

——————. 1928. The spiritual problem of modern man. In *Collected works,* 10. Princeton: Princeton University Press.

——————. 1928. The relation between the ego and the unconscious. In *Collected works* 7. Princeton: Princeton University Press.

——————. 1931. The secret of the golden flower. In *Collected works* 13. Princeton: Princeton University Press.

——————. 1954. Letter to Pastor William Lachat. *Letters 2: 1951–1961.* Gerhard Adler, ed. Princeton: Princeton University Press, 1976.

——————. 1961. *Memories, dreams, reflections.* New York: Vintage Books, 1966.

Kacirek, S. 1980. *L'énergétisme jungien.* Doctoral dissertation. Université de Paris VII.

——————. 1980. Le concept de libido selon C. G. Jung. Des métamorphoses et symboles de la libido à l'énergetique psychique. *Cahiers de Psychologie Jungienne,* No. 26.

Kacirek, S. and Gagey, J. 1987. L'axe énergétique et la psychanalyse. In *Psychanalyse à l'Université.* Paris: Presses Universitaires de France.

Kernberg, O. 1967. Borderline personality organization. In Michael H. Stone, ed., *Essential papers on borderline disorders,* New York and London: New York University Press, 1986.

——————. 1975. Narcissisme normal et narcissisme pathologique. *Nouvelle Revue de Psychanalyse,* No. 13.

Laplanche, J. 1984. La pulsion et son objet-source: Son destin dans le transfert. *La Pulsion pour quoi faire?* Paris: Association Psychanalytique de France.

Satinover, J. 1985. At the mercy of another: Abandonment and restitution in psychosis and psychotic character. In N. Schwartz-Salant and M. Stein, eds., *Abandonment.* Wilmette, Ill.: Chiron Publications.

Schwartz-Salant, N. 1988. Before the creation: The unconscious couple in the borderline personality. *The Borderline Personality in Analysis.* Wilmette, Ill.: Chiron Publications.

Primary Ambivalence toward the Self: Its Nature and Treatment

John Beebe

This then is the formula which describes the condition of the self when despair is completely eradicated: by relating itself to its own self and by willing to be itself the self is grounded transparently in the Power which posited it.

Soren Kierkegaard, The Sickness Unto Death

To offer a program for handling the borderline personality in analysis is perhaps to succumb to the seductive notion that one is going to be able to bring a seemingly endless clinical discussion to a satisfying resolution. This expectation is, however, no more exacting than that of the borderline patient: that the therapist should finally achieve a per-

John Beebe, M.D. is a member of the C.G. Jung Institute of San Francisco, where he is editor of *The San Francisco Jung Institute Library Journal.* A graduate of Harvard College and the University of Chicago Medical School, he did his psychiatric residency at Stanford University Medical Center and his analytic training at the C. G. Jung Institute of San Francisco. He is the editor of *Psychiatric Treatment: Crisis, Clinic, and Consultation* (1975) and *Money, Food, Drink, Fashion, and Analytic Training; Depth Dimensions of Physical Existence* (1983). He has a private practice in San Francisco.

The author wishes to acknowledge the help of Herbert Wiesenfeld in researching and digesting the literature of psychoanalytic self-psychology; of Mara Sidoli in making clearer the viewpoints of Michael Fordham and other London analysts; of Anna Spielvogel in insisting upon the collective cultural background; and of Adam Frey in feeling the emotional sequence through.

fect relationship to what has so far never been comfortably related to, bringing to a halt all the oscillating ruminations over this imperfect relation. Indeed, the only way I can approach this topic is with the unreasonable hope of bringing my own anxious ponderings over borderline issues in analytic work to an end.

Possibly other analysts have repeatedly wondered if certain patients, certain areas of the mind, and certain aspects of themselves will ever be able to enter the healing matrix of the analytic process that has been so triumphantly validated by other patients, other areas of the mind, and other aspects of themselves. I know I have. Again and again, I have brooded over the fate of psychological constellations that perennially approach and then avoid the transforming experience that analysis can be; and their haunting presence like beggars at the gate of personality transformation has driven me to such expiatory measures as extending my own analysis, searching the writings of colleagues, and trying to accept with self-forgiveness the limitations of my analytic resources.

Experience has forced me to respect the subtle purposefulness of difficult human transactions. Yet, I remain dismayed by the perverse drive of an energized complex that will not enter treatment but will not forsake it either. It is this ambivalent characteristic that for me is the hallmark of the complexes we call borderline when we meet them in analysis: what is borderline is the way they relate to the analytic process. Where other complexes in their purposive persistence seem to be seeking the Self as their core of meaning and become eventually comprehensible as ways through which the intentions of the Self have been expressed, these "borderline" complexes absurdly approach and avoid the Self in a Self-disqualifying way, making a travesty of the analyst's efforts at unraveling their meaning. When a patient is possessed by such a complex, we can well speak of a "borderline patient," although we should always remember that it is a quality of the *complex* and not of the person that causes borderline behavior within the therapeutic relationship. Such complexes induce a state of mind in the patient that I feel must be addressed before any really transformative work is possible. I have chosen to call this unconscious attitude primary ambivalence toward the Self.

Sometimes this ambivalence is an attitude that seems to grip the totality of the patient; sometimes it seems to belong to only a part, but its persistent power can bring analytic work to a seeming standstill and render the analyst's normally impossible job intolerable, for all analysis (as indeed all satisfying progress through life) depends on acceptance of the Self. The usual patient who comes to psychotherapy is in a demoralized state and has to be encouraged to find trust in the Self, and usually it develops that the condition is only secondary to a more fundamental trust in the person's own being having become lost. Secondary ambivalence toward the Self is relatively easily resolved, and the patient is soon able to accept the healing ministrations and guidance of his own instinct for individuation. Affects, dreams, intercurrent life experiences, and the relationship to the analyst all start to work for the patient again, as the Self performs its functions in healing cycles of integration and deintegration. Despite the usual complement of difficulties, the work proceeds in an atmosphere of basic acceptance of the effort to ground identity in the purposive activity of the Self.

For the person caught in primary ambivalence toward the Self, however, the ground itself of therapeutic effort is unsure. Not only the analysis, but the unfolding of the individual's life generally seems to offer continuous evidence of the dubiety of God.

I propose here to illustrate the way this fundamental ambivalence makes its presence felt within the analytical transference/countertransference as well as some ways in which the therapeutic relationship may be handled as the vehicle for its resolution. I will be deliberately schematic, suggesting in a sequence of twenty "steps" the interpersonal moves by which the ambivalence toward the Self is acted out, recognized, and finally resolved within the context of a relationship to an analyst. Obviously, these are steps in the imagination of an analyst interested in process: the complete sequence of resolution, if it exists, is not one that most patients will traverse with a single analyst. Nevertheless, these steps provide a way to organize the countertransference experience and therapeutic fantasy of therapists interested in knowing where they are during deep work with difficult patients. The steps also are a guide to places within the therapeutic relationship where different kinds of interventions belong, and they suggest a rational basis for locating contexts where the theoretical contributions of various analysts may be usefully applied. Throughout, the reference point will be the way the patient relates to the analyst or analytically oriented therapist who is trying to foster a relationship to the Self. As we shall see, the therapist's well-intentioned efforts in this role can arouse deep resistances in the patient for which the therapist must be prepared to assume responsibility if the patient is to be helped. In the early steps, as the ambivalent relationship is being established, it is necessary for the therapist to try to understand its impact on the patient, and to help the therapist in this effort I will draw extensively at first upon the contributions of theory. Theoretical inferences have helped me to clarify what dreams and feelings reported sometimes only hint at when this kind of therapeutic relationship is first being formed. Self theory, in particular, has helped me to make sense of what would otherwise be a totally bewildering experience: an extremely positive transference that is nevertheless characterized by intense resistance.

The First Step: Choice of a Selfobject

The intense ambivalence characteristic of borderline transference will not be directed toward just anyone. The person selected will be someone who is experienced as self-enhancing, but in such a way that the patient does not entirely feel separate from this important person. Early on, the person chosen, like any internalized *object* of the patient's libido, will be the focus of intense fascination and the target of fantasies of dependence, aggression, and desire. But this intensity is further compounded by what the psychoanalyst Heinz Kohut (1984) was the first to make clear: that there is only partial differentiation of self from object because the other person is being used to shore up the self of the subject. Kohut chose the term *selfobject*, without a hyphen, to refer to a person used in this way by the patient and spoke of the patient's transference to a therapist used in this way as a *selfobject transference*, one that thrusts the therapist smack into the subjectivity of the patient. The result is that the therapist feels vitally connected to emotionally charged shifts in the patient's self-experience.

Kohut's followers have established that the patient's subjective sense of self normally has three essential features: affective coloration, stability over time, and structural cohesion. The patients who will develop borderline transferences within the intersubjective field of the analysis have moderately severe disorders in their sense of self. In this kind of patient there is not only the negative affective coloration (feelings of low self-esteem) one would expect from almost any analytic patient, but also temporal instability of the self (experiences of identity confusion and fleeting fragmentation), and, frequently, lack of cohesion (rendering the patient vulnerable to structural fragmentation and protracted disintegration). It is to solve these problems that the patient turns to a selfobject (Brandchaft and Stolorow 1984).

It is important for the therapist to realize at the outset what it means to be chosen as someone's selfobject. Of the selfobject, Paul Ornstein has written:

Such an object is related to only in terms of the specific, phase-appropriate needs of the developing self, without recognition of the object and its own center of initiative. (1978, p. 60)

The earliest selfobject is the *archaic selfobject*, which bears considerable similarity to Michael Fordham's *self-objects*, belonging to the intrapsychic experience of earliest infancy—proto-objects organizing the experience of caretakers on the basis of archetypal schemata or models whose "imagery is not differentiated from the objects themselves, and represents the needs of the infant that a mother meets and satisfies" (Fordham 1976, pp. 19–20). But in Kohut's view the selfobject role in psychic functioning is not restricted to this archaic selfobject existing before self and object differentiation has taken place. The self-object is not just some very early form of the usual object, which will eventually be experienced "objectively": it is a subjective dimension of the never-outgrown experience of having another person shore up one's self (Kohut 1984, p. 49). There is no selfobject without some connection to the self, and the selfobject is not a person, but a personified function. The self-selfobject relationship refers to an intrapsychic experience, not an interpersonal one.

The self-selfobject relationship is, however (and this is Kohut's all-important discovery), an intrapsychic phenomenon that takes place in an intersubjective field shared between two persons. This opens the door to a discussion of what a therapist performing the selfobject function feels within this relationship, for the selfobject role is experienced by the enhancing individual in an entirely personal way. The therapist being used feels related to the patient's self with subjective intensity and gives an embodied reality to the selfobject function. The therapist's real feelings and behaviors in this role become an essential part of the patient's process of recovery of self.

Certainly, as the self-psychologists have emphasized, the therapist's emotional reactions become linked to phase-specific needs of the patient and to the feelings of past persons who have incarnated this selfobject role. It is possible, as Ernest Wolf (1986) has pointed out, for the analyst to be an archaic selfobject, a mirroring selfobject, an idealizable selfobject, an alter-ego selfobject, an adversarial selfobject, and—in all these roles—a failing selfobject; and much of this feels like, and is, a revival of the past in which the analyst is participating. Although concern for the self's welfare goes with the territory of becoming someone's selfobject, the analyst must not manipulate the self-experience of the patient by giving "good" selfobject responses and avoiding "bad" ones, but should instead take seriously the effect on the patient of all behaviors in the selfobject role. The analyst will often talk to the patient, reflecting back through interpretation and ongoing commentary what the effect on the self seems to have been of something the analyst has said or done. This interpretive approach strengthens the patient's awareness of the self as a vital organizing center responding emotionally to the successes and failures of selfobjects who can enhance its functioning. Such awareness of the self ultimately leads the patient to greater willingness to attend to its needs as well as more effective use of selfobjects. But so far this self-psychology approach to analysis, for all its innovation, does not seriously challenge the traditional view of the analyst as the reactive member of the transference dyad, whose interpretations and interventions are centered in the experience of the patient, to which the analyst conscientiously defers.

But the selfobject role is one that also gives the analyst a heightened personality within the transference. From a Jungian perspective, I find it valuable to grant this personality the status of a psychological reality, making the selfobject into a living person incarnated by the analyst, with needs and feelings to be taken seriously. The analyst must then defend the needs of the selfobject alongside those of the patient. Incarnating the selfobject function means not only reifying the selfobject but making this figure someone the patient must reckon with. When, in the steps that follow, I describe initiatives taken by the selfobject, I am referring to the analyst's willingness to act with integrity from within the selfobject role. This starts with the recognition that one's own idiosyncratic reality as a person plays a part even in the patient's unconscious decision to let one be a selfobject.

Often the literature on the selfobject role seems to suggest that the analyst's own qualities have relatively little to do with the way the patient uses the analyst. Yet the person chosen for the role will usually be someone the patient can feel close to, who has demonstrated a capacity for empathic participation in the patient's world, and whom the patient can respect. Indeed, the relationship often starts so well the therapist may not realize that what the patient sees is not exactly the therapist. For often there is an element of synchronicity in the process by which the patient arrives in just this therapist's office; and the analyst feels in some coincidental way related to the patient's history or life situation. With patients for whom this sort of transference unfolds, the relationship has at its outset a numinous quality, a sanctified sense of special rightness. To the analyst, as the person employed to stabilize and enhance development of the patient's incomplete sense of personal self, will quickly be attributed qualities of the transpersonal Self; and one may well believe, given the felt connection to the patient, that this is in a way deserved. One feels, as therapist, that one was meant or destined to help this patient, a sort of divine-right countertransference from the start. The analyst notices that empathy seems unusually easy with this new patient, despite a history of previous difficulties in this area; it is easy to experience the patient's emotions as one's own and to know, at this early stage, how to deal with them for the patient. Often the analyst basks in the glow of the patient's gratitude in the face of such helpful participation in the patient's unconscious life. Yet reverence for the analyst is sometimes accompanied by a strangely discrepant feeling, also imbibed from the patient, of awe or terror—the patient's reaction to being in the presence of the Self incarnate. And with failures of empathy this terror is replaced by an even more intense rage, which the analyst will experience viscerally as a physical attack, a feeling that turns out to be not dissimilar from that of the patient in response to empathic failure. The two partners to this selfobject transference are in an increasingly uncomfortable, emotionally continuous field that envelops them both.

Brandchaft and Stolorow have been careful to point out that "what we call 'borderline' is *not* . . . a pathological condition located solely in the patient. Rather, it refers to phenomena arising in an intersubjective field—a field consisting of a precarious, vulnerable self and a failing, archaic selfobject" (Brandchaft and Stolorow 1984, p. 342–43). The challenge for the therapist is to try to be an effective selfobject during these times of difficulty for the patient:

> It is true that the selfobject ties formed by those patients who are called 'borderline' tend inititally to be far more primitive and intense, more labile and vulnerable to disruption, and therefore more taxing of the therapist's empathy and tolerance (Adler 1980, 1981; Tolpin 1980) than those described by Kohut as being characteristic of narcissistic personalities. Furthermore, when the selfobject ties of a patient with a moderate to severe self disorder are obstructed or ruptured by empathic failures or separation, the patient's reactions may be much more catastrophic and disturbed, for what is threatened is the patient's central self-regulatory capacity—not merely its affective tone (Adler 1980, 1981; Stolorow and Lachman 1980). Nevertheless, when these patients' archaic states and needs are correctly understood, they can be helped to form more or less stable selfobject transferences, and when this is achieved, these so-called borderline features recede and even disappear. So long as the selfobject tie to the therapist remains intact, their treatment will bear a close similarity to Kohut's descriptions of analyses of narcissistic personality disorders (Adler 1980, 1981). . . . When the selfobject tie to the therapist becomes significantly

> disrupted, on the other hand, the patient may once again present border-
> line features. . . . [W]hether or not a stable selfobject bond can develop and
> be maintained (which in turn shapes both the apparent diagnostic picture
> and the assessment of analyzability) does not depend only on the patient's
> nuclear self pathology. It will be codetermined by the extent of the thera-
> pist's ability to comprehend empathically the nature of the patient's archaic
> subjective universe (Tolpin 1980) as it begins to structure the microcosm
> of the therapeutic transference. (Brandchaft and Stolorow 1984, 344)

What these followers of Kohut do not make entirely clear is why
the experience of the analyst's empathy in the role of selfobject is so
powerful. To understand this better one has to turn to a Jungian author, Edward Edinger (1973), who has pointed out that empathy par-
takes of an essential attribute of the transpersonal Self, an attribute he
calls *acceptance*. An understanding of the psychological meaning to the
patient of acceptance is essential if one is to follow what ensues later in
the selfobject transference, when such acceptance occasions violent
ambivalence. Taking an archetypal perspective, Edinger makes explicit a
point that the self-psychologists with their personalistic standpoint have
had to leave unclear, that the empathic behavior of a selfobject has the
important effect of eliciting a projection of the transpersonal Self:

> Patients with a damaged ego-Self axis are most impressed in psycho-
> therapy by the discovery that the therapist accepts them. Initially they can-
> not believe it. The fact of acceptance may be discredited by considering it
> only a professional technique having no genuine reality. However, if the
> acceptance of the therapist is recognized as a fact, a powerful transference
> promptly appears. The source of this transference seems to be the projec-
> tion of the Self, especially in its function as the organ of acceptance. At
> this point the *central* characteristics of the therapist-Self become promi-
> nent. The therapist as a person becomes the *center* of the patient's life and
> thoughts. The therapy sessions become the *central* points of the week. A
> center of meaning and order has appeared where previously there was
> chaos and despair. (p. 40–41)

This "central" quality is an archetypal characteristic of the transpersonal (big *S*, Jungian) Self, which is the ultimate source of all healing. It is the Self, as mediated by the selfobject therapist, that nourishes
the development of the personal (little *s*, Kohutian) self to provide
affective color, temporal stability, and structural cohesion to the personality.

> The Self as the center and totality of the psyche which is able to recon-
> cile all opposites can be considered as the organ of acceptance *par excel-
> lence*. Since it includes the totality, it must be able to accept all elements of
> psychic life no matter how antithetical they may be. It is this sense of the

acceptance of the Self that gives the ego its strength and stability. This sense of acceptance is conveyed to the ego via the ego-Self axis. A symptom of damage to this axis is a lack of self-acceptance. The individual feels he is not worthy to exist or be himself. Psychotherapy offers such a person an opportunity to experience acceptance. In successful cases this can amount to a repair of the ego-Self axis which restores contact with the inner sources of strength and acceptance, leaving the patient free to live and grow. (*Ibid.*, p. 40)

Edinger, writing in the early 1970s, does not employ the concept of the personal self that the psychoanalysts around Kohut have developed; so he is forced to fall back on the Jungian ego to describe the part of the patient nourished by contact with the transpersonal Self. This makes it sound as if the response to the Self is a conscious one, capable of being influenced by re-education at the conscious level. In fact the crucial experiences in the relation to the Self are not ego-experiences but self-experiences, affects not under control of the conscious mind and not always easy to hold in awareness without the support of the analyst's willingness to hear them out and vicarious participation in them. What Edinger calls the ego-Self axis, Kohut calls the self, and what Edinger calls damage to the ego-Self axis, Kohut calls a self disorder. Analysis itself as a discipline is only beginning to develop a differentiated language for the internal object relationships it has long sought to sort out for .patients. Given what has been accomplished in the past fifteen years, I think that these postmodern analytic schools— psychoanalytic self psychology and analytical psychology—are ready to make use of each other's concepts, and that it is possible now to distinguish self from ego in terms of experienceable needs, and Self from self in terms of their relative roles in the integration of personality. It has become possible to see the self as the organ of personality that seeks the Self and to realize that the task of psychotherapy is to strengthen the former, so that the healing possibilities of the latter may be better utilized. (For extensive discussions of the relation between little-*s* self and big-*S* Self, see Ekstrom 1984; Gordon 1985; Redfearn 1985.)

When an analyst is chosen by a patient as selfobject, it is for the purpose of having the analyst mediate the self-Self relationship. Sensitively employed (Book 1988), the analyst's empathy shores up the self, and it is through the self that the Self is made accessible. The selfobject function is a stand-in for the accepting Self; intrapsychically the self-object strengthens the patient's self by behaving like the Self. Once constellated in the transference, the Self will be the ultimate maintainer and strengthener of the self, to the degree that the patient can accept and honor the Self. But for a long time, and certainly at this initial stage of the work, the selfobject is the all-important representative of the Self, and it is toward this object that the patient's self will express all its desire, and all its doubt, with respect to the Self.

The patient may well be dismayed by the affects that the therapist's presence and behavior stir up, and for a long time these affects may be disowned. The analyst knows of their existence only because they are felt for the patient. These reactions come particularly in response to the analyst's failures of empathy, especially failures to live up to the patient's ideal image of the analyst and to register and accurately mirror back the felt meaning of the patient's experience. The patient's involuntary reactions to the analyst's failures of empathy are not perverse, willful, tyrannical, or "evil" behaviors on the part of the patient's ego; they are signs that the self of the patient is reacting to separations from the Self, as mediated by the therapist in the role of selfobject. An enormous step in treatment is reached when the fact of the self-selfobject relationship can be acknowledged openly between patient and therapist. This recognition can foster the patient's discovery of the self-Self relationship.

At this first step in the therapy of a patient with a damaged relation to the Self, the rages and anxieties of the self must be taken seriously, and recognized (as Kohut has taught us to do) through their displacements and disguises, such as depression, withdrawal, and apathy. Although usually occasioned by some empathic failure of the therapist in the role of selfobject (and resolvable by the therapist's unembarrassed objective acknowledgement of such failures), the affects of the self turn out to signal a healthy recognition by the patient of a separation not just from the selfobject but from the Self as well. The point for the patient is that the self has somehow been failed. The therapist's job is to promote increasing consciousness of such affects; this fosters integration of the self as it reaches toward the wider Self.

The Second Step: Ambivalent Treatment of the Selfobject

The great question in understanding the borderline transference/countertransference situation is why the self-selfobject relation, once it has been established as a consequence of the patient's experience of the therapist's empathy and of the therapist's willingness to take seriously empathic failures within the ongoing work, fails nevertheless to restore harmonious self-Self relations. Why, if the therapist has been allowed to incarnate the Self, can this therapist-Self do so little to console the patient and further the patient's life? I think here we are forced to recognize a strongly-defended, paranoid piece of the self that is ambivalently connected to any strongly empathic selfobject, confusing and undermining the self-selfobject relationship. It is this trickster aspect of the self that gets worked through with the analytic therapist in the nineteen steps that follow the establishment of a selfobject transference.

This trickster corresponds to the castrating aspect of the anima and the envious side of the animus, which seek to undermine rather than to enhance the relation to the Self. Much of what Kohut calls the self is expressed in the Jungian literature in terms of the imagery, mythology, and dramatic behavior of the archetypes Jung named the *anima* and the *animus*. Just as in Kohut's language the "bipolar self" uses a selfobject to extend its range and become a truly overarching, personality-integrating structure, so in Jung's vision of the psyche the anima/animus "syzygy" of archetypes uses personal relations to achieve, finally, a bridge to the great transpersonal Self. One of the "poles" of Kohut's self, the "grandiose exhibitionistic self," displays a need for mirroring quite suggestive of the demanding vanity of the anima archetype; and the other pole, the "idealized parental imago," places expectations on a selfobject for model behavior that are reminiscent of the exacting standard-setting of the animus. Like Kohut's self, both anima and animus act badly when their needs are not met, yet despite their seeming narcissism both archetypes have as their ultimate aim not coercion of selfobjects but connection to the wider, overarching Self. Jung's vision of the reality of the anima and animus as dramatic, mythological figures of unconscious life allows them to have, like goddesses and gods, a dark, ambivalent side missing in Kohut's description of the bipolar self. The dark side of these figures and of the little-*s* self is well characterized by the trickster figure that appears in many mythological traditions. The mythological tricksters, with their violation of sacred precincts and disregard of their cultures' central values, personify primary ambivalence toward the Self, and the quality of the self-selfobject relationship that develops within a borderline transference can be quite reminiscent of the behavior of Hermes toward Apollo or Satan toward God. The therapist who found the patient an unusually responsive subject may now well feel that a sociopath has entered treatment.

This defiant aspect of the self makes its first appearance early in life, and many therapists have found it helpful to associate the patient's difficult behavior not with gods, but with the upsetting behavior of developing infants. Many analysts have observed that patients in the midst of a borderline transference put their therapists through what toddlers put their mothers through during the process of separation-individuation.

The classic observation of toddler behavior, as well as the connection to borderline transference, has been made by the psychoanalyst Margaret Mahler (1975) and her co-workers. She noticed that around 18 months toddlers "chose not to be reminded that at times they could not manage on their own." This period was "characterized by the rapidly alternating desire to push mother away and to cling to her," a behavioral sequence Mahler calls *ambitendency*. Mother would be used as an extension of the self in ways that seemed to deny the painful awareness of separateness and of any direct need for her, such as "pulling mother's hand and using it as a tool to get a desired object" or "expecting that mother, summoned by some magical gesture alone, rather than with words, would guess and fulfill the toddler's momentary wish." On the other hand, there were moments when the child would express "sudden anxiety that mother had left, on occasions when she had not even risen from her chair!" And there would be frequent "moments of a strange, seeming 'nonrecognition' of mother, after a brief absence on her part." And mother would tend to react "adversely to her separating individuating toddler":

> The mother's reaction at that time was quite often tinged with feelings of annoyance at the toddler's insistence on his autonomy, at this wanting, for example, to tie his shoelaces without help, and so on. "You think you can manage on your own? All right, I can leave you to your own devices, see how you fare." Or, "A moment ago, you did not want to be with me. Well, now I don't want to be with you." (Mahler, Pine, and Bergman 1975, pp. 95–96)

All this is normal developing infant—and mother—behavior, but because so much of it is relived in the transference/countertransference with borderline patients, some analysts, including Mahler, have postulated an original wounding to the patient during this "rapproachement subphase" of separation-individuation. The "borderline" pathology is then interpreted either as a fixation at this stage of development or a regression to this stage under the pressure of later conflicts. Indeed, with less secure toddlers, Mahler was able to find evidence of an infantile neurosis, with the apparent acting out of a conflict of ambivalence indicated by "coercive behaviors" designed to force the mother "to function as the child's omnipotent extension" alternating with "signs of desperate clinging."

In children with less than optimal development, the ambivalence conflict is discernible during the rapproachement subphase in rapidly clinging and negativistic behaviors. . . . This phenomenon may be in some cases a reflection of the fact that the child has split the object world more permanently than is optimal into "good" and "bad." By means of this splitting, the "good" object is defended against the derivatives of the aggressive drive.

The two mechanisms that Mahler found in these neurotic infants— "coercion and splitting of the object world"—are also, she noted, "characteristic of most cases of adult borderline transference" (*ibid.*, pp. 107– 108).

Henry Parens (1979) has placed this "first conflict of ambivalence" even earlier in the sequence of separation-individuation. He sees it originating during the subphase when the ten- to fourteen-month-old toddler is first "practicing" autonomy and engaged in a "love affair with the world" (Greenacre 1960). With a "biological upsurge of the aggressive drive" the infant is expending every effort to "control and master the environment." The mother is then perceived as "the most frequent obstacle to the gratification of these autonomous strivings" and there is "a battle of wills between child and mother" (Parens 1979, pp. 285–87). Since the child does everything possible to get around the mother to explore the environment, and the mother bends her efforts toward subverting the will of the child so as to protect the child's body and the breakable things in the environment, the mythological aspect is a battle that pits trickster against witch: both tend to fight dirty. However, the infant not only directs hostile aggression toward the mother who tries to frustrate its explorations: the infant also turns to that very mother seeking comfort and the cessation of unpleasure. Thus the developing infant is forced to seek comfort from a frustrating and enraging figure, and this, Parens feels, is the source, at the beginning of the second year of life, of the first conflict of ambivalence. This may become the engram for all later conflicts of ambivalence and a potent source for complications in the attitude toward selfobjects and therefore the Self.

As a Jungian analyst, I regard the "drive to activity" (Jung 1960, par. 240), rather than the aggressive drive of psychoanalytic authors, as the factor that first mobilizes the ambivalence conflict. This drive is present from birth onward as part of the Self's push to enter the world—what Michael Fordham calls *deintegration*—but many mothers and fathers meet it with less-than-optimal acceptance; so they not only frustrate the behavior of the exploring child but also repay the exploratory attitude with condemning rejection. This communication from a parent who finds it difficult to tolerate tension amounts to a message from

the world that the Self's own unfolding developmental plan is unacceptable. At an early stage, this attitude is, I think, incorporated into the self
of the child so that part of it becomes aligned against the Self. Though
not the earliest possible such alienation, it is a formidable one. The
symbolism of dreams of adult patients in analysis includes many images
of this attitude within the self, and associations often trace them to in-
trojections of the original mother's prohibitive animus, an image in
which aspects of the early father may be included. It seems quite likely
that during infancy, even as a conflict of ambivalence toward the internal representation of the mother is taking shape, an introjection of
parental ambivalence toward the developmental process causes tensions to rise. Thus a split may appear in the self at a very early age. One
part of the self seeks the selfobject's validation for its ever-increasing
drive to activity and rages at it when the needed validation is not supplied. Another part of the self identifies with the tension-fearing parent,
becoming upset when the selfobject does seem to go along with the
Self's deintegrative agenda.

Deintegration can also complicate ambivalence toward selfobjects
by arousing defenses used by the primal self (baby's original self-Self
wholeness) to ward off not-self objects (Fordham 1974). Mara Sidoli
mentions a patient whose actual birth took 48 hours. As an adult in his
30's he dreams that he is in a leather bag that keeps opening and clos-
ing rhythmically. Outside are objects like feet, claws, and teeth which
try to get at the dreamer, who realizes that he can use his arms, "which
are hard like a winged shield to pull in the front to cover the opening."
This seems to symbolize an autistic barrier (Tustin 1986) in the patient,
who, as Sidoli puts it, is "fighting with all his capacity the deintegrative
process of the primal self." She sees the patient's attitude toward his
own cycles of integration and deintegration as having been conditioned
not only by the circumstances of his birth, but also by the the behavior
during infancy of a very disturbed mother who "persecuted him by
impinging in his vital areas or leaving him totally unprotected" (Sidoli,
1987, pp. 9–10).

As this example shows, deintegration is an autonomous activity of
the Self that may be hard for the self to accept, even if consciously one
decries the stagnation of limited integration at a lower-than-optimal
level of development. Unconscious fear of deintegration is an attitude
that can be traced back to the very beginnings of life, perhaps even to
the womb. The primal self of the infant is naturally geared to cycles of
integrative and deintegrative activity (Fordham 1976). To facilitate the
newborn baby's entry into the world of object relations, this primary

integration in which self is indistinguishable from Self must break down as the Self gives up some of its contents to projections onto the parental figures. (For example, the Great Mother archetype is projectively identified within the personal mother so that bonding can occur.) The baby is left as a much less whole, much less powerful self, subject to now all-powerful selfobjects. This deintegrative activity breaks up original self-Self identity and greatly threatens the security of the subjective self, which can be restored only by the behavior of empathic selfobjects and by new cycles of integrative activity.

The normal anxiety occasioned by deintegration throughout the life-cycle can be readily demonstrated clinically (Maduro 1985), but for some unfortunates the selfobjects turn out to be so essentially persecuting that the individual feels, from earliest infancy, unsafe and betrayed by the Self that gave up its integrative power to them. Deintegration becomes associated with painful experiences of *dis*integration at the hands of unempathic selfobjects. I know of one woman who was born at home, upon which her father's first act was to slap her mother for giving birth to a girl and not a boy; and of another whose entire original culture, Nazi Germany, was experienced from her earliest days as persecuting. For both of these women, cultural background was the basis for development of an ambivalent attitude toward the Self's deintegrative activity, and they both clung fearfully to what they could rescue of the primary integration at the expense of the freedom to participate in life.

It would seem that the Self dictates conditions of existence that the self cannot always accept. Whether in alliance with less-than-ideal selfobjects, in defiance of them, or both, the developing self can divide itself against the Self, producing a formidable obstacle to the healthy unfolding of personality. Not only deintegrative activity but even integrative activity is hampered by inability to move with the Self. In the midst of deep analytic work, negative attitudes toward the Self will surface as subtle resistance to the selfobject transference. The person chosen as selfobject by the individual who has not resolved primary ambivalence toward the Self will inevitably be treated ambivalently.

Whatever the infantile roots of the conflict, this resistance to the selfobject transference will be expressed with all the sophisticated resources of the adult patient, and with the subtly undermining, double-binding quality of the trickster archetype that has been summoned as the patient's main defense against the inexorability of the Self. Sometimes the resistance has more an adolescent than an infantile feel to it, and of course the trickster is a major archetype of the adolescent personality. Adolescence is a time of regression to early conflicts, when (as Blos puts it) "primary ambivalence . . . invades the adolescent's relations to objects, to symbols, to ideas, and to the self" (1979, p. 29) Once the selfobject transference has been established and its healing potential demonstrated, the analyst begins to experience a push-pull between one part of the patient that feels good about this state of affairs and another that does not like it at all. It is as if something in the patient were saying, "If this is true, I will have to thrive, and I can't do that."

The Third Step: The Selfobject Recognizes the Fact of the Ambivalence

The analyst is in a double bind. The intense self-selfobject transference makes it very difficult to experience anything but positive value from the patient, yet there is a sense of mounting anxiety, depression, or rage as therapeutic efforts are met with a mixed response of gratitude and suspicion. One feels strangely distanced by the patient, who continues to make it clear in a number of verbal and nonverbal ways that the analyst is both important and respected. It is not uncommon for an analyst to develop a chronic feeling of despair, as if caught in a bad marriage from which there is no escape. It is important that analysts experience this numbing effect of being related to ambivalently; this is precisely the way activity of the Self was paralyzed. Our goal, however, must be to restore our own vitality: the living autonomy of the patient's Self is at stake.

While up to now the analyst's main emotional tool has been willingness to participate in the ongoing relationship, and cognitive tool the capacity to formulate theoretically the relationship that is being established, now the analyst must take a less reactive stance within the transference and begin to take the initiative in making interpretations and interventions. This more active stance starts with the inner act of recognizing the situation in the therapy for what it is, a threat to the selfobject's emotional survival; on the basis of this recognition the analyst then takes steps to ensure the survival of the analyst-Self. Where the first two steps are reactive ones that may occur quickly, but take long to explicate and formulate in cognitive language, the next, proactive steps can be described succinctly, but may take an analyst a long time to feel the way to. They are interventions that test the patience, the resilience, and the courage of the analyst, and although they should not be executed in a brusque, heroic spirit of righteousness, they can nevertheless feel like brave interventions that put the relationship with the patient on the line. Throughout what follows, the analyst will be working hard at the timing of what is communicated to the patient, trying to match what is said and done with what the patient's associations, dreams, and affects indicate the patient is ready for.

The Fourth Step: The Selfobject Communicates the Fact that Ambivalent Treatment Has Been Occurring

It is essential to recognize that the patient does not realize the analyst is being treated ambivalently. From the patient's perspective, the analyst is a figure of admiration and awe, and frequent feelings of rage or fear on account of the analyst's importance are not a sign that the analyst is being devalued. What is not apparent to the patient is that part of him or her does not like having the self-selfobject relationship in place. Therefore the analyst must say something like, "Sometimes it feels like you welcome my presence in your life, and other times it feels like you're pushing me away. I think the reason is that I've become very important to you, and part of you feels very good about that while another part of you doesn't like it at all."

The Fifth Step: The Patient Recognizes the Ambivalent Treatment of the Selfobject but Attempts to Continue the Ambivalent Relationship

Most patients will attempt to counter the analyst's confrontation with an intellectually sophisticated psychological retort: "Well, isn't some ambivalence part of any relationship?" Even if the analyst repeats to the patient, "My point is that a part of you doesn't like having someone like me in your life at all!" the patient will go only so far as to get in touch with strong negative feelings toward the analyst. This feels to the patient like working harder in therapy, but the negative projection behind the negative feelings is not withdrawn, and the analyst experiences little emotional relief. Instead, the patient feels entitled to continue the ambivalent relationship: "My ambivalence is all right as long as I know about it." The distress of the analyst seems irrelevant to the patient, who does not appreciate that it signals how the therapy has ground to a halt. The analyst, the patient seems to imply (and may directly state), is there to accept the patient's transference: "Don't take it personally." At this point, in the face of disqualification of the analyst's experience and its deep significance to the work, the analyst may begin to hate the patient (see Winnicott 1949).

Some analysts will try at this point in a treatment to introduce nonverbal modalities like body work, painting, or sandplay; or to use verbal symbols in less structured ways than interpretation, such as storytelling, dream analysis, and active imagination. Often such methods do evoke healing symbols from areas of the Self that the patient can accept, and the experience of transcending effects may be helpful in evoking a more cooperative attitude from at least part of the patient. As many Jungian analysts have noted, remarkable solutions can be presented by the unconscious when words are avoided. Mediating these positive experiences, the analyst demonstrates a resilience in support of the Self that can be a good model for the patient. Usually, however, such methods serve, with very ill patients, mainly to strengthen the already healthy part of the self, leaving an area of profound ambivalence still in need of a definitive confrontation.

Confrontation at this point, like shifts to other modalities, should not be used as a substitute for patience. Simply holding the therapeutic environment as it is over time is frequently enough to constellate a transformation of attitude; what seems fixed turns out to have the capacity to change. It is only when the patience and resourcefulness of the analyst are absolutely at an end that further intervention is indicated. (Again, with some very difficult patients, one can reach this point very quickly, sometimes within the confines of a single analytic hour.)

The Sixth Step: The Selfobject Refuses to Cooperate with the Ambivalent Relationship

This is an essential intervention, but one that comes hard to many analysts, who do not feel entitled to take a stand against the patient's pathology. To do so involves risking the entire relationship. Yet to truly serve the self-selfobject link at the core of the therapy, analysts cannot allow themselves to be kept in a paralyzing double bind. To go along with this double bind is not only to experience distress, it is to collude, as selfobject, in denying the Self any real role in the patient's life. The analyst-Self may therefore have to say that the treatment cannot continue unless the analyst's basic working conditions (Levene 1982) are met. Chief among these is the analyst's overall ability to "breathe," but they may well include the patient's attention to such practical issues as dealing fairly with the fees for treatment; observing reasonable limits on extra telephone calls, staying after the appointment is over, and visiting the analyst's working (or living) space unannounced; accepting the analyst's vacations without excessive scapegoating of them; assuming responsibility for keeping and changing appointments; and withdrawing suicidal, homicidal, and other physical threats to the therapy. More subtly, the analyst must insist on being allowed to be him or herself, within the obvious constraints of the therapeutic role.

At this point in the treatment, analysts will sometimes seem to be putting their own comfort above that of patients. Yet in fact by taking care of "selfish" considerations, analysts guard the interests of patients, which are not served by their getting away with literal or psychological murder of the analyst-Self. There must, however, be no revenge taken upon the patient, rather the minimum necessary should be done to assure the emotional and physical survival of the analyst. The gamut runs from simple limit-setting to suspending the treatment, and the analyst may be forced to disclose more than once to the patient when internal limits are being exceeded which place the treatment at risk. At this point in the treatment, the analyst may have to say, "I am not sure if I can work with you or not," or "I cannot continue with you unless you agree to . . . ," or "For my own efficacy in the relationship, I am requiring that you . . . ," or, finally, "I would rather not see you until you are of truly one mind about working with me."

This step may come surprisingly early on in the treatment of a seriously ambivalent patient, and may even turn out to be part of an initial hour, if enough movement takes place fast enough; but whenever it occurs, the analyst must be ready to risk the promise of the self-selfobject relationship by confronting directly the ambivalence that has surfaced toward it. In making this sort of intervention, the analyst must be scrupulously careful that the patient understand that limit-setting is done to protect the integrity of the present analysis and not out of a global judgment that the patient is "unsuitable for psychotherapy." (One may have to refer the patient to another analyst to establish one's neutrality on this issue.) There should also be evidence that, having tested the selfobject capacities of the analyst to their limit, the patient has achieved a sense of selfobject constancy, so that an internal security will remain even if the analyst withdraws.

Obviously, wherever possible the analyst will continue seeing the patient, but with a shift in the way the selfobject role is handled. For instance, the analyst does not actively attempt at this point to be empathic or to acknowledge empathic failures. Instead, the empathic act of the moment is to recognize the patient's need to resolve the ambivalence before any further "self nutrition" can be accepted. The analyst is a somewhat static image of the selfobject potential, while the patient decides, with the analyst's consultative help, what to do with it. The memory of the analyst's active behaviors in the selfobject role is enough to keep that possibility alive for the patient.

Even if the treatment comes to an end or is transferred to another therapist, the analyst does not stop being a symbolic selfobject, and the patient does not forget that ambivalence toward the selfobject has yet to be resolved. The analyst must therefore not abandon the role assumed in the patient's life, and in any dealings with the patient must remember the fact of the unresolved selfobject transference. Therapeutic attention, however, whether in the context of continuing psychotherapy or not, must be sharply focused on whether the analyst is truly wanted in this role and is, as therapist, allowed to function in it.

The Seventh Step: The Patient Decides that Ambivalent Treatment of the Selfobject Was Not Justified

Because the analyst is unwilling to participate any longer in an ambivalent relationship, the patient begins to question his or her behavior. It dawns on the patient that the push-pull directed at the analyst has been excessive, that the analyst has been "jerked around" and manipulated in undeserved ways.

This realization involves feelings of remorse; the patient regrets the ruthlessness shown toward the selfobject, recognizing that a valued relationship is at risk as a consequence. Fear of permanent object loss actually motivates the patient to give up some of the ambivalent attitude. There is a shift in the kind of anxiety directed at the analyst at this point, a shift from persecutory anxiety to depressive anxiety. (This corresponds to a move from the paranoid-schizoid position to the depressive position in Melanie Klein's terminology [1952].)

As a consequence of this shift the patient is willing to experience shame and fear, while previously the analyst was asked to carry these feelings. The shame is at disappointing the selfobject; the fear is of not getting the selfobject back. This means a period of intense depressive anxiety for the patient, which the analyst will not immediately be able to relieve. The relationship must stay at risk, because the patient cannot guarantee that any relief offered by the analyst will not be met with renewed ambivalence. In other words, the patient has not yet accepted dependency on the selfobject (and behind the selfobject, the Self). Yet at least the patient has begun to wonder why the selfobject has been treated so badly.

The analyst must ensure that someone is available to receive the patient's remorse so that the patient does not become isolated with it, which can be dangerous. If treatment has been interrupted as part of the analyst's strategy of noncooperation with ambivalence, it is important that there be some other therapist available. The analyst who has terminated with a patient should not be surprised to receive at this time a letter or phone call expressing remorse, with or without a request to return to therapy. Yet if there is any indication that ambivalence toward the self-selfobject relationship is still in place, the analyst should confine selfobject behavior to hearing the remorse, refusing to continue therapy. If the patient has not terminated, the analyst must not take expression of remorse as a signal to return to full functioning in the selfobject role, for the patient has still not indicated that the analyst can be accepted as such without ambivalence.

The stance of the analyst during this step is simply to wait and listen. There is little point in agreeing with the patient that ambivalent behavior is bad; such intervention has a moralistic tinge, and humiliates the patient by seeming to suggest that at last the patient has seen the folly of his ways. Forgiving the patient is similarly gratuitous, and may backfire. It is unempathic of the patient's need to experience negative feelings toward the selfobject *as wrong but present anyway*, and the failure of empathy may occasion in the patient with still low self-integration negative feelings that are quite justified, confusing further exploration of unjustified negative feelings toward the analyst.

The key is that the patient get a chance now to notice that excessive negative feelings have been directed toward the analyst, to regret this, and to wonder what to do with these feelings.

The Eighth Step: The Patient Decides out of Respect for the Selfobject Not to Use the Selfobject to Process Negative Feelings

The patient's first solution to the problem is a moral effort rather than a psychological one, and it involves an ethical attempt not to upset the analyst further. To get a patient to take this step, an analyst must have acted meticulously during the preceding steps, or the patient will not respect the analyst enough to make the moral effort and will simply go on to another analyst at this point. The selfobject a patient is willing to change for is the one who has carefully attended to the needs of the patient's self (carefully acknowledging the inevitable failures) at every point along the way, so that it is clear if things have gone badly that it is because a part of the patient did not want such a selfobject, not because the selfobject has really failed the patient. And, even after withdrawing from active efforts to care for the self of the patient in the face of ambivalence, this selfobject will not have forgotten the symbolic importance for the patient of previous efforts. For an analyst who has been this kind of selfobject, the patient is finally able to forego cruel projections and experience the excessive negative feelings directly. Experienced without displacement onto the analyst, these feelings quickly come to the fore as an active dislike of self and Self.

Obviously, this is a very dangerous period, in which the patient may become despairing and suicidal. Neither existence nor fate seem propitious, and the patient may verbalize malignant insights: "I'm not a good person." Here the patient is experiencing the negative self-Self relation, and for the present it is best for the analyst to let this communication stand.

It comes out that the patient dislikes all of the spontaneous manifestations of the unconscious Self. The patient dislikes primal affects, especially shame, and may be ashamed of being ashamed; hates the growth process, with its pressures toward change and new object relationships; resents dreams, with their often critical content; and is frightened and hostile in the face of synchronistic events, like auto accidents, bus breakdowns, and bad weather, that seems to mirror the frequent fragmentation of the patient's life. Although defending the analyst, patients may express considerable bitterness toward other selfobjects who have failed them; and often direct anger at the Self is voiced in the form of fury at God, or statements like "Life stinks."

A much more insidious form of this problem (and a phase in which some patients may get stuck for a long time) is what Barry Proner (1986) has called "envy of the self," in which the patient may report anxiety aroused by "good experiences, good links and the undeniable knowledge of good parts of himself" and evidence a need to render such good experiences of the Self inaccessible or irrelevant to day-to-day existence (p. 277).

At this point, an analyst may want to make some rebuttal (and almost every therapist will do this at least once), but often the best strategy is just to hear the negativity out. Letting the patient experience the fact (and the force) of the negative feelings toward self and Self gives the patient a chance to see how self-undermining they really are.

The Ninth Step: The Negative Feelings toward the Self-self Appear to the Patient Excessive and Inappropriate

It now begins to dawn upon the patient that the real problem is the negativity itself. Just as earlier something became wrong about asking the selfobject to carry all the negative feelings toward the Self, now something starts to feel wrong about the feelings themselves. To be mad at God is perhaps to go too far? Why is one being so hard on oneself? Why *couldn't* one's own life be better? Not infrequently at this point in the work, there is an enantiodromia, a reversal of attitude. Some of the behavior of the analyst earlier on is recalled now and directly identified with. Sometimes a patient will have a religious conversion at this point, or at least begin to explore a community whose orientation is toward the Self. From this new vantage point, the possibility of a good connection to oneself seems suddenly like a relief, and the ambivalence that has up to now made this feel threatening starts to seem suspect. The analyst is now seen as someone who knew this could happen all along, and nostalgia for this selfobject grows.

The Tenth Step: The Negative Feelings toward the Self-self Are Found to Have a Basis in Toxic Introjects of Family and Culture

With the increased value placed on the selfobject, some of the philosophy of self-acceptance characteristic of the Self archetype appears. The patient begins to experience that something within us that takes us as we are—whatever our race, psychological type, sex, sexual orientation, or physical characteristics—and posits that we try to realize ourselves *within* these parameters, not in spite of them. This discovery of the Self's point of view casts into shadow internalized voices from the past who have doubted the patient's right to particularity. Such voices become increasingly suspect. Beginning to see how specifics of individual selfhood were undermined by original family members and a culture which found them unacceptable, the patient may now recall with bitterness maternal attempts to curtail the drive for activity and manipulate the experience of shame, and paternal pressure to internalize collective prejudices against, commonly, introversion and homosexuality. The patient weighs these early parental interventions against the mounting affective evidence of what the Self intends in these regards. As the Self is accepted, many particulars of a patient's individual selfhood become clearer, such as sexual orientation, psychological type, and religious attitude. Much of the chronic bitterness and rage disappear as patients begin to accept their inner natures; the sourness turns out to be rage from within at the failure to be accepted by oneself.

The psychological idea of the inner nature, which appears at this time, is a sign of the developing self-Self connection. It carries a feeling-tone of conviction in startling contrast to earlier ambivalence. The Self is sometimes symbolized in dreams by the fish, the most instinctive of animals, and it is felt as something within which unreflectedly knows where it is going. Now the internalized, persecuting selfobjects who in earlier life did not like the unfolding pattern that the infant and adolescent unmistakably exhibited (the inner nature is more disguised during latency) begin to seem less like authorities to be obeyed and more like toxic introjects to be dumped. Within the self these toxic introjects—which have up to now split the self and compromised the relationship to the Self, creating the "borderline" condition of chronically incomplete selfhood—are disowned. Sometimes this is accompanied by an outer break with the parents or other aspects of the original culture.

The Eleventh Step: The Patient Now Approaches the Selfobject for the Purpose of Self-enhancement

During the previous step, the patient has been strengthening the self by purging it of internal resistances to the possibility of a healthy self-Self relationship. The idea of the Self is now a psychological reality, and the rudimentary self-Self connection actually makes the self-selfobject relationship with the analyst more attractive, because the patient can approach it from a position of relative strength, since it is not the only possible basis of self-acceptance and nourishment. The patient feels ready now for rapprochement with the analyst, who must be able to meet the renewed attempt at contact with friendliness, whatever the ultimate decision about renewing or intensifying therapy. At this point the patient's use of the analyst is no longer classified as borderline but rather as narcissistic (Adler 1981).

The Twelfth Step: The Selfobject Responds to the New Approach Positively

Although the analyst may be wary of the patient as a consequence of the earlier experience during the ambivalent phase of the transference, leftover feelings of counterambivalence turn out to be remarkably easy to digest once this stage of the work is reached. Finding it easier than expected to respond positively to the patient's re-approach and behaving again as an enhancing selfobject, the analyst experiences little resistance from the patient. A decision is reached as to whether or not to reopen the old process in earnest, and the analyst's decision is respected. At this time a more satisfying termination is possible; if the two do decide to take up the work again, there is a new honeymoon as the patient allows the analyst to do the job of taking care of the self.

The Thirteenth Step: The Patient Tries to Control the Selfobject into Behaving Only Enhancingly

Soon, however, a new difficulty emerges. Where before the patient would not allow the analyst to feel good about performing the self-enhancing selfobject function, now the patient will not let the analyst out of that role. Disappointment is expressed when the analyst does otherwise. As one patient put it to me when I temporarily stepped out of the empathic position in the transference which I had held for several years, "That's not the John Beebe I know." The patient is in the throes of a narcissistic transference, and the analyst begins to feel trapped in the role of the perfect selfobject. When the analyst's empathy is not perfect the patient will not disintegrate as before, but a kind of brooding depression settles in and waits for the analyst to come around. When the analyst is hard at work and on target, the patient reciprocates by working hard, and there are frequent expressions of gratitude as well as much apparent therapeutic progress. But the analyst is exhausted at the end of a therapeutic hour, which feels like a marathon in which the therapist had to be "on" the whole time. It becomes clear that the patient and analyst can work together, but not play or relax. For this restriction of the possibilities of the relationship the analyst feels a subtle resentment of the patient, different in quality from the earlier countertransference hatred. (This resentment can cause analysts to fantasize about, and sometimes act on, ways of curtailing their practices, where it would perhaps be better to analyze the patient's narcissism that is making one work too hard.) Therapy is progressing, but it is far from satisfying.

The Fourteenth Step: The Selfobject Expresses Resistance to Being Controlled, to the Point of Behaving Like a Persecuting Object

Now the analyst may become passive-aggressive toward the patient—make vaguely insulting remarks, come late to sessions, forget appointments, and in other ways assert the prerogative not to be perfect, knowing that the patient will not directly complain. The analyst is usually puzzled at behaving this way; there is a sense of perversely sabotaging a hard-won working relationship for insufficent reason. Eventually the patient may confront the analyst in a fair but firm fashion that seems entirely reasonable, and the analyst will feel guilty and then angry, perhaps directly attacking the patient for being so exacting.

The analyst has fallen victim to a new double bind, in which it is it impossible to leave the working relationship and yet impossible to endure any longer functioning only as a self-enhancing selfobject for the patient. The analyst wants to be free also sometimes to oppose or deflate the patient, should the need arise. As the analyst enters this stage of the work, the question may frequently come from inside, "Why can't you simply be a good technical analyst?" The answer is, "Because that role has become impossible; it's too restrictive."

The Fifteenth Step: The Selfobject Stays in the Relationship but Insists on the Right to Be Imperfect, an Autonomous Self with Its Own Center of Initiative

Aside from the writings of Harold Searles (1986), there is very little in the psychoanalytic literature about this role in therapy, and perhaps this is a wise omission, for it can be dangerous for an analyst to insist on complete emotional independence before the patient is ready to do without a therapist in the selfobject role. There is a lively Jungian (and existential) tradition of analyst independence, which can be used, quite wrongly, to support inappropriate narcissism in an analyst; but at this stage some analyst narcissism at least is required to stand up to the narcissism of the patient. Jung's tradition of being himself can usefully be invoked here.

In my own work, I often prepare the way for my show of independence later by using self-disclosure and humor in the early stages of the transference. This helps the patient get used to the idea that there really is another person in the room. This fact can come as something of a shock to a patient when the day for its full realization comes. Not to display one's independence to patients sufficiently ready for it, however, is to rob them of the chance to experience the Self without any mediation from the analyst whatsoever. It is an important experience for both partners in the analytic enterprise to discover that the patient can survive quite well a totally unempathic hour, a sudden cancellation, or a period of time spent more on the analyst's needs than on the patient's. Asserting separate personhood in these ways is a matter of subtle timing on the part of the analyst, and ought not to be a deliberate technique but rather something that, when truly needed by the analyst, is allowed to happen. Meeting selfish needs is a prerogative of the analyst that must not be used licentiously. Perhaps it is best accomplished in the playfully thieving spirit of Hermes, stealing just a little of the patient's time, and with that god's light touch (Stein 1983). This tricksterish behavior of the analyst as the analysis anticipates its close is symmetrical to the tricksterism of the patient near its beginning.

The Sixteenth Step: The Patient Grants the Selfobject Autonomy out of Love, although Continuing to Want Connection with the Now Autonomous Selfobject

At this point, narcissistic control of the analyst is at last relaxed, and the analyst can breathe more easily. The patient moves toward what an older psychoanalytic language called "object love," and what we might now call the mature use of a selfobject. If we recall Ornstein's definition of the selfobject, "an object . . . related to only in terms of the specific phase-appropriate needs of the developing self, without recognition of the object and its own center of initiative" (1978, p. 60), it is clear that an autonomous selfobject is not the same thing at all, and the ongoing need for enhancement of the self will often have to be met outside the therapeutic relationship. The self is by this point not so resistant to the wider source of the Self, and it can turn to the unconscious and to outer reality to find symbols to serve as roots for the flowering of the inner world. This is a time of active planning for the future development of personality, and the patient needs the analyst simply to be there to see the fun, rather as a developing three-year-old likes to have mother, *not* interfering, beside him as he plays.

During this phase of the work, it is not uncommon for patients to develop a philosophy, describe some current project in great detail, explain a new body of knowledge to the analyst, or bring in creative work for the analyst to see. There is a definite increase in the use of transitional objects at this time, and the relation to the analyst changes as the transitional phenomena, including the now more readily accessible unconscious life, become more important than the interpersonal phenomena which so dominated earlier steps of the work.

The Seventeenth Step: The Former Selfobject Makes a Space for the Patient's Own Self-solacing Capacity to Come Forward

During this period the analyst ceases to be a selfobject and becomes again just an analyst. It is a subtle period in the relationship, when the analyst is testing the hard-won privilege not to be only and always a solacing selfobject to the patient, but there is nothing passive-aggressive in the analyst's giving up of this role at this time. The analyst makes a space, listens, and responds, but does not assume responsibility for the moment-to-moment welfare of the patient's self. The partners still sometimes feel separations from each other with mild anxiety (and occasional transitions, such as the end of some hours, can be jarring) but there is a sense of the capacity to metabolize these affects occasioned by emotional distance. A certain grace begins to appear in the way the two let each other go.

Both partners are beginning to realize that they can truly maintain their identities without each other. For the analyst this may be a time of mourning the patient, or more precisely, the role the analyst has played in the patient's life. There is a giving up of the sense of special connection to the patient, who becomes just one more valued person in one's practice, no longer someone inside the analyst all the time. Sometimes the fantasy surfaces of having given birth to the patient, who begins to notice things about the analyst's office or person that have not been taken in before, as if for the first time the analyst were being seen as a truly separate person, part of the new world the patient is exploring. This exploratory activity is solacing for the patient.

The Eighteenth Step: In the Absence of the Selfobject, the Subject Now Begins to Discover the Possibilities of the Autonomous Self

The need for solace, once established in the psyche, never disappears, but the development of personality opens up resources to meet this ongoing need. At this point in the work, the Self is more than a blueprint or a ground plan; it takes on texture and substance and begins to furnish and flesh out the developing personality. Now the reality of the psyche may become clear. Painting affective states, active imagination, solitary work on one's own dreams, and sessions with the I Ching have meaning and value as part of the rich "symbolic life" that Jung describes so credibly in his autobiography (1963).

The emergence of this style of work makes it clear that the self-Self relationship has become conscious, a path to be followed. The need for a self-selfobject relationship is correspondingly less, although a residual role for the former selfobject bears witness to the fact of ongoing personality transformation. Perhaps the last projection to be withdrawn from an analyst is that of the magus, mediator of the archetype of transformation. (One remembers that in *The Wizard of Oz*, Dorothy believes right up until the end, and even after she knows that the "wizard" is only a mortal from the Midwest like herself, that he will be able to take se her all the way home.)

The Nineteenth Step: Mature Acceptance of the Subject by the Former Selfobject

Up to this point, the therapist has been on guard with the patient, recognizing and fearing the patient's liability to dependency. Even in the recent steps of mounting autonomy for the patient, the analyst has secretly been holding his or her breath, wondering how long it will last. Now all at once the analyst relaxes and takes a renewed interest in the patient, who is suddenly a person, interesting in a new way as someone who could even, by dint of his or her independent access to the Self, function as a selfobject for the analyst.

Because the patient has a slant on the Self that is new, the analyst will develop some selfobject transference to the patient at this point. This is a true transference and not a countertransference, for its point is to widen the analyst's own access to the Self. To the degree that the analyst has a self-deficiency, it may create a compulsive tie to the patient. Obviously, this is a time when premature termination, injudicious involvement with the patient, and other complications based on the analyst's transference must be guarded against. It is quite important for the analyst to be in touch with his or her own vulnerability in this regard and be willing to return to personal analysis when the patient's access to Self creates the awareness of continued need. It is also important to let the patient go, as the new-won self has business in the world.

At the same time, it is equally important that the analyst admit now what both patient and analyst know, that the tables have turned, and that for the first time the patient has something to offer the analyst besides money and the satisfaction of a cure. I have found it helpful to the patient to acknowledge at this point in the work the value to me of the patient's hard-won access to the Self as well as what I find fresh or enviable in it. Also, discussing these feelings is the best way for me to avoid acting them out later on.

When the analyst acknowledges the value of the patient, the original meaning of the self-selfobject relationship, with its sense of magical significance, is recalled and confirmed as an anticipation of what has come to pass in reality. At this point, it is usual for the termination of therapy to take place. The patient works through the residual transference to the analyst in the knowledge that the analyst too has been affected by the Self the patient uncovered; this makes it clear to the patient that the analyst is not the Self. The analyst's transference to the patient, if persistent, is usually resolved by finding the patient within—

the still-unanalyzed part of the analyst that could benefit from further work.

The Twentieth Step: The Former Patient Takes On the Ambivalent Selfobjects of the Past, Performing a Positive Selfobject Function for Them

Earlier (in the tenth step) the individual felt so wounded by parents or others that a break was made with them, and their subsequent requests for contact were fended off. Now, secure in the knowledge of connection to the Self, the individual realizes that these former selfobjects are not simply persecuting, but also seeking the individual's help, and that a transformation in the relationship could be beneficial to both sides. Remembering that even the analyst saw in the patient a selfobject, the individual accepts that these difficult others may be able to benefit from the individual's access to the Self. The former patient is aware of being to them what the analyst was at the start of the analysis, an ambivalently accepted selfobject. It will be necessary to accept them, to call them on their ambivalence, and to grant them access on the basis of their ability to give up destructive ways of relating. The former patient may discover that this time it is possible to survive their ambivalence and to start them on their way to a more accepting relation to the Self.

References

Adler, G. 1980. Transference, real relationship and alliance. *International Journal of Psychoanalysis* 61:547–558.

——————. 1981. The borderline-narcissistic personality disorder continuum. *The American Journal of Psychiatry* 138:40–50.

Blos, P. 1979. *The adolescent passage: Developmental issues.* New York: International Universities Press.

Book, H. 1988. Empathy: Misconceptions and misuses in psychotherapy. *The American Journal of Psychiatry* 145:420–424.

Brandchaft, B., and Stolorow, R. 1984. The borderline concept: Pathological character or iatrogenic myth? In J. Lichtenberg, M. Bornstein, and D. Silver, eds., *Empathy II*, pp. 333–357. Hillsdale, N.J.: The Analytic Press.

Edinger, E. 1973. *Ego and archetype.* Baltimore: Pelican Books.

Ekstrom, S. 1984. Self-theory and psychoanalysis: The evolution of the self concept and its use in clinical theories of C. G. Jung, D. W. Winnicott, and Heinz Kohut. Doctoral dissertation, Union for Experimenting Colleges and Universities: Universities Microfilm International.

Fordham, M. 1974. Defenses of the self. *Journal of Analytical Pyschology* 19:192–199.

——————. 1976. *The self and autism.* London: Heinemann.

Gordon, R. 1985. Big Self and little self: Some reflections. *Journal of Analytical Psychology* 30:261–271.

Greenacre, P. 1960. Considerations regarding the parent-infant relationship. *International Journal of Psychoanalysis* 41:571–84.

Jung, C. G. 1960. Psychological factors determining human behaviour. In *Collected works,* 8:114–125.

————. 1963. *Memories, dreams, reflections.* New York: Pantheon.

Klein, M. (1952). Some theoretical conclusions regarding the emotional life of the infant. In *Envy and Gratitude & other works 1946–1963,* pp. 61–93. New York: Dell Delta Books, 1977.

Kohut, H. 1978. *The search for the self.* New York: International Universities Press.

————. 1984. *How does analysis cure?* Chicago: University of Chicago Press.

Levene, H. 1982. The borderline syndrome: A critique and response to recent literature on its etiologies, dynamics and treatment. *The San Francisco Jung Institute Library Journal,* 3/3:22–32.

Maduro, R. 1985. Abandonment and deintegration of the primary self. In N. Schwartz-Salant and M. Stein, eds., *Abandonment.* Wilmette, Ill.: Chiron Publications, 131–156.

Mahler, M., Pine, F., and Bergman, A. 1975. *The psychological birth of the human infant.* New York: Basic Books.

Ornstein, P. 1978. Introduction to *The search for the self,* op. cit., pp. 1–106.

Parens, H. 1979. *The development of aggression in early childhood.* New York: Jason Aronson.

Proner, B. 1986. Defences of the self and envy of oneself. *Journal of Analytical Psychology* 31:275–279.

Redfearn, J. W. T. 1985. *My self, my many selves.* London: Academic Press.

Searles, H. 1986. *My work with borderline patients.* Northvale, N.J.: Jason Aronson.

Sidoli, M. 1987. Infancy and childhood: A Jungian vertex, Unpublished manuscript.

Stein, M. 1983. *In midlife.* Dallas: Spring Publications.

Stolorow, R., and Lachmann, F. 1980. *Psychoanalysis of developmental arrests: Theory and treatment.* New York: International Universities Press.

Tolpin, P. 1980. The borderline personality: Its makeup and analyzability. In A. Goldberg, ed. *Advances in self psychology,* pp. 299–316. New York: International Universities Press.

Tustin, F. 1986. *Autistic barriers in neurotic patients.* London: Karnac Books.

Winnicott, D. W. 1949. Hate in the counter-transference. *International Journal of Psychoanalysis* 30:69–75.

Wolf, E. 1986. Selfobject transferences: An overview. *Psychiatric Annals* 16/8:491–493.

Formation of and Dealing with Symbols in Borderline Patients

Hans Dieckmann

From the beginning of my analytical work I have always been especially interested in and touched by the highly charged emotional symbols that emerge from the unconscious of borderline and psychotic patients. In this article I do not want to give a purely theoretical presentation of this subject, thus I would like to underline and clarify my reflections with some case examples. But before going into them I would like to present the main hypotheses on which I base my reflections:

1. Based upon my experience with patients who show early disturbance—whether borderline or cases of psychosis—we often find many archetypal symbols already present at the beginning of therapy. This experience was described by C. G. Jung (1946a) and he also used it as a diagnostic criterion.

2. According to Jolande Jacobi, the symbol—as long as it is archetypal—is an image that is presented to consciousness. I would prefer to say that it is the *experiencing* of the archetypal structure per se pre-

Hans Dieckmann, M.D., is currently president of the International Association for Analytical Psychology. He lives and practices as a Jungian analyst in Berlin, West Germany. He is the author of many articles and books, among them the standard textbook, *Methoden der analytischen Psychologie* (1979), and *Twice-Told Tales: The Psychological Use of Fairy Tales* (Chiron Publications 1986).

sented to consciousness. This process of experiencing is partly deter-mined by cultural background on the one hand and by the personal ex-perience of one's own life history on the other (Jacobi 1959). In her work, "Indivisibility of the Personal and Collective Unconscious," Mary Williams advanced two theses: "Nothing in the personal experience needs to be repressed unless the ego feels threatened by its archetypal power," and "the archetypal activity which forms the individual myth is dependent on material supplied by the personal unconscious" (Will-iams 1963). Both points underscore my hypothesis.

3. If we start from a differentiated, and in the great archetypal sym-bols, personified, part of the two great basic complexes—i.e. the father and the mother complex—the archetypal symbol presented to con-sciousness corresponds to a part of the complex's core. This was de-scribed in detail for the mother complex by Erich Neumann in *The Great Mother* (1955), and I tried to expound it for the father complex in an as yet unpublished work. We can, I think, derive nearly all other complexes from these two, as Eberhard Jung did in his work on the "Grand Inquisitor" (1971), which develops from the negative senex figure of the father archetype.

4. This complex core dominates the psyche and a more or less un-stable ego and leads, as Edward Whitmont described (1969), to the fundamental mechanisms of projection and identity. *Identity*, as dis-tinct from *identification*, is a completely unconscious condition which reaches much deeper. Reducing it to a simple formula, we can say that the patient is unconsciously exposed to the constellated complex, in-cluding its archetypal and collective components. I would like to em-phasize that this does not exclude the other defense mechanisms, such as active splitting (Kernberg 1975) and projective identification (Klein 1946), which are characteristic of these patients.

5. While I was still closely following Jung's conception (a similar one can be found in Freud by the way) in my book *Träume als Sprache der Seele* (1978) and took the view that the dream symbol is a transmit-ter of meaning and that it spontanously comes into being in the uncon-scious, in recent years I have started to have doubts about this based upon my practical analytical work. I still agree with Jung that the symbol makes it possible to visualize and realize contents which could not be represented in another or better manner than through such an image. It translates the abstract world of instincts into a vivid image and lets it become a psychic event which provides the instinct with a meaning and direction. I think, however, that there are symbols that undergo development and that there are creative processes—similar to those

Shulamith Kreitler (1965) described for the conscious creation of symbols—in the unconscious as well which undergo a development long before the symbol emerges. In the ongoing course of an analysis, the symbols continue to be worked through in a partially conscious, partially unconscious manner, and, in my opinion, all functions play a part—processes of thinking and of feeling as well as sensation and intuition. I differ in this regard from Kreitler's experimental examination in which she presumed that only the rational processes of thinking were required for the creation of symbols. I therefore suggest not speaking of the symbol as a transmitter of meaning which spontaneously "comes into being," but rather as one which spontaneously "appears" in the consciousness. In my first case presentation I will try to illustrate this with an example in which I will trace the first attempts to form a central archetypal symbol in the initial dream back to the personal history of childhood.

6. I start from the concept that in the specific analytical situation transference and countertransference play an important part in the formation of symbols. There is, however, no other explanation for the fact that patients who change analysts, especially when changing from one school to another, often react with a quite considerable change in their dream symbols. Differentiated patients in particular often mention this difference with astonishment. If we leave out of consideration the hypothesis of obliging dreams, which I feel to be quite shallow, for I cannot imagine that such a helpfulness of the unconscious could be maintained throughout a whole analysis, I could imagine that the unconscious of different analysts speaks to different, or to other, parts of the patient's psyche. Examinations of transference and countertransference done in Berlin, especially the works of Blohmeyer (1980) and myself (1980), clearly describe how strongly the analyst's unconscious affects the process in the patient's psyche, and speak decidedly against the hypothesis of obliging dreams.

Now I would like to clarify and discuss these theoretical hypotheses about symbols with a case example concerning a 35-year-old patient who started analytical therapy because of disorders in forming attachments to others, depressions, and symptoms of depersonalization. (It was only at the 100th hour that she wrote me a long letter confessing that she also suffered from a considerable sensitive delusion of reference in which system I was already integrated at that time.) She had never been so decompensated that she had to be treated in a mental hospital or that she could no longer do her job as a secretary in a company.

C. G. Jung, as can be seen from his early work on dementia prae-cox (1907), would have classified hers as a functional psychosis—especially as there was clearly a releasing situation to which I will refer later. In 1958, in his last work on "Schizophrenia," he reported that when he stopped working in a hospital and started his private practice, to his astonishment he found such compensated or latent psychoses much more often than he had expected—in a ratio of 1:10 in fact. To-day we call such symptoms "borderline," but it is worth asking whether the old psychiatric diagnoses such as "functional psychosis," a term which was proposed by Jung, or the various serious neuroses with early disorders which are today all included in the quite diffuse group of borderline cases, were not described in a better and more adequate manner by the old terminology.

A careful examination of Jung's works on schizophrenia reveals that he always treated such cases and some of them even quite success-fully. But only since the Freudians have dared full-scale treatment of these disorders as well as the classical neuroses have the borderline terminology and these specific problems become so popular. It was certainly a serious failing of the Jungian analysts not to have taken and sufficiently developed Jung's clinical works concerning this field.

But let us return to the patient, Karin. During the whole first pe-riod of her therapy a serious negative father complex represented the central problem. Her father was a bricklayer and an extreme alcoholic who came from a family of alcoholics (her grandfather as well as great grandfather were alcoholics). She was the second child, born after a brother who was three years older than her. Because her mother had intended to leave the father before she had become pregnant again, Karin had been unwanted, a fact which, from her earliest childhood, she had been cruelly reminded of by her mother, who had treated her very coldly and disapprovingly. Karin had therefore *nolens volens* a closer relationship to her father. She had to pick him up at the pubs every Friday night, or at least go there in order to take the housekeep-ing money away from him.

When he was completely drunk the father had eruptions of aggres-siveness at home and hit the mother and the brother. The child Karin was the only one who could calm him down a little by making him fried potatos and putting him to bed. During her puberty it even came to sexual allusions, which made the father more and more threatening and disgusting for Karin. When he was sober he, like most alcoholics, of course also exhibited a soft, emotional, caring side. But this became evi-dent only in the further course of the analysis when she had come to a certain reconciliation with his figure. At first he was only horrible, disgusting, and very frightening.

Immediately after the first interview she brought the following initial dream to analysis:

Dream: *A tiger has escaped from his cage through an open door. Detlef, my son, and I are fleeing from him. Suddenly we stand in front of the empty cage, a long room. There is a door in the bars. It is open and we go through it. Terribly afraid that the tiger could return, we run through the long cage to the other end, where we leave it through another little door. We lock the door of the cage with a key which we keep holding in our hands. We now go to a little anteroom and look through the window. We are still terribly afraid. Suddenly the tiger is coming. He is very big, terrible and fascinating. He does not take the same way as we did, but directly approaches our door. He wants to go into his cage, but we have locked the door and hold the key in our hands—what are we to do? Suddenly the keeper comes and shouts, "Who has got the key?" I throw the key to him. Now the tiger goes past us and disappears behind the door. The keeper talks to him in a reassuring manner, and we hear how he locks the door.*

In her 1972 monograph on "The Borderline Syndrome," Christa Rohde-Dachser pointed out that the initial dreams of these patients often contain motifs and symbols which are severely self- and world-destructive, an observation applicable to Karin since the tiger not only threatened her with complete destruction but her only child also. These motives of the initial dream are of course connected with the enormous aggressive destructiveness which lies in the psyche of these patients and which they cannot control. In most of the cases—as it was with my patient, too—it is not even directly repressed or completely unconscious but is coped with by the more archaic defense mechanism of active splitting.

So in the first period of the analysis I, too, could change moment-by-moment from a good, protecting, and helping guardian to an evil tiger threatening to tear her apart. I do not want to go into these problems in detail, but I would like to refer especially to the symbol of the tiger which, according to Karin's description, definitely had mythological traits. I would like to deal with this symbol with regard to its status in the current situation as well as to its genesis, its further development during the treatment, and its relation to countertransference.

Her associations regarding the tiger came only very hesitatingly but they all referred to her father's alcoholism, about which she spoke most of the time during these first sessions. That the tiger referred to the father was also shown by a later dream from this first period of treatment in which she was in her parents' house together with her child and her mother, and the three of them waited anxiously for the tiger to come back while trying to protect themselves from him.

The great energy which lies in this powerful archaic animal—it spontaneously reminded me of the sabre-toothed tiger of the Paleozoic era—certainly has some more components. In the dream he is locked up in the cage after a short escape to freedom; this points at the systemized delusion Karin had withheld until the 100th hour and which contained such strong destructive energies. The systematized delusion referred to another field—to the patient's own sexuality. Here again there is a certain relation to the father as the daughter's first erotization in puberty, as we have already noted, came from him.

The systematized delusion had the following releasing stimulus: Karin's husband was a Dutchman who had volunteered to work in the former German Reich during the war and stayed there afterwards. In the first years after the war he had worked as a tennis instructor, but after he had married he completely stopped working because of a relatively slight tuberculosis. My very efficient patient provided for the family and in addition they got some welfare money. After a short time the husband became impotent, and Karin helped herself by masturbating on the toilet to satisfy her sexual urges. While masturbating one day, she was surprised by her husband, who became very morally indignant with her. From that time on he continually kept a watch on her, even drilling a hole in the bathroom wall in order to observe her. (These events were real and not delusional. Since the husband had applied for an analysis through public assistance, documents of his anamnesis existed which proved that he had himself reported these events.)

Shortly afterwards Karin's sensitive delusion of reference broke out at her place of work. As she no longer dared to masturbate at home, she began masturbating in the washroom of her company when the urge became too strong. When she left the toilet she met a worker who smiled cordially at her. She experienced this as a malicious grin, believing that he knew she had masturbated and was making fun of it. Step by step she developed a paranoid system in which all her colleagues and her boss knew about her practice and continually hinted at it. It became so extreme that she interpreted certain traces in the dust on the stairs as hints which revealed her misdemeanor. By the time she told me about her systematized delusion, I was already part of it. She thought I had spoken to her boss, asked him for his sympathy for her, and promised that she would mend her ways. Since then the atmosphere in the company had improved a little and she was not exposed to so many torments any more. But this improvement did not last of course. The good father changed again into the evil one, and she reproached me for having told her dreams—especially the sexual ones—to all her colleagues.

Thus, in the symbol of the tiger two great fields were drawn together: the potential for strong aggression inherent in the alcoholism of her father, and her sexuality. In his *Symbols of Transformation* (1952b), Jung pointed out that images of wild animals like lions and tigers in the unconscious of women often point at the sexual instinctual dynamics which cannot be dominated and which are beyond the control of the ego. In this connection a historical amplification seems to me appropriate. At the time of the Emperor Augustus tigers were for the first time transported to Europe and became known. They were used for gladiatorial fights in the ancient Roman arena, but later were incorporated in artistic representations, especially paintings on vases, where they are harnessed to the chariot of Amor or Dionysus. Thus they are regarded as the companion animals of the two gods who symbolize precisely those fields which created the greatest difficulties for my patient.

How was the constellation of this symbol influenced by the transference situation? Every analysis is directed at the unconscious and seeks to mobilize it. Because this is the unknown part of the personality and the patient feels exposed to a mysterious medical procedure which is to a large extent unfamiliar, dreams tinged with fears and anxieties are not that astonishing at the beginning of a treatment. Futhermore, Karin was confronted with a male analyst in this situation. With her severely negative father complex and very negative experiences with her father and husband, it is no wonder that, in spite of the friendly atmosphere, she experienced me as split into two sides: on the one hand as a very threatening tiger and on the other as a helping guardian.

But why an animal? At that time I was not much older than Karin and to her unconscious I must therefore have appeared as a potential sexual partner. But the instinctual—animal—part of her sexuality was extremely repressed and under an extreme moral taboo because of her prudish education, something which was starkly expressed by her delusional symptoms. But she must also have felt from the countertransference a much more permissive attitude and atmosphere regarding these fields than that to which she had previously been accustomed. We also had a cat in our home which related well to the whole family and moved freely in our apartment, including my treatment room. The patient had never had any animals, and her attitude toward them was rather fearful and negative. These facts, too, might have played a part in her unconscious choosing a dangerous big cat as the first symbol in which the unconscious appeared.

In her examinations of the conscious formation of symbols, Kreitler proves that they are found in a gradual process with the help of certain other categories. She distinguishes among 10 different categories which, however, need not be examined here in detail. In decreasing order of occurence (with 1 and 2 nearly equal), the most frequent sequences are:

1. scene—metaphor—symbol
2. metaphor—symbol
3. interpretation—metaphor—symbol
4. scene—symbol

In this connection it is quite interesting that in Karin's childhood history there was an experience which was obviously connected with the formation of the symbol. It was of course brought up much later in the analysis and even if not directly repressed it had more or less fallen into oblivion. At a thanksgiving party when she was between five and seven years old, she had performed a dance together with other children in which she had the leading part. She danced the role of a sunflower, was dressed up as a sunflower, and held a big sunflower in her hand. With this dance she was very successful with all the adults and children and for a long time afterward people commented to her about it. It was a very impressive and special experience in her childhood. The sunflower has exactly the same colors as the tiger and in the happy dance of the thanksgiving party there is also the Dionysiac element which we find in the Roman representation of the tiger pulling Dionysus's chariot. Here we have a positive side of the energy symbolized by the tiger: expansiveness, movement, creative play, and a happily successful representation through a dance. What a pity—one could say—that all this had not been developed in Karin but rather repressed and had therefore gone to waste and become frozen. It was only in analysis that she regained at least a little part of it.

Taking into consideration Kreitler's examination, this scene from her childhood represented the precursor from which the symbol of the initial dream developed. It is of course only a hypothesis to assume that the unconscious proceeds just like the conscious mind when forming a symbol, but I think that it is quite plausible. In Karin's case the series of categories would be:

1. *scene:* sunflower dance from childhood;
2. *metaphor:* the tiger is understood as father;
3. *symbol:* beyond its interpretation as father, the tiger takes on a deeper meaning associated with an animal—elementary power which unifies positive and negative aspects.

This showed even more clearly in the further course of the analysis. As previously described, a sufficient holding (Winnicott 1958) was established at about the 100th session following a positive transference dream in which she was cordially received as a guest at our house. She then could find enough confidence in me to tell me in a long letter about her delusional system. A short time after this confession she spontaneously started to express her inner world through a series of pictures whose production covered a period of two years.

The first picture of this series was again closely connected to the central symbol of the initial dream. In the foreground it showed Karin herself as a dancer in the midst of surging mists. She turned toward a yellow sun which she worshipped. In the background on the same stage was a man who opened a curtain. He was dressed as a magician. Through the open curtain a world could be seen lying behind it. In its sky were the moon and stars, which shone on the landscape.

The sunflower dance of her childhood was clearly recognizable in this picture and there was even a real sun in the sky this time. The paternal male figure was no longer a guardian who had to lock up something very threatening, but rather a magician whom she associated with the analyst pointing at another world. Through the symbols of moon, stars, and landscape, this world had clear traits of a positive Magna Mater. Two things had obviously happened. On the one hand, the symbols of the father archetype had constellated positively. And on the other, there was the sun as the ancient positive and life-giving symbol of divinity which she worshipped in a ritual dance. There was the senex in the figure of the wise magician who pointed at a world and a possibility of experience which were until then denied to Karin because of the psychic "non-existence" of her personal mother. The symbol of the tiger was itself no longer there, but, as we will see later, it did reappear.

A short time before this, there had been another tiger dream in which the tiger moved about freely in the living room of her parents' house. She herself, her mother, and her son desperately and anxiously tried to find shelter from him in another room. The tiger still seemed to have characteristics of the father and he did not appear in an anonymous place any more, but, rather had broken into her personal sphere. Since this dream occurred a short time before her confession, it may be assumed that the symbol had lost something of its threatening character. In the dream at least she could let it come close to her and at that point there might already have been a vague presentment that this symbol and the vital powers it embraced had still some other sides than only the one of the torn apart and tearing Dionysus Zagreus.

About one year later she had a dream which was decisive in the further development of the symbol in the analysis. In this dream the patient danced along a whole series of cages holding wild animals, and while doing so she was guarded and protected by an older man who watched her without intervening. All these animals were big cats and again the majority of them were tigers. Each time she danced into a cage she was painfully pounced upon by the animal in it, and each time she had an orgasm. Finally, after having left the last cage, she sank to the ground completely exhausted but also happy. There was still a little fear in the dream but much less than in former ones, and the positive dimension of experience prevailed.

We can clearly see how the positive, dionysiac side of the erotic-sexual experience in a transpersonal form could be accepted here by the dream ego. It is also important that here again there were cages, i.e., enclosed and protected places for orgiastic experience. The figure of the senex, too, belongs to this connection, as he obviously supervised the whole event and seemed to be able to intervene in a helpful manner when difficulties arose. As with borderline cases and psychoses—of which I will speak later—the symbols of the complex core have a very high charge of energy. They always threaten to inflate the conscious ego, which often is very unstable. I think that this danger was avoided because of the protected place in which the instinctive action took place. In "Psychology and Alchemy" (1952a) Jung described a dream in which the dreamer was touched by a reptile during the course of his attempt at "becoming." Jung connected this animal base of life with the totality of the innate unconscious, which is to be unified with consciousness. In order to carry out this transformation one has to let oneself to be bitten by wild animals without running away from them. This means being able to expose oneself to the instinctual impulses of the unconscious without identifying oneself with them or running away from them. In my book, *Dreams as Helpers with the Problems of Life*, I described a similar dream which came about at a decisive turning point in the therapy of a neurosis. Interestingly enough, the delusions in the patient's consciousness changed in a manner exactly parallel to the development of the symbols. After her confession, and after having painted the first picture with the sun and moon symbols, the patient started an argument with her boss at the company, whereupon she was dismissed. As she was very efficient and diligent, she had no difficulty in immediately finding a new job where she was even better paid. In this way she broke out of the delusional masturbatory atmosphere of her old company as well as the delusion that all around her could tell by looking at her that she had masturbated and persecute her because of it. Instead, she then developed the systematized delusion that she had become homosexual. She reproached the analyst for having turned her into a homosexual. In fact, she had some dreams of a homosexual character. Since dream and reality were not sufficiently separated from each other in her experience, for her it meant that she really was a manifest homosexual, for which she utterly despised herself. (I should stress that this all took place at a time when male homosexuality was still punishable by law in West Germany and lesbianism was much more taboo than today.)

Then, for the first time in the analysis, Karin manifested aggressions against her mother. And she also experienced deep feelings of envy toward her brother, to whom her mother had always given preference. She could express her deep indignation as well at the fact that her mother had told her with such cruelty that she was a completely undesired child. At the same time, her father gained more positive traits, and she remembered some situations in which she got along with him very well.

The next phase started after her dream of the cages. She could accept her sexuality then, and the passive delusions which referred to it disappeared completely. But in its place she now discovered that everyone she looked at on the streets, in the subway, in her workplace, or in a shop blushed. When I asked her why that happened, she said, "They think I am a woman who throws herself at them." She simultaneously began for the first time to doubt the reality of her delusion. She heard an inner voice saying to her: "It cannot be like that. Either the others are all crazy or I'm crazy. But as all others cannot be crazy, I am probably crazy." This last symptom is obviously an erythrophobia projected onto other persons. Behind these symptoms are predominantly latent aggressive tendencies and tendencies toward self-abandonment. It seems to me that a new relation to the people about her, in which now also men were included, opened up for her. This was confirmed by the further course of the therapy. Looking at Karin's different systematized delusions from the perspective of her ability to make contact with and relate to other people, one could outline the sequence in which the different delusions followed each other:

1. masturbation—I relate only to myself. I am totally alone and do not want any contact except with myself.
2. homosexuality—I try to establish a relationship with another woman.
3. erythrophobia—I also include men in the circle of persons to whom I want to relate.

This scheme is not intended to be a shortened explanatory formula for these three terms, which are of course much more inclusive in their contents. It is only an attempt to view the sequence of symbols in this patient from a particular perspective.

Only at the end of her therapy after several years this symbol reappeared in a very changed form. In contrast to her earlier withdrawal into a defiant silence, Karin had very aggressively argued with me. These strong aggressions reminded me again of the tiger who was tearing apart and often they were very hard to bear in the countertransference. The patient painted—or better she let come into being on paper—a lotus surrounded by yellow beams of light. In its center were the moon and stars in the middle of a red circle. According to her explanation the yellow beams represented the setting sun. The systematized delusion had disappeared in the meantime. With the symbol of the lotus, the self constellated as a symbol of wholeness, a psychic wholeness in which the wild animal is obviously included.

In contrast to Kernberg (1975), I could never decide, when working with borderline patients or cases of psychosis, to introduce an analytical rule forbidding strongly aggressive verbal attacks on the analyst. Kernberg is certainly right in stating that in such cases the likelihood of a countertransference aggression increases to the degree to which these patients have a very good intuition which enables them to grasp and hurtfully exploit vulnerabilities of the analyst. According to my experience, however, it is better to bear and endure these aggressions. I prefer to use countertransference aggression to show that I am angry or hurt in a convenient moment. But when so doing, I simultaneously try to convey to the patient that he cannot completely destroy our relationship with his uncontrolled aggressiveness. I think the borderline patient needs to encounter at least one person who not only can understand him, but who can also accept his tiger.

Before coming back to the problem of the complex core and its symbols, I would like to say a few final words about this patient's therapy. More or less by chance I saw her again after 20 years when she

needed a short consultation because her son was in the phase of separation from her. All these years she had not developed any systematized
delusion and she had made it without any further therapy, something
which, according to my experience, occurs only rarely. But it would be
presumptuous to state that she had become sane. She remained quite a
paranoid personality. After her separation from her husband—though
she never succeeded in breaking off all contact with him—she did not
succeed in establishing a stable new relationship. Still, I think that the
therapy gave her a lot and that without treatment she probably would
have ended up in a mental hospital or completely isolated herself from
the world. She also would not have been able to successfully raise her
son without having him fall victim to serious neurosis.

I would now like to deal with a question which concerns the
libidinization of the central symbols of a complex core. Of course I
here understand libido in the sense of analytical psychology as an
unspecific energy. Most of the analysts of the Freudian school start from
the idea—influenced by the new findings on ego-psychology—that the
borderline syndrome can be etiologically attributed to a specific disorder of the ego which has affected the whole system of the psychic
set-up. Together with others, such authors as Kernberg (1975), Green
(1975), Jacobson (1964), and Modell (1963) hold this opinion. Other
authors, such as Wollberg (1968), come out against this conception of
an ego deficiency, since it could encourage therapeutic nihilism. It is
presumed on the contrary a relatively stable ego can exist which is
disturbed only by a highly differentiated pattern of defense reactions.
The cognitive functions and perception are especially affected by it. But
Wollberg's concept focuses primarily upon disorders of the ego structure acquired in early childhood and makes only passing reference to
the possibility that certain constitutional weaknesses of the ego structure could also play a part.

Following Jung's lead, I come back to a concept which I mentioned
initially. I think that the energetic power of the complex which appears
in the symbol dominates a more or less unstable ego. In all his works
in this field, Jung dealt with a problem to which the Freudians paid
practically no attention. Time and again he raised the question: "Is there
a noxious element unknown to us in the genetic codification [in the
beginning Jung presumed that there was a chemical or hormonal in-
fluence] which provokes an intensified activity of the unconscious?" In
such a situation an ego which actually is "normal" and sufficiently developed would be overwhelmed and inflated by the powerful energy of an
unconscious complex. I think we as analytical psychologists should

again take up and follow this idea. This question is certainly all the more important considering that—as any experienced analyst knows —we meet a lot of patients who do not react to serious or very serious early disorders with borderline symptoms or a psychosis at all. There are many cases of simple neuroses where a long and differentiated analysis reveals early disorders which equal or exceed those of borderline patients in their quality and quantity. I would even presume that there are a great number of so-called "sane people" in our society who suffer exactly the same early disorders but have never fallen clinically ill or shown any conspicuous symptoms or needed therapy.

In as early as 1907, in his work on dementia praecox, Jung stressed that these emotional complexes have an enormous power. He pointed out that such complexes have the same constellating effect on the remaining psychic activities as acute affect. Everything that suits the complex is accepted and all the rest is excluded, or at least inhibited. As a demonstration of this mechanism, he cites the familiar example of religious ideas. Today we recognize that this mechanism can be found not only among the convinced religious people but in politics, science, technology, and economics as well. Are we perhaps all borderliners, or do we all have a borderline patient within us who appears time and again in our consciousness with his complex-obsessed ideas? (I have dealt in detail with this highly offensive idea elsewhere (1987).)

In the same essay of 1907 Jung discusses the possibility that the correcting voices which can be found in some of these patients might represent break-ins of the "repressed normal rest of the ego complex." This would also correspond to the observation that prematurely demented people can function with sufficient normality again when it comes to a serious physical illness. In all these cases there must already have existed a sufficiently structured ego complex. Today, of course, we know from our psychosomatic knowledge that these serious physical illnesses represent repressions into the somatic. At this point the theory would be contradicted, because if the borderline patient is able to repress so strongly that he can work with a much more mature defense mechanism than he ought to have developed, there must be something wrong about the whole theory.

In this connection, the voice Karin heard telling her that the others could not all be crazy and that there must be something wrong with her own perception seems to support the argument that more mature parts of the ego complex can arise in certain situations. One could of course raise the objection that this voice she heard was due to the success of the therapy in facilitating a bit of ego-formation or maturation. But one can as easily argue the opposite and advance the hypothesis that the success of the therapy lay in the fact that the patient had been enabled to follow this voice and that the energy of the pathogenic complex had diminished. I will come back to this later since the energy invested in the complexes and their symbols is an important part of my thoughts.

In the preface to the second (1914) edition of the "Contents of Psychosis," Jung again wrote of a hereditary disposition or noxious element of unknown nature which could bring into being a non-adjusted psychological function which could develop into illness with the corresponding releasing stimulus. But already in 1919 in "Psychogenesis in Mental Disease" he described in a very detailed manner that this problem should not be dealt with in a monocausal manner—either from the psychic or from the organic side—but by reference to a multifactoral conditionalism. In his opinion most people who suffer from dementia praecox have an innate tendency toward psychic conflicts. They have an abnormal irritability (today we would rather say that it is an extreme sensibility), and their conflicts therefore differ in their emotional intensity from normal tensions. Their conflicts bring them into a state of panic and a chaos of emotions and strange thoughts. At this point we have to be aware of the fact that many of the cases which Jung described with the term "dementia praecox" would today be classified as borderline cases.

In his work on schizophrenia he described this dilemma, as he called it, in a more modern form:

> [A]re we to assume as a causal factor, a weakness of the ego-personality, or a particularly strong affect? I regard the latter hypothesis as the more promising, and for the following reason. The notorious weakness of ego-consciousness in the sleeping state means next to nothing so far as a psychological understanding of the dream-contents is concerned. It is the feeling-toned complex that determines the meaning of the dream, both dynamically and also as regards its content. We must undoubtedly apply this criterion to schizophrenia, for, so far as we can see at present, the whole phenomenology of this disease turns on the pathogenic complex. In our attempts at explanation we shall probably do best if we start from this point and regard the weakening of the ego-personality as secondary, as one of the destructive concomitants of a feeling-toned complex which arose under normal conditions but afterwards shattered the unity of the personality by its intensity (Jung, 1958, p. 269).

Jung clearly takes the view that there is an excessive strength of affect and not an excessive weakness of the ego. I took the same view in the beginning of this essay especially in my fourth thesis concerning the power or energy of archetypal symbols. I think in the case of the patient

I have described, too, one can speak neither of an excessive weakness of the ego nor of a dominance of the archaic defense formations like active splitting (Kernberg 1975) and projective identification (Klein 1975). Both of these defense formations could certainly be found in this patient, too, but they were not stronger than in cases of neurosis. I would even say that splitting as well as projective identification continue to exist as archaic forms of defense also in sane persons and that they become visible in especially affective situations. In an essay on "enemy images" (1984), I showed that it is quite common to use them on a collective level as an almost malicious sort of party game.

Apart from these archaic defences, my patient had much more mature defense formations at her disposal and the extent of her repressions was much larger. I would not say that she had a very unstable ego complex either. It is really something to withhold a systematized delusion for 100 sessions within an analytical situation. Futhermore, she was able to react discreetly to the people about her and in spite of her paranoid fears she never completely destroyed her relationships with her colleagues. Of course she warded off a lot by means of avoidance but this, too, is seen rather as a mature than as an archaic defense mechanism. I am not interested in attributing a mature ego which functioned adequately to the patient, but I would only like to question the thesis of a weakness of the ego which is acquired in early childhood in favor of an especially intense complex-strength in borderline patients.

The enormous libidinal intensity of the symbols found in the case of Karin was especially impressive but also hard to describe. There was such an energy coming from them that I really imagined the tiger's presence in the room. Sometimes we also find such an intensity when dealing with archetypal dreams or active imagination in the therapy of a neurosis. But it is rather an exception in the treatment of neuroses and the strong energetic tensions which come from the unconscious and the characteristically long periods of therapy in borderline cases differ considerably from therapy with an average neurosis.

In 1965 Rosemary Gordon dealt with the question that projective identification has not at all only negative effects but that it is capable of breaking down limits within the person concerned as well as in the object world, which can be essential for qualitative changes in the structure of the personality (Gordon 1965, 145). In the same essay she stated that what Jung understood by "participation mystique" (unconscious identity, psychic infection and inductions) were synonymous with projective identification (*ibid.*, p. 128). I have to confess that I somehow dislike the term "projective identification" and prefer the term "partici-pation mystique." It seems to me that the former is too strongly con-nected to the patriarchal hero-ego of Occidental culture and stresses the distinction (which is also an active split) between the sane analyst and the deplorably ill neurotic too much. Almost all descriptions of Freudian analysis present it as a one-sided transaction which is invested by the patient into the analyst. When a projective identification occurs in countertransference on the part of the analyst, it is in most cases seen as a pathologically disturbing process. I prefer the cross-marriage scheme of transference which Jung developed in "Psychology of Trans-ference" (1946b). According to his scheme, such processes on the lower level of the unconscious transference between the anima of the analyst and the animus of the patient are considered normal and impor-tant for therapy. In my book on *Methods of Analytical Psychology*, I too stressed the therapeutic importance of this axis (1979).

I would like to give a clear example from the therapy of a 32-year-old borderline patient. He was an "eternal" student who had already studied mathematics for 24 terms without having taken any qualifying examinations. He had been in mental hospitals several times and had been treated there with shock therapy even though his diagnosis was a serious compulsion neurosis with moderate paranoid presentational contents. He lived almost completely in a third dimension between outer reality and fantasy which was strongly mystical in its orientation. I would call it the world of a deformed *mundus imaginalis* as it was described by H. Corbin (1979). Also in many archetypal dreams which were highly charged emotionally this *mundus imaginalis* had the char-acter of an absolute psychic reality with the corresponding projective identifications into the world about him.

To one of the sessions the patient brought the following:

Dream: *It turns out that Hitler is not dead and takes over power in Germany again. As I have dark hair and a hooked nose the SS regards me as a Jew, and they throw me into prison. I am com-pletely in despair and try to affirm my innocence. I do not succeed in convincing them. Some days later an SS officer comes to my dungeon and tells me that he is now going to kill me with a shot in the neck. He pulls out his pistol and I wake up trembling all over.*

The patient was 20 minutes late and when greeting me his hands were wet with sweat. Trembling, he let himself fall down on the couch and told me that I was this SS officer and had only disguised myself as an analyst. He really expected me to pull out a pistol and shoot him. I considered it almost a miracle that he had summoned up the courage to come at all. He had obviously projected his own very aggressive maleness onto me. He now expected that I would act correspondingly and free him from his serious feelings of guilt caused by his narcissisticly overevaluated contempt for others.

At first I was very amazed and helpless, all the more so as I knew that the patient did not respond at all to reality control. But then something very strange happened inside of me. I had the strong feeling that I was a mother and held my own little baby in my arms—myself not the patient—and it was completely scared and frightened. I started to make swaying motions with the upper part of my body and to make calming completely averbal sounds. By projective counteridentification I had projected my own baby onto the patient. And it was exactly this process which made the patient calm down little by little and let him say with relief at the end of the session, "So it really was only a dream."

In such situations I ask myself if we really have to adopt all our clinical terms from the Freudians. Would it not be much more appropriate to use the term "mutual participation," which is much more suitable in terms of our theory of complex constellations in which both the analyst as well as the patient participate? Because of my experience, I simply do not believe that there is a one-sided projected identification at all, except with very schizoid analysts. It can differ very much in its quantity. The peg on which a projection hangs itself might be big or small, but there always is one. (In this connection I would like to mention that the brilliant work of Nathan Schwartz-Salant on "Archetypal Foundations of Projective Identification" (1987) has given me many precious stimuli on this subject.)

Before dealing again with the symbols, I need to make a few additional remarks concerning my basic concept. In my opinion the clinical theory of complexes has not been developed further since the time of Jung, at least not in a summary form and not with regard to the different clinical pictures. Complexes are of course often mentioned by Jungians and new complexes are quite often found and described, but not usually in their clinical relations. In most cases they are amplified and examined with regard to the variety of their symbols. These examinations certainly are very important and valuable, and I do not want to deny their value.

But I think there really is a hole in analytical psychology regarding a more modern theory of complexes which can be used in clinical diagnostics as well as in therapy by single analysts. Our trainees also need a basic instrument which enables them to understand the essentials of the complex and the widely differing courses of experience and formations within the psyche which their patients undergo. Time and again we see that in the general and specific teachings of the theory of neurosis the Jungians have to fall back upon the positions of Freudian psychoanalysis, especially when it is about the therapy of the personal unconscious. This is not only regrettable but unnecessary as the theory of complexes puts something more modern than the concept of the psychic apparatus (with its dominance of today's ego psychology where the unconscious is not sufficiently attended to) at our disposal. I appreciate the Freudian positions and their further development very much, and therefore I do not want to attack them. I am not at all opposed to taking them into account and using them. I only think that we should use our own possibilities in this field to a much larger extent.

Within the scope of a seminar held for many years at the Berlin C. G. Jung Institute, we have been dealing intensively with the burning ecological problems which today threaten the survival of mankind as a whole, and certain parallels between micro- and macro-cosmos have attracted my attention. I think that the complex organization of the human psyche is identical to the ecological systems of nature which surround us. Therefore it should be possible to develop a theory of the system of psychic complexes. I will take the two great basic complexes, the father and the mother archetype, as my starting points. I will try to grasp the cores of these two complexes in their different complex personifications by means of the scheme of pyramids presented by Jung in *Aion* (1951). I will also try to explain parts of it with the example of the case mentioned above. Both of these great complexes as well as the different elements of their cores—senex, hero, old wise woman, witch—represent systems which are connected with each other and which have in a sufficiently functional psyche, a free flow of libido.

It might seem a bit confusing that I talk about one great complex on the one hand and of several complex cores on the other. But empirical clinical experience with such a scheme of pyramids shows that, in the case of a psychic disease, only a very few archetypal points of, let's say, the father complex are mobilized or energized. In Karin's case, it would only be the mythological father animal which tears apart in the animal field and the violent senex in the human field. Futhermore, they are completely or partly dissociated from the ego complex and thus form complex cores of their own which are, so to speak, split off from the large sphere of the father complex.

These two great basic complexes must of course be confronted with the ego complex, with all its functions and conscious and unconscious parts, as a third element. It is of course connected with the complex's surface as well as with the complex cores. This results in a triangulation which might even form a kind of bridge between the schools since the Freudians are known to deal much more nowadays with the preoedipal processes that Jung pointed out very early.

This is a short and very incomplete draft of what I have in mind and have been dealing with for two years. Within our ecological working group we have especially been dealing with the nature of confrontation on a collective level in our culture under the aspects of mythology, history, and contemporary events. In a certain sense this work formed the basis of a systematic theory of complexes.

I would like to give a further example of symbol formation which also comes from a borderline patient, whose case I have presented in detail elsewhere (1971). She was a 45-year-old woman with serious depressions, states of mental confusion, and a whole series of suicide attempts. During the whole first period of analysis she was dominated by a pronounced negative mother complex. Her strong feelings of hate against her mother were accompanied by just as violent feelings of guilt. She had grown up abroad where both parents did missionary work for a very severe and restrictive sect. The mother was the second wife of the father, who already had two daughters from his first marriage, but after the death of his first wife he had left the girls completely with foster parents. In this second marriage my patient was the second of five children. As both parents were always on the road because of their missionary work, she and her sister two years older were left almost completely with native servants. When Ruth, my patient, was six years old, the family went to Europe on holiday. During this time, the mother did not stay with the children but travelled in different countries in order to give lectures on their missionary work. "To serve God," they told their daughters, "is more important than to take care of one's own children."

Finally they went back abroad, and as the two daughters became a burden, they were given without further ado to a member of their sect with whom they were to stay for the next eight years. To make matters worse, this man was a purely chance acquaintance. Ruth's elder sister did not survive this treatment. Shortly before the parents' departure, she caught a serious pneumonia and died. Ruth's remaining childhood and adolescence were nothing but suffering. Her foster mother was not any better than her own and must have had severely sadistic traits. She could finally escape from this situation only by marrying very early against her mother's will. But in the meantime she had introjected the negative mother image and was even partly identified with it, and this to such a degree that she herself bore five children like her own mother. In part she developed a counterposition by leading a real Cinderella existence in her marriage.

When I got to know her, she looked like a little grey mouse and like the incarnation of the symbol of the abandoned child to whom no attention has ever been paid. But she had—and it was surely lifesaving for her—a very strong vitality. She was furthermore endowed with an intelligence above average and a capacity for creativity which had, however, been to a large extent latent. From the beginning of the analysis, she tried to express herself and her problems in a creative manner. At first she did it in the form of long written compositions and poems, then in drawings and paintings as well as in plastic works with clay. The latter resulted in the first decisive symbol formation in the analysis.

In one of her initial dreams, she "was in a deserted house" and through a dirty kitchen she "came to a room where there were a lot of children who were all deserted, ill, and nearly starved." As I have previously noted in reference to such patients, she did not experience this dream as an event inside of the *mundis imaginalis* but rather as an outward reality which required her to help immediately. So she decided to adopt a Negro child even though three of her five were still small and she had to care for them. Of course the family did not have much money either. It was very difficult for me to prevent her from doing it. I finally succeeded only by pointing out to her the analytical rule that projects which are decisive for the patient's life can only be undertaken with the acceptance of both sides and when worked through analytically. Half a year after the beginning of the analysis, the following fantasy developed in her which returned time and again:

> I feel like I am being carried in the arms of a big, strong, and primitive man. Sometimes it is a Negro. He does not pay attention to me as a person, he only wants me as a woman. After a long fight he overcomes me because actually I want to be defeated by him. In this moment suddenly all my femininity awakes. I need this male power and I need to be overcome by the male to be able to 'come' at all. If this does not happen, I literally speaking remain dry.

I was a bit astonished by this graphic report by a patient who, up to this moment, had been quite prudish and did not speak at all about sexuality. In spite of the libidinal charge, she experienced this fantasy inside of her own inner creative activity, and shortly afterwards she started to work with clay for the first time. Of course she wanted to make the Negro, but something else happened. The patient told me about it in the session, as follows:

> My depression of the last few days has not vanished but I feel a little better. I felt like I was caught in a spider's web; I felt the need to form something out of clay. I had to overcome a strong resistance to do what I wanted to do and what could help me. I did not know how to start. Of course, I thought all the time of my beautiful black man and how to form him. But I was simply blocked. So for half an hour I just kneaded the wet clay and looked at the forms which came into being. I saw heads of animals. I felt the fresh clay and finally I did not think anything at all. Then I suddenly noticed how the figure of a child came into being out of this earth. This child had a toothache. He ran to his mother and hid his head between her breasts. Today this suffering child is still inside of me.

She brought this figure along with her to the session and I have to admit that I was very astonished about the artistic form and the strong expression it had. It was the first plastic work she had ever made in her whole life. In contrast to the dream—she said it herself—this time she experienced the ill child as her own inner figure. The comforting mother who can take the ill and deserted child which she has in herself in her arms, and who no longer has "dry" breasts, had developed in her own inner world and was now experienced by her consciousness as an important symbol.

This symbol obviously was not formed spontaneously. But it needed half an hour of intensive psychic work to put aside the figure of the Negro which dominated her consciousness. Only then the process gradually started in which she let the symbol of the positive mother archetype with the child come into being out of the material. With Ruth, just as with Karin, the symbol took up an early experience from childhood without which I could not imagine its formation. This kind of mother figure corresponded to an Asian foster mother who had taken care of Ruth during her first six years. She became very clearly recognizable in the figures Ruth formed later. To her astonishment these had Asian traits, but I had to draw her attention at it. Only afterwards, in a relatively late period in the analysis, the figure of this foster mother which had been repressed returned again to consciousness. Thus, we have here a process of symbol formation similar, almost identical, to that in Karin's case.

In literature, there are countless definitions for the symbol. There are anthropological, theological, mythological, artistic, and psychological ones. The psychological definitions in particular differ enormously and derive certain elements from all other fields, but I would like to keep to C. G. Jung's definition, which I however changed a little and which brings up one question which is clinically very important: does the symbol become a symbol only when it is accepted or experienced as such by the consciousness? Is it really—as I described it for Karin's case—first scene, then metaphor? Does the tiger become a symbol only when he appears in the picture as sun and senex and later when Karin goes through the cages? Or is it rather that the tiger is already a symbol in the initial dream and that even the sunflower dance is already one? Does not all this inner experience have enormous effects on the consciousness and psyche, effects which only a real symbol can provoke?

One can surely answer all these questions in the affirmative, and so it might be better to talk not of symbol formation or creation, but of the process of becoming conscious of or recognizing a symbol. This seems to be of the greatest therapeutic importance, especially when dealing with borderline or psychotic cases. Let's look again at what happened when both patients understood from their consciousness the symbol as metaphor or almost as a sign. For Karin the tiger was potentially the strongly aggressive, drunken father of whom she was enormously afraid. As a child she had to know how to handle him and be his guardian. Now her dream ego allowed her to flee from him and she withdrew into silence, fear, mistrust, and defiance. Although she surely needed this period, I had some difficulties in considering it a positive regression. I rather felt that the mobilization of the complex reinforced her resistance in the initial phase. With Ruth the situation was quite similar. The metaphor of the ill child which appeared in her dream almost led to an adoption of a Negro child and thus to a reinforcement of her masochism which was nearly irreparable. Her resistance expressed itself in her absolute wish to act out. She filled up whole sessions with trying to convince me.

But in the moment when each of them became conscious of the existence of inner symbols and could understand tiger and child as such, their condition changed. Karin's systematized delusion, which had been rigid up to then, began to flow, and Ruth became able to turn toward the people about her and to a certain degree forego acting out. From our analytical knowledge, we cannot simply say that symbols will have their healing effects anyway no matter whether we understand them or not. Such an attitude, which only sees the prospective sides of the symbols which come from the unconscious, could be more dangerous than helpful when working with severely disturbed patients. Symbols not only have a healing character but can also block therapy or considerably aggravate a condition if they are wrongly understood.

(Actually there is nothing which cannot be abused by resistance and defense for their purposes—even the symbol.)

Obviously symbols can only become active within the transcendent function when the defense system is loosened up to an extent which allows symbolic understanding and experiencing into consciousness. One could express it even more carefully and speak of the permission to experience and understand in another manner than the one that corresponds to the hitherto complex-fixated scheme. This facilitates the growth of libido, which then is available for the ego complex and consciousness. But of course not all of the libido which was previously bound in the complex is transferred to consciousness by the analytical process—assuming it is successful—to be at the disposal of the ego complex. If we take Karin's tiger seriously as a real inner tiger with all the power and energy which a tiger has, as Hillman does phenomenologically in his dream book (1979), the result of our therapy would be a sort of superman whose consciousness would have a very huge potential of energy at its disposal. Especially borderline and psychotic patients can teach us that there are enormous energies in the complexes. In successful analytical processes still another thing obviously happens in the unconscious which I would call a distribution of energy. Every symbol always keeps, as Verena Kast puts it, a surplus of meaning (1986).

A last tiger dream which Karin had shortly before she finished analysis may clarify this. At that time, after four years of therapy and over 500 hours of treatment, she felt—relatively—fine and was more or less able to cope with her life alone. In this dream she stands in a circus arena which has a fence around it for the dressage with wild animals. Through a passage three tigers enter the arena. She is afraid of them and shrinks back to the exit. Through this exit the tamer enters the arena and indicates she should leave it while he holds the tigers back.

There were not any more great changes after this dream, but it became more and more clear that her analysis was going to finish. As we see in this case, the symbol had not dissolved at all but remained just as it had appeared in the initial dream. Now, however, an experienced man in a protected room handled these animals and knew how to treat them. In the dream, she could experience with the corresponding respect and distance the positive and negative, destructive and creative elements of this mythological father animal. Although Karin did not understand this dream and neither could nor wanted to interpret it, it still meant very much to her and she recalled it quite often until the end of therapy. In the meantime her consciousness had developed quite an understanding and respect for symbolic experience.

When looking at both of these case presentations of the development of a symbol, it seems to me that something happened which could be compared with the regeneration of an ecosystem which has been overgrown and poisoned by one single species. In Ruth as well as Karin, at first one single complex was dominant. In Karin's case it was the negative father complex, and in Ruth's the negative mother complex. These determined to a large extent all the modes of behavior and experience of not only the conscious ego complex but the whole psyche. In the course of the therapy a shift of energy, and therefore a mobilization of other complex cores, occurred. In the case of Karin we have the following image:

At first the unconscious mobilized a mythological father animal which also potentially contained positive elements of the father archetype but which could not yet be accepted by consciousness. Then, through the picture she painted, the white or positive magician was brought up as the sun, as the one who brings light, as a big circle. With his anima the white magician obviously points at the archetype of the earth, which belongs to the Magna Mater, and at the female big circle, the moon in the starry night sky. In the next step, which is again accompanied by a positive fatherly senex figure, a direct contact with the animals which rend and tear apart occurs. This results in an acceptance of sexuality and of Dionysiac experience and in an increase of personal memories of the father, among which there are also positive ones as well. The personal father is not only black any more but becomes black and white. Finally the figure of the animal tamer appears which, in my opinion, is to be classified as an archetype of a culture hero because he is able to tame animal powers and to use them in a creative manner.

I have followed this line here only for a certain complex cores which belong to the father archetype and have only hinted at the "bridge" to the mother archetype. (Of course, this has also been extensively treated.) With the help of this bridge and reporting other dreams of the patient and changes of her experience, one could prove how the mother archetype, too, was filled in its different complex cores, or to put it in a better way, how it was included in this circulation. Although I have gone into the formation of the symbol in greater detail when presenting the case of Ruth, in her case the same could be recognized. In the field of symbols the dominating negative personal mother was supplemented by an archetypal positive mother figure, a Demeter-Kore symbol, in which mother and daughter melt together. The event which provoked the formation of these symbols was the search for her own femininity in a transpersonal sexuality which the unconscious did, however, seem to reject and look for its own ways instead. Only much later in Ruth's therapy, when she remembered the Asian foster mother, did an upwelling of positive personal experiences with "mothers" occur. Her own mother remained negative throughout the whole therapy even though at the end Ruth did not hate her any more but could understand her to a certain degree. I will not go into detail here, but in this therapy the different symbolizations and personifications of the archetypal cores of the mother or father complex were also filled and mobilized in a libidinal manner. In this case, too, a distribution of energy and division into different complexes with which the ego could get contact occurred.

In his *Aion* (1951), Jung developed in his scheme of pyramids a structure of the archetype of the self. The four pyramids drawn there are finally brought together in the form of a circle. This circle could be understood as a big system which embraces the whole psyche. In my opinion the same or similar schemes of pyramids can be developed for the cores of the mother and the father archetypes. But one should, however, also introduce personal elements into them—if this is not a "crimen laesa majestas." This point I base on Mary Williams's (1963) statement on the "Indivisibility of the Personal and Collective Unconscious" which I set out more in detail in the beginning of this article (1987). I also discussed in detail (1986) elsewhere whether it is useful or not to include in the theory certain personal elements which belong to very early childhood into the core elements of a complex instead of restricting them only to the surface of the complex.

I consider such schemes of pyramids as systems for the father and mother archetypes useful because they can show us in the first interview and at the beginning of a therapy which personification of the complex core is energetically mobilized and which parts are left blank and are therefore not experienced. In the course and at the end of a treatment, these schemes can show what could be filled up, enlivened, and opened to be experienced in therapy. (A scheme for the case of Karin is shown in Figures 1 and 2.) In her case, in the beginning there existed only the negative father and man, i.e., the lower point of transition between the first and the second pyramid. Through the mythological father animal of the third pyramid, which is situated relatively deep in the unconscious, and a more negative senex figure of the second pyramid (guardian) the father god and the positive senex (sun and magician) were mobilized in the first pyramid. Through the positive

Figure 1. Example of the Father Archetype
Karin at the start of therapy.

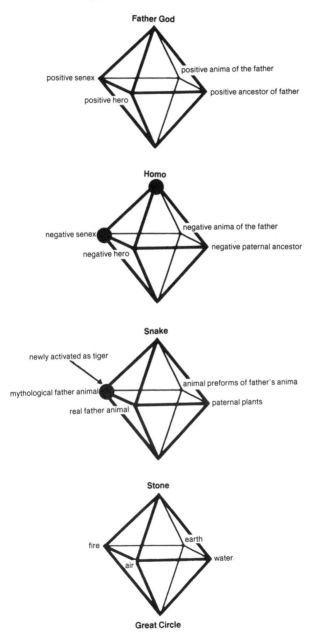

Figure 2. Structure of Archetypes
Karin at the end of therapy.

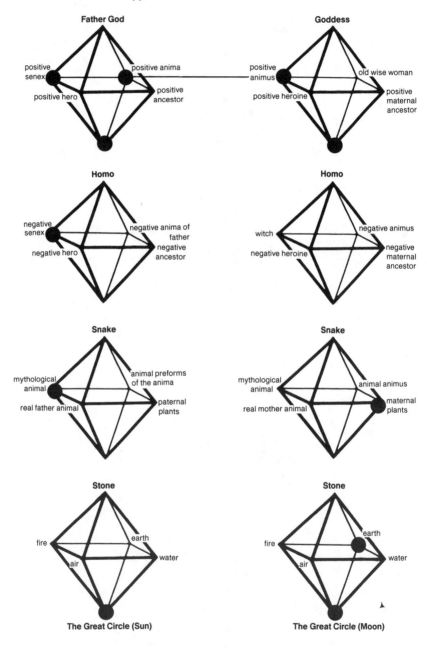

anima of the father this led to an activation of the mother archetype and at the end a positive hero figure appeared. As far as I can observe it in this case, the relation to the layer of the fourth pyramid, which is the deepest, remained unfilled. This might be the background for the fact that Karin kept a strong paranoid element in her personality.

References

Blohmeyer, R. 1980. Die Konstellierung der Gegenübertragung beim Auftauchen archetypischer Träume. *Übertragung und Gegenübertragung in der analytischen Psychologie*. Hildesheim: Gerstenberg Verlag.

Corbin, H. 1979. *Corps spirituel et Terre celeste*. Paris: Buchet/Chastel.

Dieckmann, Hans. 1971. Symbols of active imagination. *Journal of Analytical Psychology* 16/2.

——————. 1978. *Träume als Sprache der Seele*. Fellbach: Bonz Verlag.

——————. 1979. *Methoden der Analytischen Psychologie*. Olten: Walter Verlag.

——————. 1980. Die Konstellierung der Gegenübertragung beim Auftauchen archetypischer Träume: Untersuchungsmethoden und Ergebnisse. *Übertragung und Gegenübertragung in der analytischen Psychologie*. Hildesheim: Gerstenberg Verlag.

——————. 1984. The enemy image. *Quadrant* 17/2.

——————. 1987. On the theory of complexes. *Archetypal Processes in Psychotherapy*. Wilmette, Ill.: Chiron Publications.

——————. 1987. Der Mensch und seine Angst. *Vortrag im südwestdtsch.* Rundfunk.

Gordon, Rosemary. 1965. The concept of projective identification. *Journal of Analytical Psychology* 10/2.

Green, A. 1975. Analytiker, Symbolisierung und Abwesenheit im Rahmen der psychoanalytischen Situation: Über Veränderung der analytischen Praxis und Erfahrung. *Psyche* 29:503.

Hillman, J. 1979. *The Dream and the Underworld*. New York: Harper and Row.

Jacobi, Jolande. 1959. *Complex, Archetype, Symbol*. Princeton, N.J.: Princeton University Press.

Jacobson, Edith. 1964. *The Self and the Object World*. New York: International Universities Press.

Jung, C.G. 1907. The psychology of dementia praecox. *CW* 3. Princeton, N.J.: Princeton University Press.

——————. 1914. Contents of psychosis. *CW* 3.

——————. 1919. On the problems of psychogenesis in mental disease. *CW* 3.

——————. 1946a. Analytical psychology and education. *CW* 17.

——————. 1946b. Psychology of transference. *CW* 16.

——————. 1951. Aion. *CW* 9/2.

——————. 1952a. Psychology and alchemy. *CW* 12.

——————. 1952b. Symbols of transformation. *CW* 5.

——————. 1958. Schizophrenia. *CW* 3.

Jung, Eberhard. 1971. *Der Grossinquisitor in Analytische Psychologie*. Basel: Karger Verlag.

Kast, Verena. 1986. Die Bedeutung der Symbole im therapeutischen Prozess. *C.G. Jung und die Medizin*, Heilung and Wandlung, ed. Zürich: Artemis Verlag.

Kernberg, Otto. 1975. *Borderline Conditions and Pathological Narcissism*. New York: Jason Aronson.

Klein, Melanie. 1946. Notes on some schizoid mechanisms. *International Journal of Psycho-Analysis* 27:99-110.

——————. 1975. *Envy and Gratitude*. London: Hogarth.

158   THE BORDERLINE PERSONALITY IN ANALYSIS

Kreitler, Shulamith. 1965. *Symbolschöpfung und Symbolerfassung*. München: E. Reinhardt Verlag.

Modell, A. 1963. Primitive object relations and the relationship to schizophrenia. *International Journal of Psycho-Analysis* 44:282.

Neumann, Erich. 1955. *The Great Mother*. Princeton, N.J.: Princeton University Press.

Rohde-Dascher, Christa. 1972. *Das Borderline-Syndrom*. Bern: H. Huber Verlag.

Schwartz-Salant, Nathan. 1987. Archetypal foundations of projective identification. *The Archetype of the Shadow in a Split World*, Mattoon, ed. Einsiedeln, Switzerland: Daimon Verlag.

Whitmont, Edward. 1969. *The Symbolic Quest*. New York: Putnam and Sons.

Williams, Mary. 1963. Indivisibility of the personal and collective unconscious. *Journal of Analytical Psychology* 8/1.

Winnicott, D.W. 1958. *Through Paediatrics to Psycho-Analysis*. London: Tavistock Publishers.

Wollberg, A.R. 1968. Patterns of interaction in families of borderline patients. *New Directions in Mental Health*, B. Reiss, ed. New York: Grune und Stratton.

Transference and Countertransference Mirrored in Personal Fantasies and Related Fairy-Tale Motifs in the Therapy of a Patient with a Borderline Structure

Verena Kast

Translated by David Oswald

Marcel was 25 years old when he came to me to have himself "tested." At least that was the reason which he formulated over the telephone, and I assumed he was looking for some occupational counseling. Then, when he came to see me, he immediately told me that he hated being tested, that he couldn't stand tests, and that he was actually seeking a therapist who would stay in the same place for at least ten years, for he had already lost eight therapists who had moved away. This entire situation seemed very peculiar to me, and I asked him to tell me his therapeutic experiences.

He had been seeking therapy since he was 20 because he was dissatisfied with his life and occupation. He had experienced his first anxiety crisis, which he called depression, as he was offered a responsible job (he worked for the Swiss National Railways). During the four years before starting his therapy with me, he had worked only occasionally and had committed himself six times into a psychiatric clinic, voluntarily, because he had the impression of suffering from depression. As

Verena Kast, author of several books including *The Nature of Loving,* is a Jungian analyst in private practice. She lectures at the C.G. Jung Institute in Zurich where she is also a training analyst. She is a professor of psychology at the University of Zurich.

he was telling these past experiences, it became clear that he had been abandoned twice by therapists, but that in the other cases he had given up the therapy or the therapist.

[I am going to quote important passages from our conversation, for they were tape-recorded at the wish of the client. After each session he would take the tape home with him. Once for Christmas he gave them all to me as a gift with the permission to make use of them.]

I confronted him with this poor perception of reality.

V: It appears to me that you are once again seeking a therapist in order to prove to him or her that he or she isn't worth anything, and to prove to yourself that you are incurable.

M: (He looked at me in astonishment.) I will prove to you that you are wrong. I don't want to tell you my story, I have already told it a thousand times, nobody believes me; by the way, my story is unbelievable. The doctor from the clinic will send you my patient records.

During this first session I had contradictory impressions and feelings. I was very curious. I felt a strong energy in Marcel; I also had sympathy for him. On the other hand, I felt angry with him as well. I felt an enormous aggression in him and a deep anxiety. I understood that his desire to undergo tests with me which he really despised meant that he genuinely wanted to confront himself and his life, and that he was afraid of doing so. I also assumed that he would test me at the times when he became afraid, trying to find out if I was good enough for him.

I explained to him that he would probably be testing himself and also testing me, but that I also had the feeling he was spending too much energy confronting himself and simultaneously covering up his problems because he could not yet endure the anxiety connected with them. He felt himself understood and said, "I have a little trust in you, but I have to go away now and think about it in order to know if I really want to work with you, and you too—maybe you can think about it also."

Conclusions from the First Session

Marcel was afraid of being rejected and didn't realize that he was the one doing the rejecting. He felt abandoned. I perceived very strong contradictory emotions, above all destructive aggression and fear. He was looking for help which, however, he was not able to accept. As he said that he felt a little trust, he had to leave to think about it and to consider whether he really wanted to work with me. He must have had a great fear of getting involved in a therapeutic relationship, probably a fear of fusing with me and, in connection with that of course, of being abandoned by me.

Diagnostic Considerations

His first crisis arose as he was supposed to work more independently, in a moment of separation from his colleagues. Times of separation, in which autonomy was encouraged, were experienced with very great anxiety by him. The defense mechanisms of splitting and denial were obviously present, as well as omnipotence fantasies and devaluation strategies. I will come to the transference/countertransference situation later.

Marcel returned to the clinic where he was staying at the time and instructed them to immediately send me his history. He told everyone that he had found the best therapist in the world, as the doctor later told me with a laugh. This was a matter of primitive idealization.

Marcel was diagnosed as a schizoid personality with paranoid features, possibly the onset of a hebephrenia.

Some Remarks About his Anamnesis

He was the first of two children in a very problematic family. His mother, a paranoid schizophrenic, had occasionally been hospitalized in clinics, the first time as Marcel was three years old. The father was an aggressive alcoholic. Between the ages of six and fifteen, Marcel was placed, along with his sister, in a home run by nuns. There he went through—in his experience at least—an extremely harsh upbringing. After finishing school, he worked as an unskilled laborer for the railway. He tried several times to start an apprenticeship, but when he sought out a master, he was too ashamed of his background, and invented all sorts of biographical details so he wouldn't have to tell his real history. In the patient records he was described as a liar. I think that what was happening was not lying, but rather an aspect of splitting, the negation of his history.

My diagnostic considerations led me to see Marcel as a paranoid personality based on a borderline structure. Since my explanations of his splitting tendencies did not provoke confusion in him, but on the contrary gave him a bit of confidence, I thought—without being able to positively exclude the possibility of a hebephrenia—more in the direction of a borderline organization.

In the second session he told me he had thought about whether he wanted to work with me, and had come to the conclusion that we could do extremely good work with each other and might succeed in healing him in a very short time. In any case, he said, he was determined to work intensively with me, and he wanted to prove his good will by revealing two secrets to me in confidence. The first secret was that he had an enormous fear of becoming sick. For this reason he would never touch door handles and never shake hands with anyone. This secret led me in the course of the therapy to work intensively on his body-ego, to have him consciously perceive his body, and above all to track down the power in his tensions and hidden aggressiveness.

The second secret was that the "entire world" thought his sickness was connected with his mother's sickness, but that this wasn't true.

M: It was very difficult for me as a small child when the police came and took my mother away. But it was also difficult for me when my mother spoke with people who I didn't see. That made me very anxious. But my mother is a very dear person, I like her very much. I remember how she carefully used to wash us. She washed our feet with Vim [a caustic cleaning fluid]. I am very important for my mother, I have to make sure that she takes her medication. As I told you that, I had the following fantasy: I am in the mountains, on the edge of a forest in a meadow. It is autumn, like now, there is a small river, the place is very beautiful. It is good to be alone, I don't want to see anyone. (And he added, with a threatening voice,) If somebody comes, I will beat them, especially if it's a woman.

V: Does anyone come?

M: No, nobody. This is boring. Why don't you come?

V: I don't like to be beaten.

M: You can come, but I determine the distance.

V: Agreed. I'll come closer.

M: It's now two hundred meters between us, that's good.

V: It is nice here. One is above the fog.

M (with a triumphant voice): You have got to climb down. You go into the fog. You're going to be cold.

V: You didn't like it, did you, that I spoke about the fog? I spoke about the fog because it is not possible for it to be so nice, for your situation to be so nice, so peaceful, for you to feel so good. You don't have any contact up there, and then also you told me a secret in confidence, the secret about your mother is very important for me. I can easily believe you, that you have a good relationship with your mother, but it must be difficult to live with her, to watch out for her. I don't see clearly there yet. That is the fog for me.

He listened attentively to me, then he said:

M: I will punish you anyway.

V: You punish me if I don't do what you want? Perhaps you punish when you are afraid. It makes one afraid to see a situation as it is. I can certainly understand that.

M: I am always very aggressive. I am always furious. I am always afraid. But now you have destroyed my fantasy, I will punish you. But let's go into the fog. The session is done. Don't forget my secrets.

As he spoke about the secret concerning his mother, he tried to close his eyes to the difficulties he must have had with her, and produced a very peaceful fantasy. Yet one could see his isolation, especially his problem with women. This fear of women and the aggressiveness connected to it was transferred to me. His closeness-distance problem was clearly visible: He wanted people to come close to him, but it was extremely important to him to fix the distance himself. Approaching him was like approaching a shy animal. My interpretation helped him to express his fear and to recognize that he was always furious. My explanation therefore tended to strengthen his ego. This confirmed my hypothesis that Marcel's case was the psychic situation of a person with a borderline organization, rather than the beginning of a hebephrenia.

On the transference level one also saw his tendency toward splitting. I was on the one hand someone who could share his loneliness, and therefore a good object. But if I didn't do what he wanted, I immediately became the bad object which he fought against, which he felt he must punish, an indication of projective identification combined with an omnipotence fantasy covering up his powerlessness. I myself felt a strong anger as he said to me that I could climb down into the fog and be cold. It wasn't so much the words as the way he said them, the malicious, sadistic grin I thought I perceived on his face. I interpreted this anger in part as countertransference, bringing up and expressing his own anger. Of course some of the anger was also my own, anger at men who simply take control of women.

Basically though, I understood that Marcel could endure his fears as long as he could control the people around him. Thus we were dealing with the defense mechanism of projective identification in which he experienced aspects of his own personality in the person across from him and felt he must control them, there, in order to remain "whole"—and to keep the evil portions from turning uncontrollably against him. I felt that there must be some connection with the experience of his mother being unable to control her fears and also his being at the mercy of these fears as a child.

During the five sessions that followed, Marcel spoke about his daily life, about his problems at work. These sessions centered around finding a job which he liked and which corresponded to his capabilities. In order to deal with this problem, Marcel, who was already drawing a disability pension, was assigned to an occupational counselor by the Office for Disability Insurance. He then regularly discussed with me what this counselor discovered. In this situation I had the role of the good father, while the occupational counselor was the bad father. Marcel came to the eighth session and opened it as follows:

> M: I am very dissatisfied with you. It can't go on like this.
> V: You want to punish me?
> M: Exactly! I am going to tell you a story. Do you know which one?
> V: I'm not clairvoyant.
> M: Exactly, that is the problem. You aren't even clairvoyant. You poor thing!

On the one hand, this demand to be clairvoyant amused me; on the other, I naturally asked myself what this meant. I became irritated and felt a fear growing in me which I could not explain.

> M: You are in a bad mood today. I see it well. Unfortunately I can't take your bad mood into consideration. Sorry. I have to tell you my story. I am in a cave, and you live in a farmhouse not far away from the cave. I'm alone. It is boring. I go out and I see that you are working in the garden. I ask if I can help you, and I decide that you need a fence and I construct it. In the evening you return home to your farmhouse. You invite me to come to you. I want to drink milk and you bring me milk. I want to go back into my cave, but it is cold and you invite me to sleep in your guest room. In the morning you get a telephone call, you must leave. I'm still sleeping. You write me a note. I make breakfast, we eat together after you have returned.

He looked at me attentively as he was telling this, while I was not allowed to look at him, according to an agreement between us. He didn't like it when someone looked at him. I could only look at him when he expressly allowed it. He continued:

M: You wash the dishes. I make my bed, then I go back into my cave. You can call when you want something from me. And now I'm talking about you: You are a terrible slut. You are a whore. You should have your hairs torn out, one after the other, and then be thrown into a cellar.

V: Who then has ever thrown you into the cellar?

M: There are all sorts of whores. Some are like the nuns at my boarding school, and some are the kind that want to sleep with all the men. It is unbearable that my sister is a prostitute. I can't bear it. How my mother must suffer.

V: Does your mother know about it?

M: No, I am the one who suffers. I am responsible for my sister. I was always responsible for my sister.

I explained to him that surely it had been extremely important to his sister that he had assumed responsibility for her, but that she was now living her own life and we had to accept that, even though we had reservations about whether what she was doing was good.

Commentary

Marcel had this fantasy at home, between the seventh and eighth hour. He allowed himself fantasies of the good, nourishing-mother type. I gave him milk and I had a garden. He identified himself totally with me, knowing what would happen, and also knowing what I needed. In his fantasy I needed a fence; he had need of a frame. (Perhaps he felt our relationship must be protected, or we should be more concerned about the frame of the relationship.) He retained for himself the option of drawing back into his cave, and one can of course ask why he happened to choose this particular symbol. It is a symbol of the archetype of the mother, which has the meaning of protection but also confinement. His coming to me would be a path towards autonomy.

He described his cave as a cold place, as a possibility of placing distance between the live, warm mother and himself. In his fantasy he also showed that he felt he must help me so that I could help him. Helping in order to be helped was probably one of his childhood experiences of relationship. It is also of course an experience of relationship in our society. The idea of fusion was again quite clear, but still he left me a certain autonomy. He even dared to fantasize that I would have enough trust to go away and be bold enough to come back.

If one saw the fantasy in context, then there was much trust and closeness being expressed through it. He saw me as a nourishing mother who also gave a bit of autonomy. He showed that in this relationship he could fulfill his basic human needs. He presented himself as protector, which was probably the only possibility for him to build up a relationship. After obviously embellishing this fantasy at home, he came into the hour and told me that he was not at all satisfied with me, demanded of me that I read his mind. I think we are again seeing the splitting here. He fantasized only the good aspect, and I imagine that he greatly feared I would reject him with his fantasy, or that the wish to fuse with me as the good mother would become too strong.

Let's return to the dialogue which took place in the hour. As if he had not spoken about me, which was of course correct since I was at this moment primarily a transference object, he suddenly wanted to do so now and became very aggressive. He accused me of being a whore, which by itself was quite strong, who deserved to have her hairs torn out one by one—for me, a sadistic image. These images could also have been hinting at sexual fantasies which he hadn't dared express. By tearing out my hair, I think, he also wanted to rob me of my erotic power. I had already in various ways become very dangerous to him.

I didn't interpret the progress which expressed itself in the fantasy, nor did I mention the splitting which was tangible in the situation. In hindsight, I think that I should have done that. By suddenly talking about his sister, which by the way revealed another secret, namely that she was a prostitute, he showed that he was also projecting his sister onto me.

In the following sessions he spoke a great deal about his sister. He tried to understand why she was a prostitute. While speaking of her, he also spoke of his sad experiences in the home. He described himself as someone who was constantly in a desperate rage. On the one hand, I shared his feelings of being full of rage. On the other, his childhood experiences made me very sad. One time I had tears in my eyes. He perceived that and also began to cry. When he came the next time, at the beginning of December, it occurred to him that I could go away at Christmas. He arrived wearing a very harsh facial expression and told me:

M: You made me cry last time. That will never do. I can't lose my composure. I will beat you with chains. I will tie you up with chains and beat you. I'll take an iron rod and beat you still

more. The blood will flow and the blood will flow. . . . I will
drive you on before me like one drives an animal.
V: Stop. I have enough. I can't stand it.

I was very afraid and was tempted to react in similar fashion, with
equally primitive sadistic means. I was afraid for my life. I said to myself
that at any moment he could draw a pistol out of his bag and kill me.
And I thought about how I would disarm him. As these thoughts were
going through me, I looked at him and his face showed a great fear. It
became clear to me that I had to protect him, because he was at least as
afraid of me as I was of him. I told him my insight and explained to him
that he had expressed very archaic aggressive and sexual drives which
would naturally create an enormous fear in me also. I told him I could
understand that he was feeling this rage and that he was afraid of these
wishes, but that I also thought our relationship was good enough for
him to be able to express his fantasies. Yet, I told him, as a woman I
couldn't bear it when he treated me like that.

M: Excuse me please. You know, it's not me who made these fantasies, it's a very big man who made them.
V: Can you see this man in your fantasy? (I explicitly said "in your
fantasy" because I had the feeling that he was confusing reality
and fantasy.)
M: This man is big, a bit like a giant, very serious, very demanding.
He wants me to not cry, to have a good job, to not be afraid, to
do everything like the other young people.
V: You feel rather terrorized by him.
M: Yes. He terrorizes me, he doesn't help me. Never in my life
has anyone helped me. My father was always drunk, I had to
protect my mother from him. He didn't help me. He was
satisfied that I was with my mother. When I was 18, he reproached me for not having a good job. But what should I do
when this man terrorizes me and when I then terrorize you?
V: Next time, tell me immediately when this man starts to terrorize
you. And we'll try then to understand what makes you afraid.
You terrorize when you're afraid, and you're afraid when you
fear you'll lose me, like when Christmas vacation is coming up.
And then I think, one must watch this man well, perhaps we can
tame him.

Commentary

My feeling of sadness brought us very close to one another, perhaps also brought him close to himself. He was afraid of being swallowed by soft feelings, and on the other side of being carried away by archaic impulses which he could not master. That was why he created an omnipotence fantasy. My intervention was probably not very professional. I didn't stop to think whether that was really a good moment to point out to him my real existence outside of his system, but my reaction was the only possibility for me. His reaction was interesting. He made a distinction between his ego and this big man who terrorized him. I think his ego was born in this moment.

In this context one has to think about the role of the father in the separation-individuation phase of the child, a phase which is so important in the formation of a borderline structure. In other words, to emancipate the child from the influence of the nourishing and protecting mother, the father must help the child in the separation phase. But Marcel's father hardly seems to have done that. And I imagine that his absence had the consequence that Marcel developed a mythical father image, equipped with all the aspects which he thought masculine, and also equipped with a sacred power, but "evil."

Hypothesis about the Phenomenon of Splitting in People with a Borderline Structure

When the child has to separate from the mother or from the person who can evoke the mother archetype, the child has to transitionally experience this person as "evil," otherwise this separation cannot take place. This causes anxiety in the child. The father would now have to be the model of a person who has separated himself but still not lost trust in the good mother, who can therefore build up a relationship to her again. The father would have to be the one who unites the two poles, the two archetypal possibilities, the two aspects of the same power. If the process of identification with a father who has survived this separation is impossible, this development becomes more difficult. The feelings that the mother is now evil remain in force if the father does not enable the transition into a more autonomous phase, where the good and the bad feelings about the mother can exist side-by-side. If the negative feelings dominate, the child has to deny them in order to save the feelings for the good mother. This is achieved by splitting. With Marcel, this father figure was missing. It had not yet come to life up to this point in the therapy.

Transference and Countertransference with Marcel—Summary

In the fantasies at the beginning of Marcel's therapy one can see the characteristic manfestations of the transference with borderline patients as described by Rohde-Dachser (drawing on Kernberg), which are basically:

- A magical kind of hope in the therapy and in the person of the therapist
- A diminished ability to differentiate between fantasy and reality
- Very aggressive-toned episodes of transference of mistrust and an extensive fear of being rejected
- Abrupt changes in the feeling-tone of the transference, all the way to a transference psychosis.

We react to these transferences with special, typical countertransferences:

- Many different feelings of countertransference in the same session
- A subliminal aggressiveness
- Mechanisms of projective identification are likewise activated in the analyst. Ancient fears, archaic fears, and aggressive drives are activated and turn against the analysand.

The feeling of closeness on the one hand and my refusal to accept his transference on the other had the effect on Marcel of causing him to distance himself from a big man who terrorized him. This experience moved me to think about the father role. On the other side, there now was the matter of dealing with this man. Marcel could always describe being basically afraid of this man, but then we could get no further. In one such situation, the fairy tale of Blue Beard occurred to me, and I told Marcel the tale. (See end of article.)

Having a fairy tale pop into mind in a certain analytical situation is a special form of countertransference. By telling the tale, I was indicating that I was prepared to move this inner man into an intermediate realm of our relationship, into a realm where we both could relate to him. At the same time, the personal history, the personal suffering was placed in a larger context where it was mirrored in an experience which people have always had to go through. A fairy tale in addition has the great advantage of showing an attitude with which a corresponding problem area, in this case the activities of Blue Beard, can be approached.

Marcel listened very attentively, quite in contrast to his usual habit, for he normally didn't like it when I spoke. He said at the end that it really was his story, it really was just such a Blue Beard with whom he was always fighting. (He soon found out that it was actually the brothers at the end of the tale who could fight against him.) Marcel emphasized that although his big man didn't actually have a blue beard, he easily could have one. Relating Blue Beard to this male figure clearly raised one perspective for interpreting this fairy tale. It was a matter of putting a stop to Blue Beard's activities, and if one observed the end, where the brothers confronted Blue Beard and put him to death, then it was clearly a matter of converting destructiveness into potent aggressiveness.

It occurred to Marcel that Blue Beard must have been a very powerful man, also a very rich man, but that women couldn't endure being around him. He felt that the fantasies that he had already had were very similar to those fantasies described in "Blue Beard." In the projection onto this fairy tale, then, he could try to come to grips with these fantasies. He found this Blue Beard to be sadistic. He sharply condemned the women who got involved with him, for, as he said, they did so just because of the money. Marcel felt what is clearly expressed at the beginning of the fairy tale—that all the women have a bad feeling and don't want to get involved with Blue Beard at first, but don't take this bad feeling seriously.

He was torn, and he vacillated back and forth between anger at these women and anger at Blue Beard. We talked about how Blue Beard didn't dismember the women until they knew his secret. Marcel became very agitated and said he would kill everyone who knew his secret. It was very important to preserve his secrets, and he was very upset at the idea that someone could get at his secrets. I emphasized then that I was speaking about Blue Beard, not about him, and Marcel calmed down.

The tale had the effect of something like a triangulation. Problems that had manifested themselves in our relationship were now seen in the fairy tale. In the fairy tale he could recognize his problem but nevertheless only let it come as close to him as he could bear. The tale accompanied us about half a year. We talked again and again about his everyday life, about the apprenticeship which he had begun, and every so often, in fragments, the Blue Beard tale was mentioned. Marcel thought about it, talked again about the corpses, saw himself dismembered, and also talked now and then about how women made him so afraid that he felt he must dismember them.

After several weeks, these corpses became uninteresting and he began to be interested in the behavior of the youngest daughter.

It had been clear to me for some time that my attitude was the same as that of this young woman who no longer got tangled up with Blue Beard but turned to another power and hoped for the brothers. I experienced the second part of the fairy tale as always present, even when Marcel was speaking about Blue Beard and the corpses. I always knew, so to speak, that the woman was not to get herself entangled in that, nor, however, should she be naive about Blue Beard's destructiveness.

There are different versions of the Blue Beard tale. In a French version there is a little gray man living upstairs in the castle to whom she hurries and looks for protection. In a Spanish parallel, the girl calls to Maria, the pure one. In other versions the woman turns to a power which is directed against Blue Beard and which above all is more comprehensive than Blue Beard, who is defeated and removed. In our variant, the heroine turns to her sister. The sister would be the side in her which isn't under the spell of this Blue Beard. And this sister is now the mediator to the valiant brothers.

This passage was always present for me and helped me, and presumably the analysand also, to maintain some distance from the Blue Beard theme. Working with the fairy tale, as working with fairy tales actually always does, enabled him to come to grips with his problem, yet also to simultaneously distance himself from it so that it didn't paralyze him. As he began to be interested in the heroine, I asked him to imagine the sun shining and the green grass growing. He himself came upon the fact that this was a great contrast with the death chamber down in the castle. The expression "death chamber" seems appropriate to me, for there is of course a death god hidden in Blue Beard. By relating the fairy tale to the individual problem of the analysand, this aspect was hardly taken into consideration. Then I asked him to see the grass growing and the sun shining and at the same time Blue Beard whetting his knife. He succeeded in imagining both images together and holding the tension. Soon then the brothers appeared to him, the valiant brothers, whom he described with great love.

The appearance of these brothers was something he longed for, and as they caught Blue Beard on the porch steps and killed him, Marcel breathed a sigh of relief and was convinced that he had also finished off the Blue Beard in himself. During the time we were working on the tale, hardly any transference attacks occurred. When I came too near to him with a statement and he wrinkled his forehead, I referred to the fairy tale.

Work on a fairy tale, I think, actually becomes a transitional object in the sense intended by Winnicott. A small child will clasp, say, her stuffed rabbit to herself when she is alone, and this rabbit is a symbol for the mother, for the feelings connecting her with the mother, and for the relationship to her—a symbol for well-being and also for the ability to comfort and care for oneself. In the same way, a symbol can be a transitional object and work on the symbol can be work on the transitional object. This work on the symbol can sometimes take the place of working directly with the transference/countertransference relationship, and in Marcel's case it seemed appropriate since we had to keep the wild man out, yet still deal with him. This work on the fairy tale can, however, also be understood as an endeavor which points to something standing behind the relationship, behind everyday reality, points, in the last result, to that sustaining primal ground which is accessible in the symbol, and particularly accessible also in the fairy tale. I see in this context the elements of the collective unconscious which carry us, which are available to us in fairy tales and myths, and which we make available to others for working through a problem.

The brothers in this fairy tale continued to be very important for Marcel. He fantasized about them. He thought about how these brothers could help him, how they could behave in certain situations, and sometimes he succeeded in tackling such situations instead of destructively attacking them, and he was pleased about that.

Three-and-a-half Years Later

Transference and countertransference have, of course, changed very much during the course of therapy. Marcel still has the tendency to tell me fantasy stories. It is easier for him to tell about his problems in this form.

He has finished his apprenticeship, found a position, friends. He has also canceled the pension that he had been receiving. He has a lot of success with girls, but his relationships last only for a short time. He often tells these girls some made-up story about where he comes from, gets tangled up in contradictions, and when they point these out, he becomes enraged. Marcel has the desire to punish these girls, but he knows why he doesn't do it—he thinks about Blue Beard.

One of Marcel's fantasies from this phase:

I am on my meadow. It is the meadow from the first fantasy.

In my view the meadow is a symbol of his personality, of his being at home with himself, but also an aspect of the protecting mother with whom he can fuse and from whom he can separate when he wishes.

I am in my small little house. It is spring. [In reality also it is spring.] I am there with Kathrin, a young girl whom I have known for three weeks, and with two colleagues. An ambulance drives past the house. I look to see whether my friends see it. Roger sees it and says, "They will come take all of us away." I answer, "That is ridiculous, and even if they do take us, Kast will come get us out of the hospital again." The ambulance, however, didn't even stop at our house but drove on past. I start to argue with Roger and tell him that he is always trying to set the whole world into panic.

After telling me this fantasy, he reported that his mother has been committed to a psychiatric clinic again, that this worries him, and that he is discussing it with the doctors. He simply has the feeling there must be more that can be done with his mother than just giving her medication again. He says that he began to yell at the doctors, and I ask him to see this event in the context of his fantasy. In the fantasy it is of course very clear how afraid he is of becoming sick like his mother, and that his two colleagues, whom he normally experiences as the valiant brothers in the sense that they defend him, would not help him anymore.

What does the transference look like now in this fantasy? The trust which he has in me is evident. Occasionally he also demands that I be the good mother who protects him from all problems, including the ones with his own mother which set off his anxiety about suffering a similar fate. He can have trust in me and be at the same time enraged. That doesn't bother him. I am simultaneously a good and a bad object—that's why one can have trust. He doesn't need to possess me anymore. I also no longer have to appear in his fantasies; it is enough that he thinks of me. I am no longer a part of his fantasy. His fantasy of fusion is still there, but this is probably necessary for him to be able to bear the feelings of abandonment which he always experiences when he makes a step. What appears crucial to me is that I can exist as good-bad mother. But he also has colleagues at his side who help him (even though one of them is very anxious) and a young girl is also there.

Without coming to grips with Blue Beard and without the support of his apprenticeship master, who cared for him in the manner of a good-enough father, this development most likely would not have been possible.

Blue Beard

There was a man who had fine houses, both in town and country, a deal of silver and gold plate, embroidered furniture, and coaches gilded all over with gold. But this man was so unlucky as to have a blue beard, which made him so frightfully ugly that all the women and girls ran away from him.

One of his neighbours, a lady of quality, had two daughters who were perfect beauties. He desired of her one of them in marriage, leaving to her choice which of the two she would bestow on him. They would neither of them have him, and sent him backwards and forwards from one another, not being able to bear the thoughts of marrying a man who had a blue beard, and what besides gave them disgust and aversion was his having already been married to several wives, and nobody ever knew what became of them.

Blue Beard, to engage their affection, took them, with the lady their mother and three or four ladies of their acquaintance, with other young people of the neighbourhood, to one of his country seats, where they stayed a whole week.

There was nothing then to be seen but parties of pleasure, hunting, fishing, dancing, mirth, and feasting. Nobody went to bed, but all passed the night in rallying and joking with each other. In short, every thing succeeded so well that the youngest daughter began to think the master of the house not to have a beard so very blue, and that he was a mighty civil gentleman.

As soon as they returned home, the marriage was concluded. About a month afterwards, Blue Beard told his wife that he was obligated to take a country journey for six weeks at least, about affairs of very great consequence, desiring her to divert herself in his absence, to send for her friends and acquaintances, to carry them into the country, if she pleased, and to make good cheer wherever she was.

'Here,' said he, 'are the keys of the two great wardrobes, wherein I have my best furniture; these are of my silver and gold plate, which is not every day in use; these open my strong boxes, which hold my money, both gold and silver; these my caskets of jewels; and this is the master-key to all my apartments. But for this little one here, it is the key of the closet at the end of the great gallery on the ground floor. Open them all; go into all and every one of them, except that little closet, which I forbid you, and forbid it in such a manner that, if you happen to open it, there's nothing but what you may expect from my just anger and resentment.'

She promised to observe, very exactly, whatever he had ordered; when he, after having embraced her, got into his coach and proceeded on his journey.

Her neighbours and good friends did not stay to be sent for by the new married lady, so great was their impatience to see all the rich furniture of her house, not daring to come while her husband was there, because of his blue beard, which frightened them. They ran through all the rooms, closets, and wardrobes, which were all so fine and rich that they seemed to surpass one another.

After that they went up into the two great rooms, where were the best and richest furniture; they could not sufficiently admire the number of beauty of the tapestry, beds, couches, cabinets, stands, tables, and looking-glasses, in which you might see yourself from head to foot; some of them were framed with glass, others with silver, plain and gilded, the finest and most magnificent ever were seen.

They ceased not to extol and envy the happiness of their friend, who in the meantime in no way diverted herself in looking upon all these rich things, because of the impatience she had to go and open the closet on the ground floor. She was so much pressed by her curiosity that, without considering that it was very uncivil to leave her company, she went down a little back staircase, and with such excessive haste that she had twice or thrice like to have broken her neck.

Being come to the closet-door, she made a stop for some time, thinking upon her husband's orders, and considering what unhappiness might attend her if she was disobedient; but the temptation was so strong she could not overcome it. She then took the little key, and opened it, trembling, but could not at first see anything plainly, because the windows were shut. After some moments she began to perceive that the floor was all covered over with clotted blood, on which lay the bodies of several dead women, ranged against the walls. (These were all the wives whom Blue Beard had married and murdered, one after another.) She thought she should have died for fear, and the key, which she pulled out of the lock, fell out of her hand.

After having somewhat recovered her surprise, she took up the key, locked the door, and went upstairs into her chamber to recover herself; but she could not, so much was she frightened. Having observed that the key of the closet was stained with blood, she tried two or three times to wipe it off, but the blood would not come out; in vain did she wash it, and even rub it with soap and sand, the blood still remained, for the key was magical and she could never make it quite clean; when the blood was gone off from one side, it came again on the other.'

Blue Beard returned from his journey the same evening, and said he had received letters upon the road, informing him that the affair he went about was ended to his advantage. His wife did all she could to convince him she was extremely glad of his speedy return.

Next morning he asked her for the keys, which she gave him, but with such a trembling hand that he easily guessed what had happened.

'What!' said he, 'is not the key of my closet among the rest?'

'I must certainly,' said she, 'have left it above upon the table.'

'Fail not,' said Blue Beard, 'to bring it me presently.'

After several goings backwards and forwards she was forced to bring him the key. Blue Beard, having very attentively considered it, said to his wife,

'How comes this blood upon the key?'

'I do not know,' cried the poor woman, paler than death.

'You do not know!' replied Blue Beard. 'I very well know. You were resolved to go into the closet, were you not? Mighty well, madam; you shall go in, and take your place among the ladies you saw there.'

Upon this she threw herself at her husband's feet, and begged his pardon with all the signs of a true repentance, vowing that she would never more be disobedient. She would have melted a rock, so beautiful and sorrowful was she; but Blue Beard had a heart harder than any rock!

'You must die, madam,' said he, 'and that presently.'

'Since I must die,' answered she (looking upon him with her eyes all bathed in tears), 'give me some little time to say my prayers.'

'I give you,' replied Blue Beard, 'half a quarter of an hour, but not one moment more.'

When she was alone she called out to her sister, and said to her:

'Sister Anne' (for that was her name), 'go up, I beg you, upon the top of the tower, and look if my brothers are not coming; they promised me that they would come to-day, and if you see them, give them a sign to make haste.'

Her sister Anne went up upon the top of the tower, and the poor afflicted wife cried out from time to time:

'Anne, sister Anne, do you see anyone coming?'

And sister Anne said:

'I see nothing but the sun, which makes a dust, and the grass, which looks green.'

In the meanwhile Blue Beard, holding a great sabre in his hand, cried out as loud as he could bawl to his wife:

'Come down instantly, or I shall come up to you.'

'One moment longer, if you please,' said his wife; and then she cried out very softly, 'Anne, sister Anne, dost thou see anybody coming?'

And sister Anne answered:

'I see nothing but the sun, which makes a dust, and the grass, which is green.'

'Come down quickly,' cried Blue Beard, 'or I will come up to you.'

'I am coming,' answered his wife; and then she cried, 'Anne, sister Anne, dost thou not see anyone coming?'

'I see,' replied sister Anne, 'a great dust, which comes on this side here.'

'Are they my brothers?'

'Alas! no, my dear sister, I see a flock of sheep.'

'Will you not come down?' cried Blue Beard.

'One moment longer,' said his wife, and then she cried out: 'Anne, sister Anne, dost thou see nobody coming?'

'I see,' said she, 'two horsemen, but they are yet a great way off.'

'God be praised,' replied the poor wife joyfully: 'they are my brothers; I will make them a sign, as well as I can, for them to make haste.'

Then Blue Beard bawled out so loud that he made the whole house tremble. The distressed wife came down, and threw herself at his feet, all in tears, with her hair about her shoulders.

'This signifies nothing,' says Blue Beard; 'you must die'; then, taking hold of her hair with one hand, and lifting up the sword with the other, he was going to take off her head. The poor lady, turning about to him, and looking at him with dying eyes, desired him to afford her one little moment to recollect herself.

'No, no,' he, 'recommend thyself to God,' and was just ready to strike . . .

At this very instant there was such a loud knocking at the gate that Blue Beard made a sudden stop. The gate was opened, and presently entered two horsemen, who, drawing their swords, ran directly to Blue Beard. He knew them to be his wife's brothers, one a dragoon, the other a musketeer; so that he ran away immediately to save himself; but the two brothers pursued so close that they overtook him before he could get to the steps of the porch, when they ran their swords through his body and left him dead. The poor wife was almost as dead as her husband, and had not strength enough to rise and welcome her brothers.

Blue Beard had no heirs, and so his wife became mistress of all his estate. She made use of one part of it to marry her sister Anne to a young gentleman who had loved her a long while; another part to buy captains' commissions for her brothers, and the rest to marry herself to a very worthy gentleman, who made her forget the ill time she had passed with Blue Beard.

Gender and the Borderline

Andrew Samuels

Introduction

When my son was in his mother's womb, an amniocentesis was performed to check for chromosomal defects. One consequence of this test is that the sex of the fetus becomes known. Parents may ask for this information or may elect that it be kept a secret; we felt uncomfortable being the only members of the prenatal team not to know, and so we asked to be told. We had not anticipated the changes in attitude, or rather the firming of unconscious attitudes, that this magician-like knowledge would bring. The movements of the fetus growing stronger each day were re-imaged by both of us. Originally dance or gymnastics, his activities became impulsive attacks on his poor mother, expressions of dissent (this reinforced by ultrasound pictures of an upraised clenched fist), daring geographical explorations.

The stereotyping was accompanied by a series of rationalizations

Andrew Samuels is a training analyst of the Society of Analytical Psychology in London and author of *Jung and the Post-Jungians*. In addition, he is coauthor of *A Critical Dictionary of Jungian Analysis*. and editor of *The Father: Contemporary Jungian Perspectives*.

I am grateful for helpful comments on the first draft of this paper from Coline Covington, David Curry, Lou King, Roderick Peters, Fred Plaut, Sheila Powell, Brian Skea, and, in particular, Rosie Parker.

about why it was better really that we were having a boy. Initially, on balance we had wanted a girl, and for the usual contemporary reason: to raise the New Woman. But another scenario was quickly written. We were old enough to make it a possibility that this would be an only child. The inevitable problem of overprotectiveness would be less severe with a boy, whom we could conceive of as playing with other kids in the street. As an only child "he" would be better able to cope with his inheritance than "she." I would be less seductive with a boy, and his mother more boundaried.

This experience provided vigorous confirmation of the immense power of the psycho-cultural matrix we call gender, and I knew that in spite of the difficulty in developing nonsexist language, I would have to go on writing about the subject in general, and the father in particular. When tasked to write about the borderline, I was pleasantly surprised to find a conjunction of interests. Later in this article the parts played by gender identity, gender certainty, and gender confusion in borderline disorder, as well as the father's role in it, are examined in detail.

Both during the pregnancy and in the months after the birth, there arose in me certain images and feelings concerning my analytic profession. My impression of depth psychology is that there was a golden age, which is now past. Grand theories seem unlikely to recur now that, after nearly a century, the broad outlines of the enterprise are firmly drawn. If that is so, then the seminal challenge presented by all-inclusive theories that force one to work out a response is lost. If our generation's job is not to be restricted to professionalization and institutionalization, it is necessary to highlight one thing we can do that the founding fathers and brilliant second-generation consolidators could not. I do not pretend in this article to add much to existing descriptions of the borderline or to notions of its etiology and treatment. What I am going to do is be *reflexive* in relation to the idea of the borderline. This means focusing on the psychology of its psychology, deliberate navel-gazing, a healthily narcissistic trip to the fantastic reaches of our discipline; which in turn means creating a postmodern psychological paper redolent with the assumption that psychology is not natural, but made by psychologists. After that, but only after that, we can turn toward the world, equipped with a rich collection of associations.

Active Interpretation: A Methodology

When analysts look at themselves, at how they behave, and think, and organize themselves, they are without knowing it also gazing at the world of psyche. The vicissitudes of depth psychology—the splits, plots, alliances, polemics, power struggles, debates—all these reveal that in their professional lives therapists and analysts are themselves participating in a mighty projection. When analysts argue, the plural psyche is speaking. Differing points of view reflect psyche's multiplicity. So the postmodern angle, scorning depth, meets up with the unconscious symbolism of psychological life.

It is necessary to work these opening remarks into a formal methodology. In this paper I look at two separate debates, one about borderline conditions, the other about gender. As we proceed, we will note a similar *shape*, a certain flavor or odor, to the debates. This is not to say that discussions of the borderline *are* discussions about gender—but it may be interesting to let the two debates interact and see what they do to each other, first in clinical terms, and then in cultural terms. Finally, there follows the deconstructive act of looking at one problematic (gender) in terms of the other (borderline). Though I advance a particular point of view, I pursue not so much the light of truth as the heat of friction.

It may be objected that this approach lacks heart in that a commitment to an idea or a set of ideas is lacking. That this is not the case can be seen in my discussion that follows on the origins of gender. Certainly, if the main plank of the article were to be *comparison*, this would be a valid criticism; but it is not. Rather, the shifting and mutable nature of ideograms like gender and borderline is respected and responded to by letting them "fix" each other. Nor do I neglect the central emotional experience of choice in relation to competing theories. However, in addition to finding a *numinosum* in what is chosen I also find something numinous in the act of choice itself. We are free to choose, choose, and choose again; conviction and flexibility both flourish. Any *numinosum* defies explanation but seems to convey an individual message, which, though mysterious and engimatic is also deeply impressive. The *numinosum* is so powerful that it orchestrates the many variables in a particular situation into one overwhelming message. This may be what happens when single themes become dominant in the thinking of certain theorists: sexuality, mothering, transference. It is this tendency for certain themes to acquire numinosity that we must thank for many of the breakthroughs in depth psychology. The difficulty is that such beliefs tend, if not to ossify, then to become so important to individual stability that when challenged one feels threatened in a life-or-death way.

When theories compete, what attitudes are possible? None seems satisfactory. We can choose between them—but that leads to blind partisanship. We can synthesize them—but that leads to omnipotence. We can be indifferent to the dispute—but that leads to ennui and a subtle form of inflation. We can be pluralistic—but that leads to fragmentation, anxiety, and confusion.

Psychological theories are for the post–golden age analyst what alchemical texts were for Jung. Our deconstruction of depth psychology parallels his of alchemy. What has motivated the whole vast project of depth psychology? What are depth psychologists doing? Just as the alchemists projected the workings of the unconscious into chemical elements and processes, caught up in the pervasive symbolism of it all, so the texts of the depth psychologist, taken as a whole, may unwittingly provide us with documents of the soul. What was intended to be *about* psyche is *of* psyche. The conscious aim may be to plumb the past for its truths, or to connect past and present, or to reveal the workings of cumulative psychopathology. But what are revealed are the central characteristics of the psyche itself. Here clashes between theories are useful, themselves containing the definitive psychic issue. Not psychological dialectics, but psyche's discourse given dialectical form. The warring theories and the specific points of conflict speak directly of what is at war in the psyche and of what the specific points of conflict therein might be. Personal experience itself exemplifies contradictory theories. Should we give primacy to environmental factors in the development of personality, or to constitutional factors, or should we attempt a synthesis of the two? Did my mother abandon me because I was unlovable? Or was she mad? Or, unhappily for me, are both true?

The texts of depth psychology constitute, in Derrida's words, a world of "signs without fault, without truth and without origin which is offered to an active interpretation" (1978, p. 292). We are forced to pay attention to those three horsemen of the poststructural apocalypse: relativity, interaction, and the absence of deep structures divorced from experience. *Everything depends on the active interpretation.* The rationale for the paper rests on the notion that the difference between creating a theory and critiquing a theory is a delusive one. As Derrida says, everything is a "free play" of signs and metaphors. For analysts, a psychological theory, or an account of some technical consideration, is a text with no natural meaning. In a sense, this is a Gnostic approach to depth psychology using analytic intuition and the knowledge locked up in our reactions and our countertransferences to the text. When we look at what Kernberg has to say about Kohut, for instance, we will see that style is content. The polemical and argumentative style of that and most psychoanalytic discourses, reflecting the competition of theories, underscores our appreciation of their suasive, rhetorical intent.

The Fascination of the Borderline

From a psychological standpoint, it turns out that one common theme in the two debates about the borderline and gender is *aggression*. You will recall how quickly our gendered fetus/baby became an aggressor in our minds; in due course, the central function of aggression in borderline conditions will also be brought in. Here I want to make an introductory suggestion: the issue of aggression may be a clue as to why borderline phenomenology is currently of such enormous interest that some will have become fed up with the concept. We live in aggressive times; nuclear weapons heighten awareness of the danger of expressing aggression. Problems with aggression and the owning of aggressive fantasy are also central to depression, and my "take" on borderline disorder is that it masks both serious depressive illness and psychosis. Thus, borderline conditions may be looked at as affective disorders involving distortions in self-image and gender identity, rather than as ambulant schizophrenia, defensively contained. What we see in borderline symptomatology may be *depression sine depressione*. None of the usual clinical features of depression are present: no retardation or delusional guilt. Instead, we see agitation, anxiety, massive despair, and nihilistic delusions of bodily decay and destruction.

Nosologically, depression in borderline conditions probably has to be seen as a form of depressive psychosis. Crucially, depressive psychosis differs from nonpsychotic depression in that the sufferer shows no signs of wanting to be rid of the condition, which is instead accepted. This acceptance is in the nature of bowing to an authoritarian inner source which says, paternalistically, that it is wrong to get well.

Continuing to probe the many reasons for analysts' current interest in borderline conditions, it is possible to see that some of these are themselves reflexive; that is, they arise from analytic self-interest. For instance, there is the desire to justify theoretically what is already happening clinically, making private and implicit theory public and official (see Samuels 1985a, pp. 267–69). Analysis has always displayed an ambivalent face toward its patients. On the one hand, it shows signs of wanting to be selective, to *vomit* out the unsuitable (symptom, patient, trainee), to be elitist; on the other hand, analysis also wants to include everyone in its therapy, the whole world even, in a gigantic act of *swallowing*. The obsessive attempts to define, list, and evaluate the characteristics of borderline conditions show this vomiting/swallowing ambiguity: who should be excluded from treatment, who might be included in it (see Gunderson and Singer 1975).

The borderline speaks to us so deeply because in it we test the limits of sanity and madness. Jung is supposed to have said, "Show me a sane man and I will cure him for you," but I prefer Chico Marx's "You can't fool me. There ain't no Sanity Clause." We know from the antipsychiatrists how impossible it is to define sanity and madness. Being sane means not being in the hospital; sanity is in part the result of social learning, not least about cultural gender expectations. Yet we do know when someone is completely crazy. The whole idea of a borderline between sanity and madness, and particularly of a personality organization (that is, people) walking that line, may be seen as our attempt to settle our anxiety about madness. We are saying: We can talk of sanity and madness (neurosis and psychosis) in a subtle and liberal way *precisely because* we have allowed for a gray area. We are also saying: Even a gray area is defined, and, once we've defined an area, we can do something in or about it, we can treat it.

Though the words are not used much on account of this subtlety and liberality of ours, the ideograms of sanity and madness have not vanished from collective consciousness. Instead, we have sought to defuse madness by evacuating its religious, demonic, mysterious connotations and replacing them with the peculiar blend of Romantic nature-worship and scientism which constitutes modern psychiatry and depth psychology. When we study and treat borderline patients, our envious fascination is with their tricksterish capacity to be "mad" without completely letting go of being sane. The borderline state is a way of going mad tactfully and without attracting too much attention. *The clever construction of the gray reinforces the secret presence of the black and white.*

The borderline person corrals the ecstasy of madness—not completely crazy, not incapable of making a point or a decision, not dead. Some of the features of borderline-personality organization unwittingly reveal the presence of ecstasy: intense affect, sometimes with depersonalization; impulsive behavior, sometimes directed against the self; brief psychotic experiences; disturbed personal relationships, sometimes exceedingly intimate and sometimes distant. This could be the profile of a saint.

Then there is the general fascination of the border as an image. Hermes was the god of borders and boundaries, and a kind of liminal creativity may be found in a state of madness not lost in the fog of absolute craziness. The borderline patient is just sane enough to *see* the archetypes rather than live them out impulsively.

Of course, there is no border. Are there ever true borders in human psychology, or only border areas, no-man's lands, demilitarized zones, joint sovereignties? At least border *areas* would be permeable, allowing for inputs and outputs. (The body comes to mind here, for it is all border area.) If border areas are permeable, then the element in psychic structure they most closely resemble is the ego. Ego (and analyst, for that matter) needs just the right amount of permeability. Too many perforations and the unconscious floods in: We lose personal and social cohesiveness. Too few, and there is a divorce from creative libido; we lose religious sensibility and the artistic instinct. *Just as there needs to be movement between ego and unconscious, so there needs to be movement between the neurotic and psychotic parts of a personality.*

Maybe the borderline is a protection. When analytical writers refer to it as a type of personality organization or as defensive they have this in mind. But on which side of the borderline lies the enemy? To continue in too martial a vein is to become unable to conceive of neurosis and psychosis *together*, of primary and secondary process together, of fantasy and directed thinking together.

What does a border, or boundary, mean in interpersonal life? It is impossible to say with certainty that the border is between people—i.e., that border is to do with separation. Intense dyadic relationships access the *mundus imaginalis*, and then the border may be viewed as surrounding the couple, or linking them—or there may be no need to postulate a border (see Samuels 1985d).

The Borderline Debate

The remarkable thing about the psychoanalytic debate concerning borderline disorder is that it is taking place at all. The whole enterprise is radically undermined by the idea that there is no such disease entity as the borderline, and that borderline phenomenology is best understood either in terms of narcissistic personality disorder or latent schizophrenia. Nevertheless, because of its fascination, the idea of borderline disorder is here to stay.

The debate revolves, as readers will know, around the names of Kernberg and Kohut. As so often is true of vicious, personalized power struggles, the protagonists have much in common. Both are reacting against fossilization of ego psychology, though Kernberg is keen to retain a place for structural metapsychology in his model. Both go beyond drive theory, particularly where it is used outside of the fabric of relationship. To the outsider, Kernbergian object relations and Kohut's formulation of the self-selfobject relationship seem to overlap.

But when it comes to the diagnosis, etiology, and treatment of borderline disorder, disagreement sets in. Kerberg's emphasis (1967, 1975, 1984) is on an innate or at least very early excess of aggression, which, coupled with low tolerance for anxiety and lack of impulse control, leads to a defensive division of the ego. Individual problems with the intensity of one's aggression are said to be constitutionally determined. Concerning psychosexual development, Kernberg observes in such patients: (a) a premature and complicated experience of the Oedipus complex; (b) an inability to distinguish between father and mother; (c) a tendency for father to replace mother as the object of dependency; (d) either or both parents seen as dangerous to sexual fulfillment. In general, the patient muddles what Kernberg sees as appropriate two-person and three-person psychological functioning. Treatment of borderline conditions is by "expressive" psychotherapy, emphasizing the usual psychoanalytic desiderata: neutrality, transference, interpretation, etc.

Kohut objects to Kernberg's reliance on the idea of conflict. Kohut regards all psychoanalytic endeavor previous to his own as marred by the emphasis on conflict (1971, 1977). This emphasis, according to Kohut, derives from the old-fashioned biological bias of psychoanalysis, and especially of ego psychology. But conflict is an external imposition onto the internal subjective world of meaning, an artificial drawing-up of the lines of battle by an outsider that contradicts felt experience within. The notion of conflict demands a "mental apparatus" within, through which the conflict takes place. Above all, conflict psychology refers to drive-related needs and wishes which may or may not be met. Kohut proposes a relational model stressing developmental needs such as those for mirroring and empathy. Interestingly, Kohut (1978) did call for conflict psychology and his self psychology to be used in tandem, a call which has not been taken up. Indeed, it was explicitly rejected by some (e.g., Wallerstein 1983). Elsewhere I have suggested that in analytical psychology there is evidence that this call has been heeded, albeit unknowingly (Samuels 1985a, pp. 128, 161–62).

According to Kohut, borderline disorders may be seen as deficits in the fabric of an evolving self caused by an insufficiently empathic, mirroring early environment. In the borderline patient, the self is in a state of permanent or protracted breakup, weakness, or distortion. It should be noted that Kohut has ceased to use a schema of subsystems, one of which might overwhelm the others. There may be different self-images or self-representations that do not fit together harmoniously, but then that is part of being human. They are all still self.

Kohut's preferred treatment for borderline conditions is, like Kernberg's, psychoanalytic in orientation. But Kohut concentrates more on the facilitation of self-selfobject relations through mirroring and empathy and less on the interpretation of conflict. In spite of Kohut's express statement that empathy does not replace interpretation, Kernberg criticizes Kohut for merely enabling patients to rationalize their anger against the parents who let them down: Kohut is charged with being supportive and educative and therefore unpsychoanalytic. Kernberg also claims that Kohut leaves no place for aggression in the analysis of the borderline patient; this because the latter downplays aggression in the etiology of the condition. In a nutshell, Kernberg's accusation is that Kohut, *qua* analyst, is a mother:

> The misinterpretation and overgeneralisation of these findings imply that, for patients in regression, it is the therapist's empathic presence—rather than his interpretation—that is really helpful; that it is the patient's identification with this mothering function—rather than his coming to terms with his intrapsychic conflicts—that is important. . . . Empathy is a prerequisite for interpretive work, not its replacement. (1979, pp. 231–32)

If we look at this charge closely, two questions come to mind. First, is Kernberg advocating analyst-as-father or merely claiming to have mother and father aspects of himself as analyst in balance? Second, is something revealed here about Kernberg's fantasy of a mother: one who makes no place for aggression? In a more sober vein, it seems that we need to discuss *the mirroring of aggressive impulses and fantasies* (see below, in the section on the role of the father in borderline-personality disorder).

In terms of depth psychology's perennial quest to find out whether something "really" happened or whether it was "fantasy," Kohut and Kernberg hold opposite positions. Kernberg's perspective is markedly internal, while Kohut's seems to be exceedingly external. Actually, Kohut has made a truly synthesizing contribution here. He says, in effect, that while the reported abuse, for instance, may not have happened, this does not mean that we are dealing solely with fantasy or wish. It is possible to experience and refer to an *actual* atmosphere of child abuse, not just psychically real for the child: the atmosphere is as real as can be. As far as I am aware, Kohut was the first psychoanalyst to make this point explicit (1983).

Both Kernberg and Kohut describe borderline dynamics in terms of an avoided psychosis. This connection to schizophrenia takes us back to the roots of the borderline concept in biologically based psychiatry (Stone 1986, pp. 5–13). Though history is important, there is a fundamental contemporary challenge here. When we consider the possibility of innate excesses of aggression or constitutionally low levels of anxiety tolerance, we have in the back of our minds a sort of delimiter of mental health and mental illness; as I suggested earlier, the borderline syndrome has an extraordinary capacity to bring such issues to the forefront of attention. But all this talk of the innate is rather cool language with which to describe *fate*. To avoid glib references to fate, it helps to tie them to precise descriptions of particular constitutions, in terms of specific psychological qualities. What the idea of innate delimiters challenges is the image of a woman or man potentially capable of doing or being anything. Later, when we talk about the problems women face in our culture, this issue will become central.

The Hereditary Factor

The specific problem this discussion of borderline disorder explores is innate aggression. Psychoanalysis as a whole entertains several ideas about aggression: it is innate; later patterns of aggressive discharge and relating depend on earlier ones; if early experiences of aggression are unsatisfactory, aggression may take a predominantly malign form in later life. Now, I do not intend to discuss the death instinct here, nor the question of cumulative psychopathology over a lifetime. Rather, what concerns me is the hereditary factor. I shall try to be consistent in my use of the terms *innate* and *hereditary factor*: By innate I mean inborn, common to all, though possibly different in degree. By the hereditary factor I mean, broadly speaking, an individual's quantity of some innate quality, determined by the family of origin.

When an idea arouses great anxiety, it is worth investigating. Interestingly, Kernberg's latest statement of his position (1984) downplays an innate excess of aggression in favor of aggression deriving from massive, very early frustration. This in effect makes aggression a *secondary* element and frustration the key dynamic. Sometimes, the hereditary factor is sidestepped and a multifactorial viewpoint advanced, usually with considerable finesse. For example, Stone suggests that while the hereditary factor will push some people towards a borderline state despite good parenting, very destructive families do it all on their own without any help from genetic liability (1986, p. 421). Of course, Stone is probably right, but what sticks out is the particular quality of anxiety produced by the hereditary factor, by the genes. Not by what is *not* in our genes, but by what *is* in them. Later, when we discuss gender, we will see the same kind of anxiety, so it may be worthwhile trying to anatomize it here.

The hereditary factor stalks the nature-nurture divide — itself a false distinction, of course. Kohut's assumption, as he tries to go beyond drive theory, is that the body-based and the biological are enemies to his kind of empathic-introspective understanding. As if the biological were not human! The concern, which I feel as well, is that we may lose our freedom of maneuver, even our freedom as persons and as analysts, if we try to ingest this hereditary factor. It is certainly the case that genetics are usually employed in a reactionary or conservative cause; therefore we are right to be worried. But, as the gender debate demonstrates, cultural and familial factors are clearly so much more powerful than genetic ones that our anxiety is more difficult to explain.

Perhaps we can best describe the kind of anxiety the hereditary factor arouses as a form of moral panic. The idea of innate aggression produces a whole variety of responses in us, ranging from scientific understanding to wise acceptance to idealistic rejection to a religious belief in perfectibility. The attitudes of Kohut and Kernberg towards the idea may be characterized as differing moral stances; they value the borderline patient differently. Kernberg is alert to the basic, intolerant attitude of the borderline individual towards aggression, aggression fundamentally bad because it threatens the self and others. But Kernberg himself identifies with this point of view in finding it difficult to conceive of a positive outcome for a mother-infant couple faced with an excess of aggression in the infant. I call this kind of morality *original morality* (Samuels 1987) because of its certitude. Kohut, on the other hand, tends to see aggression as a valid protest and an appeal for both help and rectification of the situation: aggression is adaptive, ingenious even. I term this *moral imagination* because of its pluralistic, flexible, improvisational cast.

Full human morality involves a dialectic, an interplay, the articulation of these two moral modalities. On its own, each is stultifying or unsatisfying. Original morality in isolation is heavy, intolerant, rigid; moral imagination alone is too slippery by far. Kernberg and Kohut personify two sides of a moral split generated in us by our anxiety about innate aggression and the hereditary factor.

We are frightened that we may find that *illness* is the fundament of the personality, that the archaic distortions of our complexes are themselves the ground of our being, that we are constitutionally unable to cope with ourselves, that we are inherently deviant, born in sin. The moment the innate is admitted, even in an interactional, multifactorial approach, its impact is enormous and unpredictable.

Jung's views on the causation of schizophrenia shed light on both the innate-environment question and on what we might mean by sanity and insanity. The evolution of Jung's thought reveals his uncertainty. He is clear that schizophrenia is a psychosomatic disorder, that changes in body chemistry and personality distortions are somehow intertwined. Jung did not consider borderline disorders as such, of course, but his concern to establish whether chemistry or personality was primary is directly relevant to the contemporary problem.

Jung's superior, Bleuler, thought that some kind of toxin or poison was developed by the body, which then led to psychological disturbance. Jung's crucial contribution was to establish that psyche was sufficiently important to reverse the sequence: psychological activity could lead to somatic changes. Jung did attempt to combine his ideas with those of Bleuler, however, by means of an ingenious formula. While the mysterious toxin might well exist in all of us, it would only have its devastating effect if psychological circumstances were favorable to it. Alternatively, a person might be genetically predisposed to develop the toxin, which would then invade the complexes. That schizophrenia be seen as anything other than an innate, neurological abnormality was, in its time, revolutionary (see Samuels *et al.* 1986). That its causation should be psychogenic within a psychosomatic framework (Jung's final position, 1960a, par. 553ff.) enabled Jung to propose that psychological treatment—psychotherapy—was appropriate.

Our position is different. We have trouble with the toxin!

Admitting that the constitutional and the inherited play their part, even a determining one, in the formation of (borderline) personality does not require us to give up on therapy or throw out the texts of developmental psychology. Hailing everything as archetypal is counterphobic, a reaction-formation to the hereditary factor, a blind refusal to countenance individual peculiarity and the specificity of constitution. Facing up to the hereditary factor in the level of aggression of each and every one of us makes it even more important to track the individual movement of a person with and through their inborn characteristics, with and through their fate.

The mythos which speaks most directly to the conundrum of the innate is that of Sisyphus. His ultimate crime was to try to avoid the most innate factor of all—death—and his punishment as tricky as the means he used in his futile attempt. Just when we feel free of who we always were, free of that aggressive inner runt, we have to go back to the beginning, to the beginnings. Which of us has not suddenly got much worse in the last segment of our personal analysis? Sisyphus becomes our spokesman in other ways. His original crime was to inform on Zeus for having abducted the nymph Aegina. And the strategem by which he arranges his return from Hades involves the cooperation of his wife. Sisyphus's stone rolls together images of the father, the father's sexuality, and the perennial hope that other people, one's spouse in particular, will help one to avoid the unavoidable.

On Aggression

If aggression is innate, where is it located? Do we have to locate it at all? Aggression may be reconsidered as a passion whose presence is ubiquitous in mind and body. The borderline patient, and the antagonists in the borderline debate, may then be seen in the grip of this aggressive passion and fascinated by it, respectively. *Aggression deserves the same kind of treatment which Jung gave to the sexual passion of incest.* That is, by trying to figure out what the goal or *telos* of aggression might be, we can begin to appreciate the purposive aspects of borderline disorders.

In saying that aggressive fantasy has its own *telos*, I do not intend to minimize the damaging, negative, painful, perverted, controlling aspects of aggression. However, the observation has often been made that aggressive *behavior* in the form of healthy self-assertion is a necessity for survival in both an absolute and a social sense. My concern is more with aggressive images and images of aggression.

Aggressive fantasy brings into play that interpersonal separation without which the word relationship would have no meaning. In this sense, aggressive fantasy wants to make contact, get in touch, relate; for some, mainly men, it may be the only way to relate. The same is true for internal elements and processes: aggressive fantasy enables separate images of the parents to emerge, as well as other images and inner discriminations—for example, what theory refers to as the ego-self axis. As Searles says, "at one moment a violent urge may express a striving to be free and at the next a desire to relate" (1973, p. 325). Aggressive fantasy forces an individual to consider his conduct of personal relations. When he fantasizes an aggressive response to his desires on the part of the other, he is learning something about that other as a being with a separate but similar existence to his own. Without aggressive fantasy, there would simply be no cause for concern about other people; it points beyond ruthlessness to the discovery of the reality and mystery of persons. "It is only when intense aggressiveness exists between two individuals that love can arise" (Storr 1970, p. 57). Finally, aggressive fantasy is playful at times, even humorous, a continuous cartoon of ejaculatory, exploratory enjoyment and *jouissance*—a way for *women* to be "seminal," "thrusting," and "penetrative."

Since it is composed of images as much as impulses, aggressive fantasy can be approached via its specifics. Hence Freud's paper, "A child is being beaten" (1919). And Jung who, writing about the treatment of depression, suggested that getting to the inherent fantasies leads to "enrichment and clarification of the affect" (1960b, par. 167). But it is clarification of the *image* which is needed in relation to aggression; biting is not tearing, nor smearing, nor cutting, nor punching, nor shooting, nor beating.

Aggressive fantasy, like incestual fantasy, has a refueling and regenerative function which is accentuated the more extreme the fantasy. What Jung pioneered for fantasies of incestuous sexuality in *Symbols of Transformation* (1956) should be attempted for aggressive fantasy. This would mean, for example, that aggression between persons, or the aggressive fantasy of one about the other, would not only be something about those two persons; its symbolic meaning as *coniunctio* as well as its literal potential would engage our interest. Just as with sexuality and spirituality, the transformation of aggressive fantasy tends in the general direction of its opposite: creativity and (or in) relationship.

In myth, when Kronos turns on Uranus in one of the imaginal birth moments of Western culture, he cuts off his father's genitals with a sickle, casting them into the sea. From them Aphrodite is born, the goddess of love. It is clearly no accident that contemporary depth psychologists make of the aggression-depression dynamic a central part of their theorizing. Nor is it a coincidence that Herman Hesse's counterpart to Narcissus, the one who leads a life of mind and spirit, is Goldmund, killer and fornicator.

Equipped with a re-imaging of aggressive fantasy, we might return to an examination of the hereditary factor in the borderline discussions, and to a consideration of its psychiatric-biological roots. Historically, the earliest discussion of borderline patients involved the idea of a hereditary taint (see Stone 1986, pp. 1–5). Stone decided to investigate the psychiatric histories of the relatives of borderline patients, using (mainly) Kernberg's criteria for the diagnosis. His conclusion was that

> many patients called borderline—by most of the popular definitions—appear to have a pronounced hereditary predisposition to mental illness. Often this factor is sufficiently striking to permit the clinician to make an educated guess about the patient's vulnerability, his eventual course and the type of psychotherapy and medication that will prove most effective.

Stone then reintroduces the historical perspective and continues:

> The importance of a hereditary factor in these conditions is no new discovery; it was taken for granted by the psychiatric and psychoanalytic communities until the second generation of psychoanalysts began to adopt a more linear and purely psychologic model of causation. (1986, p. 493)

As noted earlier, Stone does modify his findings slightly by referring to families so destructive they can bring about a borderline situation without any innate predisposition being present. But that surely begs the question: *Is there an effectual difference between inheritance in genetic and familial terms?*

I must confess that I was surprised to find inheritance turning out to be at the heart of the borderline mystery; my own views usually tend towards the environment-cultural end of any explicatory spectrum. What I discovered in myself working with borderline patients and these ideas is the very anxiety about the hereditary factor I have described. If something *less* than total insanity can be inherited, then maybe *everything* psychological can be. We have to entertain the idea of a "soft heredity" as well as the "hard" kind, meaning inheritance of a pattern and proportion of passions, especially aggression.

In spite of its concern with aggression, as Galenson (1986) has noted, depth psychology has contributed very little to our understanding of its normal developmental sequence. One reason for this may be that stimuli for aggression differ from those for hunger, say, in that they *seem* environmental rather than self-generated. Perhaps this is how we prefer to conceive of aggression, even when intellectually we concede its innate nature.

To illustrate the effects of parental deprivation upon aggressive development, Galenson presents an account of eight female infants in a therapeutic nursery, all from disadvantaged backgrounds and whose fathers were not readily available to them. Their very early development was unremarkable, but as they started to walk, they were abandoned by their mothers emotionally. They were often struck for being "bad," and eventually the little girls developed the habit of striking their dolls and their mothers. When these children were around 18 months, they showed an interesting pattern in relation to any adult men they encountered: "a combination of teasing and flirtatiousness. . . . Unlike the usual pattern of sexual arousal, however, the strong admixture of aggression in these children made it difficult to decide whether they were loving or attacking these men" (Galenson 1986, p. 352). What is more, the way the girls related to their mothers strongly resembled the way the latter related to men. Galenson's descriptions underscore the links between aggression and gender identity.

Stone (1981) saw things in reverse, as it were. Galenson's observations connect an aggressive mother with later gender problems, whereas Stone's opinion was that, in many instances, actual incest contributes greatly to the formation of borderline-personality organization. "Women who have been victimized in this manner, particularly by older male relatives, often develop sharply polarized and ambivalent attitudes toward men, an image of themselves as both angel and prostitute, a reckless and impulsive lifestyle, and chaotic, turbulent relationships with men, oscillating between adoration and jealous mistrustfulness" (Stone 1986, p. 422).

The material of Stone and Galenson, coupled with Kernberg's idea of premature oedipal development, supports an approach to borderline-personality disorder *via the person, image, and theme of the father*.

The Gender Debate

Some questions: Are men innately more aggressive than women? Does that explain their social and political dominance? Is there such a thing as innately masculine or feminine psychology?

In his book, *Archetype: A Natural History of the Self*, Anthony Stevens drew on the work of the sociobiologists Wilson and Goldberg to reach the conclusion that "male dominance is a manifestation of the 'psychophysiological reality' of our species. In addition [there is] genetic and neurophysiological evidence relating to the biology of sexual differentiation. . . . Patriarchy, it seems, is the natural condition of mankind" (1982, pp. 188–92).

In *Jung and the Post-Jungians*, I drew on the work of Janet Sayers to critique Stevens's position (Samuels 1985, pp. 220–22). Sayers sees those opposed to changes in women's roles as appropriating biology to their cause, and she demolishes the sociobiological case in a witty and learned way. For instance, Wilson quoted studies which showed that boys were consistently more able than girls at mathematics, but girls have a higher degree of verbal ability. Since boys are also, in his view, more aggressive in social play, Wilson concluded that "even with identical education and equal access to all professions men are likely to continue to play a disproportionate role in political life, business, and science" (quoted in Sayers 1982, p. 77). Sayers wryly remarks that it is hard to see how males' lesser verbal ability leads to their being better fitted for political life. Surely, if biology really does determine social roles, it should be the other way round?

Recently I came across the work of another academic psychologist, Gerda Siann (1985). She comprehensively surveyed the various research findings which purport to link aggression to the male hormones. She concludes that "no specific areas in the brain or nervous system have been pinpointed as controlling aggression" (p. 33) and that an overview of repeated studies shows that androgenized girls do not seem more aggressive than their peers, siblings, or mothers. Overandrogenized males do not display noteworthy dominance, assertion, or aggression in spite of the fact that their greater size would guarantee victory (they seem to be rather gentle people). What is more, Siann's careful reading of the research findings shows that castration has no effect on the overall aggressive behavior of sex offenders, save in relation to actual sexual attacks. Finally, plasma testosterone levels do not seem to relate directly to aggressive behavior. Siann's overall conclusion was:

> the evidence does not show any clear and unambiguous relationship between male hormones and the propensity to display violent behaviour or feel aggressive emotion. Indeed the likelihood of such a simple unidirectional relationship has been thrown into doubt by two additional lines of investigation. The first shows that the secretion of male hormones is itself directly affected by environmental and social variables, and the second is concerned with the speculation that female hormones may also be implicated in violent behaviour and aggressive emotion. (p. 37)

Siann also investigated the published research linking genetic inheritance and aggression. Her findings, which make interesting reading when compared to the discussion of the hereditary factor in borderline disorder, are that there is no evidence for the genetic transmission of aggression or violence (p. 39). *In sum, there is no corporeal innate factor in aggression.* The possibility remains that there is a noncorporeal innate factor—that aggression is linked to sex by invisible, psychological factors. We shall consider that possibility in a moment.

To sustain Stevens's sociobiological viewpoint, female aggression has to be overlooked or minimized. What is more, there is a confusion here between aggression and dominance. Not all human dominance is aggression. We have to consider phenomena such as altruistic or self-sacrificing behavior, conscience, the checks placed on the power of a leader, and the human capacity for collective decision-making.

As a nonscientist trying to make sense of the empirical evidence, I find it interesting to consider objectivity and even coherence in science as gender-influenced ideologies. When we speak of the hard sciences or hard facts, we are dealing with the consequences of gender-based child-rearing practices which have relegated softness and irrationality to an inferior (feminine) standing. In addition, the "masculine" cast of so-called objectivity may to some extent be an outgrowth of the need of most boys and many girls to assert their differences from their mother. The achievement of personal boundaries and optimal separation from the mother may, for some, tip over into rigidity and an accent on distance and precision—the objective attitude. Depth psychologists with such an outlook tend to be uncomfortable with transpersonal phenomena such as mystical experience, because such things cannot be understood from a distance, from outside; knowledge only comes from some kind of merger with what is perceived, which awakens latent fears of a return to the suffocating symbiosis with mother.

What follows is a more purely psychological discussion of the third question with which we started this section: Are there such things as innate masculine and, more pertinent perhaps, feminine psychologies? If there are, then could there be a noncorporeal innate factor in aggression?

Beyond the Feminine Principle

It is hard to write flexibly and fluidly about what is flexible and fluid. The danger when trying to reflect on our current preoccupation with gender is that we might become too clear and too organized—a reaction-formation to the inevitable anxiety (and guilt) we experience at finding that what we thought was solid and fixed is perforated and shifting. Humanity is not just divided into women and men but also into those who are certain about gender and those who are confused. Finding a balance between gender certainty and gender confusion is a hard task. Clinically, we see the negative effects of exaggerating either position, and working with individual patients on gender identity is a kind of preliminary to examining the collective level on a wider scale.

For gender confusions have as important a role to play as gender certainties. They contribute something imaginative to social and political reform and change. I refer to confusion and not to something like flexibility which sounds more laudable because, experientially, that is precisely what it is, no bones about it. Not for the first time in psychology can we fashion strength out of an apparent weakness. To do this, I have had to learn from women what they have been through.

In order to discuss the subject at all, a distinction between sex and gender should be made, allowing for some overlap. *Sex* (male and female) refers to anatomy and the biological substrate of behavior, should there be one. *Gender* (masculine and feminine) is something cultural or psychological, arising in part from observations and identifications within the family, and hence relative, flexible, and capable of sustaining change. Now, in some approaches, particularly in analytical psychology, a form of determinism can creep in and an invariant nature for gender be assumed, as if gender characteristics and qualities were as fixed as sexual ones. But the history of women shows that change is possible just because the social meaning of womanhood is malleable. Ignore this, as Stevens does, and the possibilities of change other than ordinary maturation and individuation are lost.

Is there such a thing as a "feminine psychology"? I will begin with a general discussion, and then consider whether there is a psychology for women alone. In a moment, I will look at the "feminine" in relation to men, and after that, at femininity and masculinity as metaphors.

Males and females do have experiences that vary markedly. But it is a huge step from this observation to the claim that they actually *function* sufficiently discrepantly psychologically for us to speak of two distinct psychologies. The evidence concerning this is muddled and hard to assess. For instance, the discovery that boys build towers and girls build enclosures when they are given bricks can be taken to show *similarity* of functioning rather than difference (as is usually claimed). Both sexes are interested in their own bodies, and possibly in the differences between male and female bodies. Both sexes express those interests in the same way—symbolically, in play with bricks. Or, put in another form, *both sexes approach the difference between the sexes the same way*. The differences that we see in gender role and gender identity can be looked at as having arisen in the same manner. The psychological *processes* by which a male becomes an aggressive businessman and a female a nurturing and submissive housewife are the same and one should not be deceived by dissimilarity in the end product.

What I am describing is not one's relation to *innate* femininity or masculinity. Rather I am talking of one's *relation to the phenomenon of difference*; then we can consider the social or cultural structures erected on the basis of that difference. This leads at once to questions of gender role (for example, how a woman can best express her aggression in our culture), but these questions need not be couched in terms of innate femininity or innate masculinity, nor even in terms of a feminine-masculine spectrum. Instead, they might be expressed in terms of *difference*. However, the difference between aggression and submission must be seen as different from the difference between men and women! Or put another way, what differences there might be between women and men are not signified by the difference between submission and aggression.

I am aware that *men* are said to have access to the feminine, or to the "feminine principle," and I used to think that such an inwardly directed view was the jewel in the Jungian crown. Now I am not so sure. If we are attempting to describe psychological performance, we have to ask why terms with gendered associations and appellations are being used at all. Otherwise we end up asserting that "masculine" aggression is available to women via their relation to the animus, or "feminine" reflection to the man via his anima. But aggression is part of woman and reflection is part of man. What is more, even current attempts to speak of a woman's aggression as feminine rather than masculine bind her as tightly as ever. Let us begin to speak merely of aggression. Gender engenders confusion—and this is made worse when gender terms refer exclusively to the psyche. When we speak of inner femininity in a man, we bring in all the unnecessary problems of reification and substantive abstraction I have been describing. We still cannot assume that psychological *functioning* is different in men and women, *though we know that the creatures man and woman are different*.

The question of difference brings us to a point where we can play back these ideas into analytical psychology. From Jung's overall theory of opposites, which hamstrings us with its insistence on contrasexuality (masculine assertion via the animus, etc.), we can extract the theme of difference. The notion of difference, I suggest, can help us in the discussion of gender. Not innate opposites, which lead us to create an unjustified psychological division expressed in two lists of antithetical qualities, each yearning for the other so as to become whole, but the fact, image, and social reality of difference itself. Not what differences between women and men there are, or have always been; if we pursue that, we end up captivated by our obsession with myth and the eternal, part of the legacy of Jung. I am interested in what difference is like, what the experience of difference is like, and how that experience is distorted in the borderline disorders. Not what a woman *is*, but what being a woman is *like*. Not the archetypal structuring of woman's world, but a woman's personal experience in today's world. Not the *meaning* of a woman's life, but her *experience* of her life. Each person remains a man or a woman, but what that means to each is immediate and relative, and hence capable of generational expansion and cultural challenge. My argument is that *paternal deficits constrict the expansion and truncate the challenge for that kind of individual we have come to call borderline.*

In both the collective, external debate about gender characteristics and the personal, internal debate about gender identity, the question of masculine and feminine is best left in suspension—even, and the word is used advisedly, in some confusion. *Gender confusion is a necessary antidote to gender certainty* and has its own creative contribution to make. This is particularly true in the treatment of borderline disorders, as we shall see. For when we consider the borderline, we will see that gender confusion and certainty are profoundly problematic when they operate in isolation from each other. *Inadvertently, those who propound a feminine principle play into and replicate borderline dynamics.*

Later in the paper, when I discuss the case of Margaret, my use of the terms *gender certainty* and *gender confusion* will become clearer. I am not primarily interested in the conventional, psychodynamic idea that gender certainty often masks gender confusion—though it certainly can. My concern is with uncovering a secret gender certainty in the unconscious—the hidden influence of the feminine principle, for instance. Such unconscious gender certainty may be present both when the surface gender identity is confused and chaotic *and* when it seems certain. In the latter case, the content of unconscious certainty is not the same as conscious certainty.

I think that what happens in borderline disorders, and probably in other conditions, is that gender certainty and confusion are kept rigidly apart, instead of being allowed to play into each other. This parallels the borderline patient keeping normal/neurotic and psychotic elements apart.

An example of gender certainty can be found in the case study written by Verena Kast (see Kast, pp. 159–176, in this issue). Later, I will give some examples from my own practice. Kast's patient, Marcel, is certainly confused about his gender and about relations between the sexes. But lurking in the background, and functioning as something more than an antidote to his experiential confusion, is unconscious gender certainty. It is this that fuels his identification with the violent giant, and later leads to the analyst's introduction of the figure of Bluebeard and the fairy tale of that name. Marcel tells us that his father advised him to get a good job, not to be afraid, and to do everything exactly like other people. He looks after his mother and sister. Even now he tells tall tales to girlfriends.

What we see is an identification with a rudimentary image or idea of masculinity, one quite unmediated by his drunken and violent father. We might even say that Marcel's gender confusion is stoked by these half-formed, powerful, idealized, archaic images of manhood. With Bluebeard as the yardstick, what chance is there for Marcel, a human being with a mixture in him of gender confusion and certainty?

It is probably fair to say that post-Jungian analytical psychology has become preoccupied with gender certainty and confusion in its concern with the feminine principle. Here I am not referring to the writings on women and feminine psychology by Jung and his early circle of followers. The problems with that body of work are well known and often stated. But in the '70's and '80's, mainly in the United States, women writing in analytical psychology set out to revise, or revolutionize, the early work. Such writers struggle to be "post-Jungian" in their attempt to critique those of Jung's ideas which seem unsatisfactory or just plain wrong, without dismissing Jung altogether.

The reason there has been a concentration on the feminine principle in recent Jungian writing is that it provides a means to celebrate the specificity of women's identity, life, and experience. In addition, the notion of a feminine principle helps make a critique of culture out of personal confrontations with it. The basic desire of feminists who are involved in Jungian psychology has been to refuse and refute the denigration of women by analytical psychology, to bring the feminine gender in from the condescending margins, and to promote an alternative philosophy of life to that expressed in the power institutions of a male-dominated society.

Taken as a whole, and I am generalizing, feminism drawing on Jung's ideas stands out mainly in two ways from the other varieties, with which I am more in sympathy. The differences stem from Jung's approach, resist eradication, and cause great difficulties. First, it is assumed that there is something fixed about *femininity*, and hence about *women*; that women therefore display certain essential transcultural and ahistorical characteristics; and that these can be described in psychological terms. Omitted are the ongoing role of the prevailing culture in the construction of the feminine and the distinction between the eternal and the contemporary. It is here that the dead weight of the heritage of archetypal theory is felt, but as the mirror image of Jung's problem; he assumed that there was something eternal about *women*, and hence about *femininity*.

I would like to pinpoint what I find problematic in many attempts to locate eternal models for the psychological activity of women in mythology and goddess imagery. When such imagery is used as a kind of role model or resource for a woman in her here-and-now pain and struggle, I follow the endeavor. But when its aim is a reclamation of qualities and characteristics which purportedly once prevailed in human society, only to be smashed by the patriarchy, then that is altogether more suspect. For it is a highly disputed point, to put it mildly, that such an era ever existed. Could this be a case of taking myth too literally? And isn't there a hidden danger here? After all, if men were to claim to be in a direct line of psychic descent from the gods and heroes, we'd end up with precisely the status quo, with things just as they are, as though they couldn't be any other way. As far as role modeling and resources go, surely an actual woman, especially an analyst, can provide these for another? The search for hidden sources of authority may be a project already flawed by the very sense of weakness and lack of autonomy it seeks to overcome.

Could the feminine principle be played in a pragmatic rather than an absolute key? If so, then its truth would be measured, in William James's words, "by the extent to which it brings us into satisfactory relations with other parts of our experience." We would have to start assembling material on the experience of difference as well as on the experience of womanhood and manhood. Sociologists and academic psychologists may have done this, but depth psychologists have not— yet. Should we do so, then in Shorter's words we would become less concerned with the image of woman and more concerned with *likeness* to that image. She says: "Likeness is consciousness of image and its embodiment. . . . It is not a question of imitation; each person becomes in part and to the measure that he (sic) is able 'like to' the image" (1987, p. 40). Or, in Caroline Stevens's words, "As a woman, anything I do is feminine" (personal communication, 1987).

The second point of disagreement between the feminism of analytical psychology and feminism generally is that much Jungian discourse on the feminine seems to be directed away from political and social action. Dwelling upon the interior and feelings is an end in itself. So, just as middle-class Victorian women were believed to be the repository of sensibility, and confined to hearth and home, in the Jungian manner of it, women in the nuclear age are meant to be mainly private creatures.

My concern is that much thinking and writing about the feminine principle opens a secret door into analytical psychology for the return, ironically, of an overstructured approach to psyche heavily dependent upon abstraction and decidedly moralistic. What I am suggesting is that much contemporary Jungian work on feminine psychology is a far closer "imitation of Jung" than was consciously intended. The intention of rectifying Jung's mistakes and prejudices has been subverted.

Trawling the recent literature, I am struck by the massive problematic signified by numerous phrases such as feminine elements of being, feminine modality of being, femininity of self, feminine ways of knowing, feminine authority, feminine assertion, feminine reflection, feminine dimensions of the soul, primal feminine energy pattern, feminine power, feminine response, feminine creativity, feminine mysteries, feminine body, feminine subjectivity, feminine transformation. I could quadruple the list; for ease of reference, I will simply cite the *feminine principle*.

Something oppressive has come into being—not because what is claimed to be the *content* of this feminine principle is oppressive, but because celebrating the feminine as an ego-ideal only leads to a simple, pointless reversal of power positions. Further, perhaps it is feminism's shadow that can make women feel inadequate for not coming up to the mark?

Gender, Metaphor and the Body

I would like to say a few words now about the literal and metaphorical relationship of anatomy to psychology in order to draw together the psychological and scientific aspects of the gender debate, and because I will bring this in again towards the end of the paper. A literal determinism seduces those who seek to make a simple equation between body and psyche; we do not really know what the relationship between them is, but it is probably indirect. The fact that a penis penetrates and a womb contains tells us absolutely nothing about the psychological qualities of those who possess such organs. One does not have to be a clinician to recognize penetrating women and receptive men—nor to conclude that psychology has projected its fantasies onto the body.

The claim is often made that a female's body possesses certain qualities and characteristics which are the basis of a specific, innate female psychology quite divorced from male psychology, which is based on the male body. Now, as I mentioned earlier, there is no problem with the idea that males and females experience their bodies as different from those of the other sex. But the argument that there are innate psychological differences between the sexes based on the body presents serious and insidious difficulties. It *sounds* so grounded, so reasonable, so commonsensical, so set apart from any social or ideological outlook. However, if psychological activity is body-based, then as the body is more or less a constant over the entire history of humanity, psychological theory can only *support* the horrendous gender situation we face today. Tied to the body, how can it be altered? It must be an inevitability and we would have to agree with Stevens when he argues that "patriarchy is the natural condition of mankind."

Of course, psychology cannot be split off from the body. But the link is on a deeper level even than that of anatomical or endocrinological distinctions. The link between psyche and body surely refers to the body *as a whole*—its moods and movements, its pride and shame, its rigor and its mess. On this level, the body in question is already a psychological entity, a psychesoma, an imaginal body even, providing a whole range of experiences. Sometimes this imaginal body provides crossover experiences, "masculine" for women and "feminine" for men. When the link between psyche and body is envisioned in terms of the body as a whole, then whether that body is anatomically male or female is less significant. I am not attempting here to deny anyone's experience of their body, nor to dispute the value of paying attention to that body. Indeed, the descriptions later in this paper of the father's relations with his children are markedly oriented toward physical experience and activity.

Why is the issue of the body as a possible base for sex-specific psychology so critical? I can make two suggestions about this. First, the whole culture versus innate gender debate is, or has become, numinous. If I have taken one side rather than advancing a multifactorial theory, it is partly because this is what I think, partly because that is my personal style, and partly because a clash of doctrines is where vitality in psychology is to be found. Though I believe I am right, it does not matter so much whether you think I am right or wrong as whether you can recognize what I am talking about. Then we share the same vertex, or overall standpoint—and can muse on the fact that it is really rather hard to be completely wrong in psychology.

The second reason the gender debate stirs us has to do with ambivalence about our constitution, that psychological makeup which we bring into the world. On the one hand, how secure and fulfilling it is to know that one is quite definitely a man or a woman! I certainly feel the need for certainty and do not mean to suggest that there are no such creatures as men and women. On the other hand, I am quite sure that anatomy is not destiny, and I am trying to work my resentment at the idea that it might be into a critique of those who tell me it is.

Which leads us back to the great problem with theorizing that is overly dependent on the body's impact on psychology. If anatomy is destiny, then what can be done to change the position of women? Women who base their quest for a new and positive meaning of femininity on the body alone inadvertently undermine their own cause. After all, definitions of women and men have always changed over time. Up until the end of the eighteenth century, for instance, representations of men in literature and drama quite often had them in tears—so different from this century, in which big boys don't cry.

It follows that animus and anima are not imaged as man and woman because they possess any masculine or feminine qualities. No —here anatomy is a metaphor for the richness and potential of the other. A man imagines what is other symbolically as a woman—one with another anatomy; a woman does the same with a man's body. The so-called contrasexuality is rather contrapsychology; anatomy is merely a metaphor. But anatomy is absolutely *not* a metaphor for any particular emotional characteristic or set of characteristics. These vary with individuals and what is at a given moment outside their conscious grasp and hence in need of being represented by a personification of the opposite sex. *The difference between you and your animus or anima is something more than the difference between you and a man or a woman.* (I do realize that I am discussing animus and anima in their personified forms, but I bring them in as illustrative of the indirect nature of the relations between body and psyche.)

I am saying that *metaphor can be as seductively misleading and one-sided as literalism.* Sometimes it is claimed that masculine and feminine are metaphors (you know, "just" metaphors) for two distinct *Weltanschauungen*, or for the typical styles of operating of the two cerebral hemispheres. Why, oh why can't we just talk of *Weltanschauungen* and hemispheres? When we bring in either masculinity and femininity *or* maleness and femaleness we project a dichotomy which exists in human ideation and functioning onto convenient receptors. The argument that masculinity and femininity should not be understood literally, having nothing to do really with bodily men and women in an actual social context, recognizes that a projection has been made, but falls far short of a successful recollection of it, certainly as far as our culture is concerned. All the other divisions we know about—rational/irrational, Apollonian/Dionysian, classical/romantic, digital/analogic and so forth—all of these exist in every human being. They cannot conveniently be assigned a gender (or sex), save by the kind of bifurcated projection I have depicted. Why do we make such a projection? Surely it is more than a question of language? It could be because we find it difficult living with both sides of our murky human nature. In true borderline fashion, we import a degree of certainty and clarity, and hence reduce anxiety, by making the projection. To sum up: in this projection lie the origins of dualistic ambitions to construct distinct psychologies for the two sexes, and of the attempt to use masculinity and femininity solely as metaphors.

The gender debate suggests that we need to question whether heterosexuality itself should be seen as innate and therefore beyond discussion, or whether it too has a nonbiological dimension. I am thinking of Freud's perception of innate bisexuality followed only later by heterosexuality. Jung views man and woman as incomplete without each other, heterosexuality as a given. In this he disallows Freud's emphasis on bisexuality as the natural state of mankind, wherein sexual identity arises from the enforced demands of reproduction and society. My argument transforms the concept of bisexuality from something undifferentiated (polymorphous or polyvalent) into a vision of *there being available to all a variety of positions in relation to gender role —without recourse to the illusion of androgyny.*

Feminist art critics have faced up to many of these problems. About the relation between the biological and the cultural, Parker and Pollock state that "acknowledging the importance of events of the body . . . is not reducible to biological essentialism, a facet of patriarchal ideology which supposes a primordial difference between the sexes determined by anatomical and specifically genital structures. How the body is lived and experienced is implicated at all levels in social or societally determined psychic processes" (1987, p. 29). Parker and Pollock go on to describe an artwork entitled *Menstruation II*, by Cate Elwes. During her period, dressed all in white and seated in a white, glass-fronted box, she could be watched bleeding. Questions and her answers could be written on the walls of the box. Elwes wrote, "The work reconstitutes menstruation as a metaphorical framework in which it becomes the medium for the expression of ideas and experience by giving it the authority of cultural form and placing it within an art context" (quoted in Parker and Pollock 1987, p. 30).

If discriminations like these are not made, then those analytical psychologists who espouse the idea of innate, body-based, sex-specific psychologies, will find themselves lined up with what is often referred to as the "New Right." New Right assumptions about sex-specific psychology tend to be based on tradition and often have a romantic appeal, but as Statham argues in her paper, "Women, the New Right and Social Work" (1987), those working therapeutically need to be aware that any such assumption can be used to promote "order" and that women's activities, in particular, may be decisively limited.

The same point is made, with a good deal of passion, by Anne McManus in the August 1987 issue of the British feminist journal *Spare Rib*. She writes:

> Feminism is flowing with the rightward tide, its critical radical spirit diluted beyond recognition. . . . A decisive shift came in the transformation of women's *liberation* from oppression, to today's *confirmation* of that oppression in a type of popular feminism which unashamedly embraces anything female. Never mind that this implies a conservative re-embracing of traditional women's roles that the original movement was all about denouncing. Now any old gullible gush practised by women is feminist, especially if it's emotive and authentic (what isn't authentic anyway at this level?) and anti–male rationality. A false dichotomy between thinking men and feeling women evacuates reason to men while women's fates are sealed, trapped again in eternal emotionality which leaves male power safely intact. Thus women are immobilised and trivialised by their very softness and tenderness, voluntarily abdicating the dirty power struggle, and *thereby* the power, to those who have it.

Connecting Passage

The opening section of this paper used a reflexive approach to review the importance and fascination of the borderline idea: it reveals to us our preoccupation with madness and sanity. Then, bearing in mind the idea that the difference between theory and critique is delusive, the debate concerning borderline disorder was examined. Aggression was identified as a major theme exciting attention and anxiety— aggression as an innate and hereditary factor. Next I presented the gender debate, in which innate aggression was again a key issue; this moved into the discussion of gender and psychology.

As I have said, the two debates, on the borderline and on gender, are not about the same thing. But the parallels between them mean that they can be played off against one another: gender and the borderline,

borderline and gender. Played off against one another by the writer, naturally. It is not an accident that the figure of the father is slowly forming in this essay, for as I shall demonstrate, the father links up the hereditary factor, aggression, borderline-personality organization, and the chimera of gender.

The Father in Depth Psychology

We have reached a very interesting point in the evolution of analytical thinking. The wheel has turned full circle, for the father was the key parent in the early days of psychoanalysis—the tyrannical, castrating, oedipal father. Then we got hooked—necessarily—on the mother; now we are coming back to the father. Still often the prohibitive father, he is also increasingly the positive father: the facilitating, empathic, mirroring father who aids imagination, creativity, and psychic health generally. Out of that patrix we see the father cropping up in the etiology of all kinds of disorders where he did not seem to have a place previously—anorexia, for example, and alcoholism (Shorter 1983; Leonard 1982). So, although the positive father shares center stage with the negative father, it is the former who may be regarded as a new element in the picture.

In a way it is puzzling that just as psychological thinking reaches the image of the positive father, cultural and social criticism should have at last caught up with the image of the negative father: patriarchy, phallocentric culture, male violence, male sexual abuse of children, male chauvinism. Perhaps depth psychologists, not for the first time, are engaged in something subversive. At the moment when the image of the father and his authority in society are under attack, we as analysts are providing balance. There is certainly a subversive element in what I have to say about the father, particularly the positive, erotic father.

In Western countries, a shift is undoubtedly taking place in parental ideals and aspirations; the implications are profound even if the change is little more than cosmetic, behaviorally speaking (see Lewis and O'Brien 1987). An apparently increased sharing of parenting functions is not, in my opinion, most important. The significant difference is that the father's *involvement* with his family, something more than merely providing for it, is coming out of the closet. Changing diapers, taking a hand in feeding, going to the swimming pool—these are symbols of a situation in which it is no longer shameful (i.e., feminine) for a man to express directly deep involvement with his family; the wrong kind of involvement too has found its way into prominence. Thus the preoccupation with incest and child abuse, which, as we would now probably all agree, is far more widespread than has been thought. My suggestion is that these statistics, like changing diapers, are not the issue. Behind the pain and guilt of actual incest lies a fascination with father-in-the-family. The newspapers and the electronic media express this with images of the father involved with his family, positively when he takes the kids swimming, negatively when he touches their sex organs in the pool.

We need to explore incest because, like it or not, incest and the father are irremediably linked (which is not to deny maternal incest). Freud and Jung split more dramatically over the incest question than over almost anything else. Freud spoke for the literal, the instinctual, the causative; Jung for the metaphorical, the psychological, the inquiry: What is it for? My aim is not to call Jung right and Freud wrong; indeed, that aspect of Freud is not essential to today's psychoanalysis. But this tension Freud and Jung personify between the literal and metaphorical aspects of incest is one still with us today, so that when we encounter clinical material it is at the heart of our reactions (see Samuels 1980).

Jung's ideas about metaphorical incest sometimes appear to be divorced from ordinary family realities. The underlying question, it seems to me, is How do we grow? We may answer it by saying that maturation is the outcome of a psychological, biological, and cultural interaction, or something anodyne like that. But, the Elephant's Child continues to ask, *exactly* how does it happen? One reply focuses on the depth aspects of relationships in general, and relationships with parents in particular. A very close identification with somebody at a higher level of psychological development (whatever that might mean) facilitates enhancement or enrichment of the personality. The idea that a person actually grows *inside* by relating to people *outside* is at the heart of psychodynamics and object relations. But what in our human makeup enables us to get that close in the first place? If you are my parent, I need to be close to you to grow, but something more than the fact of this dependence is required to make that happen between us. It does not happen consciously; neither of us can bring it about through will power alone. *The psychological function of incestuous sexuality is to facilitate the proximity of love.* Desire in a relationship guarantees its importance. This can go tragically wrong, get acted out, possess generation after generation of a family. *But incestuous desire has the function of providing the fuel for the vehicle which brings us close to other people, making growth possible: love.*

All analysts presumably recognize this in the clinical context. What is the function of the sexual transference? What is *it* for? And what is the function of the normal, reciprocal, sexual countertransference (see Searles 1959)—not neurotic, not problematic, not acted out, just recriprocal? A patient (of whatever sex) expresses desire for an analyst (of whatever sex), who cannot help but be stirred in some way. What's *that* for? What happens in a family between parent and child may also happen in psychotherapy or analysis. One vital function of sexual transference and countertransference is enabling patients to use analysts for their own growth (and vice versa). Such transference-countertransference is not a secondary eroticization of something else, such as the feeding relationship: it is absolutely primary growth stuff (see Samuels 1985c for a fuller exposition).

However, the idea that fathers might play a part in this process or in other developmental processes seems to excite resistance. In a paper, admittedly written some time ago, on borderline phenomena, Mahler (1971) records her impression—"just an impression"—that the preoedipal father has a role in the separation-individuation process. Still, as so often happens in psychodynamic writing, this role is conceived of *in relation and reaction to maternal influences*. For instance, according to Mahler the father is the "awakener from [the] sleep" of symbiosis, or the protector from an overwhelmingly suffocating mother. Now, it has to be granted that the social and psychological relations of father and child are in certain ways indirect, and I shall return to these in some detail in a moment. But this does not explain or justify the continuing marginalization of the father in the analytic literature, as if he had no pattern of relationship to his children worth exploring in its own right. Elsewhere (Samuels 1985b), I have tried to redress this imbalance; here, I should like to analyze it further.

If we are concentrating on borderline phenomena, wherein gender-identity difficulties are generally recognized, then the omission of the father-child relationship and paternal psychopathology is peculiar. To illustrate the problem: In his recent book, *Severe Personality Disorders* (1984), Kernberg's index does not include the father; and the index to the monumental *Essential Papers on Borderline Disorders* (Stone 1986) has but one reference to the father—Mahler's "impression," mentioned above. Nor are the Jungians more evenhanded. Schwartz-Salant (1982), Fordham (1985), and Redfearn (1985) have each a single reference to the father in their indices, and numerous references to mother.

It is worth trying to understand the imbalance because speculations may throw up insights about the father to be played back into practical analysis. The argument I would like to rehearse is that of the father *as* gender.

Citing the father *as* gender is intended to do more than grab the reader's attention. For gender is the psychological analogue of biological sex; as we have seen, this implies a foregrounding of the cultural dimension. As far as extra-uterine life is concerned, the relationship of father and child arises from two other relationships: the pairing of man and woman, and the primal bond between woman and infant. Please note that I am not saying that the tie of blood is irrelevant or that the relationship of father and child is less direct emotionally, or less meaningful to both of them, than is that of mother and child. *But it is signified and acknowledged in a different way because it is constructed in a different way.* It therefore carries a different set of implications. To say that the father-child relation arises from the interplay of two other relations is to recognize that it is mediate and cultural in its essence. A common connection to the mother brings the father-child relation into being. As we know from anthropology, it is not necessary for the biological father to *be* father, and there is widespread cultural variation on this. In all cultures, though, the woman who gives birth to an infant is mother. The actual presence or absence of a father does not alter the overall dynamics of the picture, though individual experience is of course affected (see Samuels 1985b, pp. 40–41).

Paradoxically, that the relationship to the father is a *created relationship* gives it immense psychological and cultural significance (hence my insistence earlier that this is not a secondarization of the father); it is the germ of an entire system of cultural organization based on kinship. For kinship is neither natural nor universal in its shape and pattern. Our concern with the psychological aspects of kinship and how they affect gender issues brings us to understand the problem analysts have with the father: *The father is too psychological.* The relationship is not a biological fact and, because of depth psychology's confused connection to biology, therapists tend not to be too confident with purely psychological facts. Working with psychological facts is a struggle, and this explains the appeal of Lacanian psychoanalysis to feminism: the psychological and cultural factors in the emergence of the child as a sexed subject are given the greatest weight (see Mitchell 1974).

A fascinating byway of this discussion is the impact the father has on the biological relation between woman and infant. Just as fatherhood arises out of the interplay of the two biological relations man-woman and woman-infant, so the process may be envisioned in reverse. The (cultural and psychological) relation to father, or its image where the father is absent, impacts on the (biological) relationship of woman and infant, converting and transforming it into the kinship relation of mother and child (remember, kinship is not natural). Here again, I am not claiming that maternal feeling is the result of the transmutation of biology into culture by the father. What I am saying is equally funda-mental, though. The cultural edifice of motherhood, which includes 90 percent of developmental psychology, can only be approached through the assumption that relations *can be* cultural and psychological. The father, in his essence cultural and psychological, is the paradigm for our capacity to regard any relationship from a psychological point of view. However, our tendency to circumscribe the mother within biology parallels the fact that there is no way to regard the father save psycho-logically and culturally. *The biological weakness of the father-child relation gives it its psychological strength.* For this relationship has to be *declared*. Indeed, whole chunks of patriarchal culture rest on this particular aspect of male vulnerability. We do not know the father as father until we can apply his psychological idea and image. The image produces a relationship purely psychological and tremendously difficult to handle. What is more, once we accept father as a cultural phenome-non, we must entertain the idea of mother too as cultural, not neces-sarily natural. As our culture decrees that motherhood *is* natural for women, it cannot afford to look too closely at the father, lest he give the game away.

It may be puzzling that when I write of the father, I make little or no attempt to distinguish between the literal and the metaphorical father. The reason for this is anything but carelessness; I used to be exceedingly careful to make the distinction. As a result, I think I lost something. Gradually, I have become aware that there are as many connections between the literal and metaphorical fathers as there are discrepancies. If it is impossible to state a general principle on which these connections rest, it should be useful to examine the "archetypal father." It is surely somewhere in the theory of archetypes that we would expect to find links between the literal and the metaphorical.

When I refer to the archetypal father, I do not suggest that human beings are born with a particular image or expectation of a father figure. The archetypal father refers us rather to whatever about the image is powerful, gripping, numinous, awe-inspiring, even religious or psychotic. The archetypal is within as people confront their images of the father, or the general image of the father. The archetypal father is not in the father at all, but in the child's perception of him (see Samuels 1985a, pp. 52–53, 261–65).

As clinicians working in an evanescent society, we are faced with the problem of evaluating the general father image to which our patients constantly resonate. For instance, when father is *said* to be about authority, inner images of father are bound to be organized around authority. In other words, the clinical approach to individuals includes analysis of the cultural stereotype. As the patient describes his or her father, the analyst is likely to think of the cultural parameters. My attitude is that whatever a culture says of the father is true in the sense that, living in a culture, our inner conception of father makes use of this cultural definition. The father image a culture generates operates as a kind of filter upon perception.

We turn now to the part played by the father in borderline-personality disorder. Please note that no attempt is being made to claim that problems with or of the father *cause* such disorder on their own. My purpose is to highlight one important theme without "knocking" other theories. That is, the part played by mother is simply not my focus here.

The Father in Borderline-Personality Disorder

Stone and Galenson (above) provide empirical support for placing the father at the heart of borderline-personality disorder, especially in women. But we should be careful lest the borderline spectrum become a tag for women. Maybe this has already happened; Stone (1981) opines that the diagnosis ratio is between two-to-one and three-to-one in favor of women. Broverman *et al.* demonstrated as long ago as 1970 the part gender-role stereotypes play in clinical judgments of mental health. By means of questionnaires given to clinicians they confirmed two hypotheses: (a) clinical judgment concerning mental health differed according to the sex of the patient, and these differences faithfully followed current gender stereotypes; (b) behavior judged healthy for men portrayed an "ideal standard of health," whereas behaviors judged healthy for women did not—there is a double standard when it comes to diagnosis.

Bearing this in mind, it is conceivable that aggression in women may look excessive if women are regarded as normally and naturally unaggressive. A diagnosis of borderline-personality disorder on the grounds of such "excess" aggression would be erroneous. On the other hand, as women possess a lifelong awareness that they are not supposed to be aggressive, the subjective experience of her aggression, and the attitude of her parents to it, may contribute to a state of excess in terms of a woman's psychic reality. Unfortunately, gender-role stereotyping has a way of becoming self-fulfilling prophecy.

An approach to borderline-personality disorder highlighting the role of the father (without denying the part played by mother) would be insipid if the father in question were restricted to the preoedipal phases of development, whether these be regarded literally or metaphorically. If we do not abandon completely the distinction between preoedipal and oedipal aspects of the father-child relation, let us be careful not to construe maturation as a process that takes place in discrete stages or phases. Development is not necessarily a linear or (chrono)logical business. For instance, as I have shown elsewhere (1982), there is a psychological sense in which three-person functioning precedes two-person functioning. Put concisely, children's recognition of and relation to the father and their discovery of the relation between father and mother make it impossible for them to continue to maintain the illusion of a fused or symbiotic relation to the mother. Intimations of threeness usher in genuine twoness.

Another justification for taking into account both the preoedipal and the oedipal father comes from the work of the Kris Study Group of the New York Psychoanalytic Institute. They studied borderline patients intensively and concluded that there is no one phase of development, no one structural defect, no one kind of trauma solely responsible for borderline disorder (Abend *et al.* 1983, pp. 222–28). The group also concluded that all the borderline patients they considered "showed evidence of severe Oedipal problems . . . [and] intense triangular conflicts." Of course, as a somewhat reactionary group of classical Freudians, they seek to downplay early object-relations theory, but it seems to me that their conclusions are amply documented and well argued. It is possible to glean something of value from this internal Freudian dispute: The insistence among disputants within psychoanalysis that borderline disorders must be either two-person or three-person illnesses points up the struggle borderline individuals face as they come to terms with the pre/post-oedipal divide, the primal scene, and in particular, apperception of the father.

This study of the father's place in borderline-personality disorder is divided conventionally: father and daughter, then father and son. This reflects differences in the experience of boys and girls. A considerable amount has been written about how the sexes' different experience of the *mother* lead to significant differences in gender and social roles and stereotypes. For example, Eichenbaum and Orbach write that

all mothers learnt from their mothers about their place in the world. In each woman's experience is the memory—buried or active—of the struggles she had with her mother in the process of becoming a woman, of learning to curb her activities and to direct her interests in particular ways. (1982 p. 31)

N. Chodorow considers the different nature of the preoedipal experiences of females to mean that a woman's sense of self is "continuous with others," which enables them to be empathic with an infant—unlike males, who are treated as an "opposite" by their mothers (1978, p. 26).

What follows is an attempt to draw together some ideas abut the consequences for gender and social roles and stereotypes of the father's relation to his children of both sexes. *There are two caveats, though. First, as I argued earlier, differences in experience do not lead to two distinct kinds of functioning, two distinct psychologies. Second, we shall have to see through that conventional division: father-daughter—sexuality; father-son—aggression (see below).*

Father and Daughter in Borderline-Personality Disorder

In my practice I have been seeing several women who occupy a cultural and psychological position somewhere between the traditional and the contemporary; I expect that this is a "borderline" problem with which my readers are familiar. Two emotions stand out: First, their sense of failure at fulfilling neither the ancient nor the modern womanly ideal, a feeling sufficiently pervasive to undercut any coherent sense of identity; sometimes the rage and frustration of failure boil over into aggressive or sexual outbursts. Second, in these patients there is an unusually great conscious and unconscious preoccupation with motherhood, whether present or absent from their lives, which heavily colors their image of femininity and gender identity. Motherhood is equated absolutely with womanhood, and whatever confusion or weakness in gender identity there might *seem* to be, the patient *knows for sure* what a women is *in principle*. She has identified and is identified with a "feminine principle"; she is mired in it. Interestingly, though, at the same time she may share the social downgrading of motherhood—at the conscious level, anyway.

Over time, I became aware of a common thread of experience in these women's relation to their fathers and troubled attitude toward their mothers. I have developed an interest in how the father, overtly different from his daughter, has something to do with the degree of success she has in coping with the eventual discovery of covert differences from her mother. These remarks on the daughter-father relationship arise from the need to root ourselves imaginatively in lived personal experience. It is this rootedness which helps to keep the so-called literal and metaphorical in articulated balance, so that the notion of transformation, central to the Jungian enterprise, does not prevent us, in Sylvia Perera's words, from "dealing with things on their own matrix level" (1985). Incidentally, I am not neglecting all the other familial relationships in this account: the focus is deliberate.

Let me begin with a clinical vignette. Margaret was eighteen when she came to see me. (All names and details have been changed.) She turned up for our introductory meeting exactly one week early and the next day her mother telephoned to ask what had happened at the session; later that evening, Margaret had taken an overdose. In fact, I had sent her away because I was with another patient, so we had had only doorstep contact. But she managed, obviously, to communicate her desperation. Margaret was the second-youngest of four children. Her mother had some experience of Jungian analysis which she put to good use interpreting her children's dreams and in other "professional" ways. Working with Margaret, I was struck by how often her mother's opinions were given voice. Above all, motherhood was the acme of womanhood and she, Margaret, was *such* a worry and a failure because of her lack of interest in things maternal, babies in general, and her younger brother in particular. We might say that Margaret knew for sure what a woman was supposed to be, and with gender certainty, judged herself harshly. The problem in analysis was how to build on her vague recognition that there is more to womanhood than motherhood.

Margaret's father was described as an alcoholic with a tendency to become violent; completely in awe of his wife, he regarded the children as her domain. His attitude toward Margaret's education was that it should fit her for marriage. In general, he was dismissive and disapproving of Margaret. Truly, the mother image held sway over this family.

Margaret's ambition was to be a writer but she could not fit this into a scale of values with motherhood at the summit; it was *either* be a writer *or* be a mother. Unconscious attempts to denigrate motherhood as a means of feeling less inferior took the form of fantasies of being a boy, and in dreams, hostility towards her mother and the *idea* of motherhood began to emerge. It took me some time to see that aggression against mother was, for Margaret, a way ahead.

Dream: *The whole family was on holiday—it might have been in Venice for there were small canals and white pavements and glass*

shops. One night S. (elder brother) murdered Mummy and K.
(younger brother) in their beds—Mummy stabbed first and then K.
who was lying next to her. I was so upset I went shopping in an
American supermarket crying really loudly, not knowing how to
contain my grief. I tried to pay for the chewing gum I had bought
but I saw the packet had been half-eaten. I tried to fill it up from
other packets. A man said to me it's good to cry.

We discussed the dream in terms of her freedom, when disguised as her brother, to slay mother and by implication the mother "trip" which had been laid on her. It did not feel right to her to limit our understanding to aggression against her personal mother. She commented that it was odd that she did not simply buy a full packet of gum as a replacement; it had to be *that* packet. She associated this with being "stuck" with who she was in outline, although new contents were perhaps possible. I threw in the idea that gum isn't nutritious, to which she responded by saying that chewing gum was vital to her concentration when painting—"Why do you always talk about food," she asked, "when I want to talk about work?" So in the transference-countertransference I unwittingly but necessarily embodied the mother seeking to limit her adult identity to that of the maternal woman.

After that dream she became depressed for a while, and prominent in the transference during the depression was a yearning for paternal acknowledgment. She said she had "lost" her father forever now, because he would have nothing to do with a mother-murderer like her, being so much under his wife's thumb. My tentative formulation is that to the extent that borderline-personality disorder is a depressive illness, the sense of mourning refers to parental deficits in the area of gender identity. In Margaret's case, gender certainty hid her emotional impoverishment; she had to become *confused* at depth before she could get free. But the very existence of certainty as a powerfully self-destructive factor within her was hidden behind a confused and androgynous persona, requiring analytical elucidation. This is a radical revision of the conventional formulation, which is content to reach the confusion.

Returning to the argument, following Jung we know that kinship libido has something to do with personality enhancement and enrichment (see above). If incest fantasy is acted out it becomes destructive, but if it isn't there at all as a sort of tangible presence in the family, in an actual family, then the growth that can occur in a daughter's metaphorical relationship with her father will not take place (or a son's with his mother, for that matter). This is the implication of the idea that sexuality fuels the device that renders relationships into the stuff of inner growth. In Robert Bly's words (1986), the divine is connected with matter. Jung's ultra-violet needs to link up with his infra-red (1960b, paras 414-20). Plain speaking about the body and about sexuality is neither prurient, titillating, nor embarrassing; it is necessary.

Now boys probably do have an easier time of it than girls, because mothers used to sexuality in relation to children are not as frightened of feelings toward their sons as fathers generally are of their daughters; I am thinking of the erotic aspects of pregnancy, childbirth, feeding, and so forth. This cultural phenomenon can readily be seen in everyday life. There are typical ways in which fathers unable to cope with the erotic involvement force the psychosexual development of their daughters into a borderline format. The first and most obvious way is actual incest. A father may not realize what he is doing, because his personality and background make it impossible for him to balance the sexual and the symbolic, the literal and the metaphorical. Nowadays, keen interest in male sexual abuse of children may put increased pressure on the father who wants to be physically uninhibited.

A brief illustration of the interweave of paternal deficit, gender certainty, and aggression comes from my work with Penny. She was referred to me as borderline and presented as a noisy, demanding, even hysterical, highly "instinctual" person. There was a history of prolonged sexual abuse—by the man next door. She reached a place in the analysis where she could see that this man had appealed to her because of a "total gulf" between her and her father. Two memories came to her, and she could not decide if they were connected: First, she saw her father in the bath with an erection. Second, she recalled her mother saying to her father, "If you do that again, I'll leave you." After these memories surfaced, she was very angry with me indeed. One session she got up and sat at the desk behind me (she does not use the couch on a regular basis). She told me what she would like to do to my head with a blunt instrument, and this became an expressed fantasy of what she *was* doing.

I knew that she was a violent woman. Penny had had military training in unarmed combat, and once, leaving a session, she had deliberately run someone down with her car. But I was not frightened; in fact, I had the most pleasant, warm sensation in my lower legs and feet, as if seated before a fire. I went on to have the vision of a small and comfortable living room in which we were both sitting. In my mind's ear, I could hear the rustle of my newspaper. I was in fact smoking my pipe. I said, "You're watching Daddy read his paper. It's pleasant. Part of you wants it to go on forever. Part of you wants him to look up and acknowledge you. The tension is what is making you angry. You're smashing my brains up because that settles the question of whether I'll notice you of my own accord." For the first time, she and I could grasp the *telos* of her exceedingly dramatic and demanding behavior. Her aggression towards father enabled her to avoid finding out what he felt about her, perhaps to avoid finding out what he was doing when her mother threatened to leave him. I had experienced an embodied countertransference which spoke both of her strategy and its difficulties (see Samuels 1985d for a fuller account of embodied countertransference and analytical visions).

Penny, like Margaret, knew what a woman was supposed to be like. She had done more than Margaret to break free of this through her life in the military, and she was older, in her late thirties. The vital assistance which her father might have supplied had been sought from the neighbor in too-literal, concrete form. The period of work I have been describing preceded what I can only describe as a classical Freudian analysis of Penny's oedipal dynamics as these were expressed in her compulsion to go out with married men not fully available for relationship. Space does not permit more on how things developed.

Listening to Penny's story, we might once again reflect that the father who bathes his daughter and the father who touches her up in the bath are two sides, substance and shadow, of that new phenomenon, the involved father. But there are many more ways for fathers to damage their daughters, and as I have been trying to show, actual incest is only the tip of the iceberg. Numerous problems met with clinically stem from an *insufficiency* of kinship libido or incestual fantasy, not an excess of it. The father who cannot attain an optimally erotic relationship with his daughter is damaging her in a way that deserves therapeutic attention. He reveals himself in so many ways: creating excessive prohibitions around her activities with boys, mocking her sexuality, making fun of her infatuations with rock stars—all part of the theme (she's growing via her closeness to Michael Jackson). If a father says, "take that dreadful poster down," and he is the kind of father I have been describing, then he may well be inflicting a certain kind of incestual damage upon his daughter. Mockery, strictness, and plain uptightness are reflected in a lack of physical involvement from the time a girl is a little baby. Lack of physical contact between father and daughter is an enormously important factor in personality disorders, whether narcissistic or borderline. I suggest that we begin to think of *an optimal erotic relation between father and daughter, and of the pathology of a failure to achieve it.* Eventually, a daughter and her father renounce *admitted* longings for each other; this mutual renunciation is an affirmation of the daughter's erotic viability.

I must stress that this *erotic playback* as I call it, is not correlated with whether or not the father is remembered as nice and understanding, though a loving father is more likely to be optimally erotic than a physically violent one. I have encountered numerous women who have experienced erotic playback from fathers who do not fit the liberal, bourgeois description of a "good" father.

My idea is that a father's very real erotic playback permits his daughter to break out of the bondage of the metaphorical equation *woman = mother.* The equation is equally binding on a woman whether motherhood is highly valued or not and is quite the most powerful element underlying the belief among women and men, gender progressives and gender conservatives alike, that there is a distinct feminine psychology. The erotic can act to liberate the daughter to begin exploring other, nonuterine female paths for herself, and maybe paths which cannot be sexed or gendered in advance: the spiritual path, the vocational path, the path of solidarity with the travails of other women, the path of integration and expression of the aggressive impulse, the path of sexual expression—the individuation of the lusty woman who can begin to think in terms of going where she wants to go and coming when she wants to come. Eventually, a positive estimation of motherhood may evolve, but on an individual basis. Erotic playback promotes the attempt to challenge the constricting aspects of the notion of a separate feminine psychology or principle. On the personal level, a tight and rigid knowledge of femininity—what I have called gender certainty—is a key element in how the lack of erotic playback deploys itself in borderline-personality disorders.

Brenda did not see her father until she was five or six because, as a German alien, he was interned in Canada during the war. Her first meeting with him, as she related it, was when she was lying in the bath, and this strange man came in, only to be introduced as her father. She said, "If you're not nice to me, I'll call you Uncle," and he immediately began to lecture her for being fresh. It seems that her father did not take the time to reintegrate himself into the family, trying instead to impose his authority on it from the outset. Her mother, who was Jewish, felt responsible for her gentile husband's fall from grace in Nazi Germany as well as for his subsequent internment. She put up with his authoritarianism for many years, before leaving him finally when Brenda was grown up.

For a long time, I had little idea why Brenda wanted analysis. My hunch was that all was not well in her main relationship, but I decided to wait and see what materialized. Gradually, it all came out. Her partner was a struggling writer, while she herself was a high-flying academic. She complained of underfunctioning in the work situation: not the intellectual work, but the administration of the department and relationships with colleagues, especially men, went poorly. She felt perpetually on the brink of a a huge explosion of rage and spoke of fears of going mad.

In presenting a dream of Brenda's, I am not communicating a breakthrough because we did not progress much in our work together.

Dream: *I'm in a large, whitish Georgian house, neglected. Neglected garden. Stairs, steep, very narrow, uncarpeted, wooden. On either side white-painted tongue-and-groove, very high enclosed small landing. A door, also tongue-and-groove, hardly visible, tightly shut. Finally, at the top, a small room—bedroom?—and beyond it an open door to the bathroom. Large bath with water in it, more like a mini–swimming pool. Cut-out black wooden seats floated in it, like clouds. To one side of the door a plastic curtain. I look behind it to find an ordinary bath. Noise from another room. I go in. A larger bedroom, light. A large bed. Many men and women intertwined. Lazy, sensual, one woman sitting back on her haunches, a man kneeling, facing her. He puts out his hand and pinches her breast—lightly—and I feel that it must be a rather painful sensation. I'm both drawn towards the scene and slightly repelled.*

These were Brenda's associations to her dream:

The house is like a country equivalent of some friends' London house; similar mixture of being a fine house but rather crumbling. The stairs— rather puritanical, narrow, white. Reminds me of C.'s [partner's] parents' sort of decoration, but also we have tongue-and-groove panels round our bed. But the way the door merges with the wall, that's definitely C.'s parents' style. That door—so firmly closed—the bedroom door of my parents' room, closed, the Saturday after-lunch (or was it Sunday?) ritual, "We don't want to be disturbed. . . " The bath—when I was about fifteen I stayed in Bremen and was taken to a country schloss. In the garden was a little sunken bath with a submerged stone bench at either end. I thought —think—that it was the height of sensuousness. The plastic curtain and bath seem rather ordinary, utilitarian. The bedroom—it was relaxed, easy, cooperative but . . . . I don't know what I didn't like. The breast? My nipples are very sensitive, when they're touched I feel vulnerable, for what starts as pleasure can suddenly become pain.

Our dialogue about the dream and associations covered three general areas. First, her parents' marriage—its exclusiveness, togetherness ("tongue and groove"), and her mockery of it ("ritual"). Second, that the bath was the "height of sensuousness" implied that her rebellious initial utterance to her father gave her pleasure of a kind. Third, and connected to this last, there is a link between sensuous pleasure and vulnerability (her sensitive nipples), as for instance when supine in the bath with the other upright. Brenda's lifelong fight with her father was their sole source of erotic playback, and it was not enough. She tried hard to keep her aggression out of her marriage and under control at work, but was consumed by terror of a catastrophic explosion. What she found difficult to face was the sense of satisfaction she attained via her aggressive impulses and fantasies. In the analysis, at least, she did not discover ways of achieving intimacy other than aggression. For when negative feelings towards me and the analysis began to surface, she withdrew, and I was unable to persuade her to stay.

In contrast to Brenda, Veronica had a stable, close, loving relationship with her sensitive, warm, and admiring father. Undoubtedly because of that the analysis was a struggle at first. Over time, in the telling, the father-daughter friendship seemed to acquire an odd flavor. It sounds trivial, but I was struck by the fact that she took her car "home" for maintenance (a long journey), and by her telling me her father always worried about whether she was warm enough. As I noted these things, I started to see that behind Veronica's calm and serene demeanor there was a tremendous and raging contempt for the whole world and the people in it. I said to myself that she was safe in Daddy's arms, safe to look down on everything and everyone.

I thought I was being patient and coping with my frustration. But obviously I was not! For Veronica accused me of being a "whirlwind," having seen me leave the office in a hurry after her session one day. Actually, whirlwind was not her own word, for it had been used of me by her boss, who had referred her to me for analysis. So, in father's arms, even then.

I decided to introduce this idea of mine about "father's arms" and her reply was immediate. When she was a little girl she used to sit in a chair and her father would stand or crouch behind with his arms around her and the chair. They called the game "castle arms." After telling me this, she opened up much more and a truly disastrous picture of her heterosexual relationships emerged. She had "carried a torch" for one of her college professors for over ten years. During that time, they hardly ever met or made love. Yet in some ways the relationship was stable; she felt whole in it, safe, and womanly. But in her masturbation fantasies, her desires were more pressing and active. This was exemplified by her masturbation fantasy of the two of us together.

For Veronica, "castle arms" fulfilled several functions: (a) she could feel an aggressive superiority towards the world; (b) her own particular version of femininity was buttressed by its arrest at a pregenital point; (c) she and her father were spared the pain of a mutual renunciation of erotic feelings, which deprived her of the springboard-into-life effect.

The various strands of this paper can come together now: There is something borderline about the belief in a distinct feminine or masculine psychology. Women suffer enormously from narrow definitions of what it means to be female, from the requirement that they be unaggressive, selfless creatures who relate, are responsive to the needs of others, and react but do not act. Gender certainty forms the oppressive heart of borderline disorder. Thus borderline-personality disorder may be regarded as a kind of protest of this requirement. True, as *mothers*, women may be extraordinarily responsive. But as *persons* women can sniff out other vistas and ways of being. Strange as it may seem, it is the young female's apperception of herself as a sexual creature, facilitated by an erotic connection to her father, that enables her to spin through a variety of psychological pathways, enjoying the widest spectrum of meanings inherent in the ideogram *woman*. The father's first fertilization helped to make the female baby; his second helps bring forth the female adult, who is then free to drop her father when and if she needs to. There would be little point in replacing a femininity that pleases Mummy with a femininity that pleases Daddy. And the female adult can, now more than ever, be a multifaceted woman-person, free not only *from* symbiotic relation to her mother, but *to* grow in all manner of unpredictable and exciting ways.

Father and Son in Borderline-Personality Disorder

There are two quite distinct but compatible ways to view the father-son relationship: in terms of intergenerational conflict or in terms of intergenerational alliance. It is the peculiar genius of Freud's oedipal theory that in it such a dual viewpoint exists. Unfortunately, as the emphasis in psychoanalysis has been almost exclusively on the prohibitive, castrating father, we have heard, as I noted earlier, rather little about the alliance with his son. Yet the interplay of alliance and conflict is crucial to any kind of organic cultural development. Indeed, conflict and competition between father and son may indicate change, progress, and vitality as well as provide a healthy check on both reaction and revolution. Overt alliance provides a framework within which all of this, competition included, can happen. Connecting past and present, for the father-son link is nothing if not historical, the image of the elder telling (almost) all he knows to youth is a compelling one. It is as if father and son strike a bargain, at least in my commonplace rendering of Freud's theory of identification. If the son gives up his claim on the mother, he will receive help with his life tasks. Only when excessively defensive does this identification lead to a submergence of the boy's individuality in the image of his father.

The castrating father of Freud's theory should not be ignored, though. For the incest taboo to be effective, and it has to be lest all culture sink into a familial miasma, the older generation has to be well-muscled. This is not the place to discuss castration anxiety in depth, but Jones's concept of aphanisis is relevant (1927). The term means the removal by the same-sex parent not only of the means to express sexual desire, *but also of the capacity to feel desire itself*. It is a brilliant attempt by Jones to verbalize what it is that the oedipal child is afraid of, and hence what gives the prohibition its power.

The reader may recall that one task of analysis is seeing how the cultural stereotype resonates with the inner images of the patient. For a son, the cultural stereotype of the father suggests a figure incarnating conscience and functioning as a repository of values and ideals. The father's function in relation to the son is to turn incestuous libido away from the mother in new directions, leading to spiritual enrichment. But the father expresses his opposition to incest in the most virulent form —castration, aphanisis, or some other terrible punishment. Thus a remarkable scenario develops. Represented in myth as a bull, a creature whose potency and virility mingle with its other terrifying and violent features, in the person of the father instinct serving spirit drives out instinct serving sex; the spirit is also instinctual, as it were. This paradox suggests that in the son's internal father image, a degree of emotion or passion is necessary alongside spirit. Many male patients, including several borderline individuals, complain that this is what their other-wise unobjectionable fathers lacked. *A passionately spiritual father is different from one whose dry concentration is on conformity; the whole flavor of prohibition is different.* The passionately spiritual father is not the same as a bully, one whose self-image rests on the defeat of his son.

The clinical material I have to offer about the "dry" father is some-what unusual. Eric was an actor. His demeanor was passive-aggressive, his ambition zero, and his value system that of a conventional English gent. Eric's mother was strongly in support of his analysis and gave him a schematic biography of his early life to show me; below are the parts of this which relate to the parental marriage. Eric was very much a mother's boy. His presenting problem was a phobia about pubic hair and violent fantasies of dismembering women and inserting their cut-off limbs into their vaginas. As Pontius has pointed out (1986), such fantasies involve the creation of a "male-female superhuman," and reading his mother's account of her marriage, one can see why Eric was impelled from within to create a replacement for it as the source of his being. I am aware that the mother's account is highly partial; that is the point of reproducing it.

(1) Advised by V.'s psychiatrist not to marry him as he was considered a depressive with psychological impotence.
(2) Eric result of only intercourse during first year of marriage, this a means only of producing a child and not of love-making, which V. considered dirty.
(3) Eric worshipped by me not only as a miracle in itself but perhaps also as a means of sublimating lack of sex life.
(4) At age six, Eric given a puppet theatre by his godfather inside which he was amazingly artistic. Said he wanted to be a ballet dancer. V., already not a full man himself, was adamant this was not what a man should do. A row followed between us in front of Eric—I had so much sexual frustration that I could be very bitter towards V. although or because I loved him so much I wanted him very badly. I had no sex life at all after I conceived T. (Eric's sister).
(5) Quite wrongly, I had to make too many decisions due to V.'s passivity.
(6) Children sent to boarding school at V.'s insistence.
(7) V. keen for Eric to enjoy sports and walks but all they did together was discuss history, which they both adored. Eric not "sporty."
(8) V. had depression and psychoanalysis all our married life (sic).

I should like to discuss Eric's situation in terms of his father's failure to use paternal reverie as a container which might facilitate the transformation of Eric's aggressive fantasies and impulses towards women into something to be integrated and, eventually, used creatively. Each of the terms *reverie, container*, and *transformation* has origins in Bion's extension of Kleinian thinking (1965). However, these terms are usually employed in relation to the mother; we do not have much idea of what paternal reverie is like.

Overall, the father-son couple work on the establishment of a *telos* for aggression, as referred to earlier in the paper. This involves the recognition, at a preverbal level, of the intentionality of aggression. Aggression cannot exist save in relation to its object, and where the object of aggression feels like the mother, the father's transformative influence has the effect of highlighting *affect* and downplaying its *target*. What is at stake is *the integrity of aggressive process*. We can put this into the language of the heroic quest: the father contextualizes heroic endeavor as something other than the slaying of a mother-dragon, for that act can lead to a metaphorical slaying of the whole creative unconscious. The father facilitates *heroic process* rather than a specific *heroic achievement*. This involves the need to expose oneself to danger not once but many times, a lifelong adventure beginning in childhood. The deliberate exposure to danger, *and not the danger itself*, is the valuable part of the son's heroic quest. If there is a victory, it is decidedly not a once-and-for-all event; it is not the sort of victory to get inflated about.

As far as the integrity of aggressive process is concerned, it does not really matter that much whether the child's self-image at any one time is that of aggressor or victim, provided he has ample experience of both of these roles and is not trapped in either. The father structures a spectrum for aggression ranging from one to the other, and because of projective identification, the victim can *become* a threatening object and vice versa. This fluidity and interchangeability are vital if aggression is to remain a benign force, capable of utilization via transformation. Generally speaking, the father aids his son in the transformation of aggression through reverie, handling, and play. Of course, in practice both parents do this, and when the mother performs the particular function of transforming aggression, she can be recognized as doing some fathering—just as fathers are often said to do some mothering. The terms *mother* and *father* are also metaphorical statements. What particularly needs emphasizing, though, is that transforming aggression is not the same either as managing it by helping a child to remain psychologically intact under the terrific internal pressure occasioned by rage, or surviving a child's aggressive onslaught. Transformation here does *not* refer to those achievements. It is an ongoing process of relatedness involving loss of egohood by both parties in order to bring to consciousness and fulfillment a psychological need hitherto unrecognized.

Throughout, this article has prepared for the linkage of the father with the transformation of aggression; that is why the questions of innate aggression and gender-specific psychology were examined so thoroughly. The father-aggression association is not biological or logical; it is partly sociological, but above all, psychological.

Let us look at one specific aspect of aggressive transformation, wherein Eric and his father failed completely. This is the shift in the quality of aggression from a manic-heroic-separation style to the aggression of ordinary oedipal rivalry. This shift requires fostering within the father-son relationship specific to that bond; lack of such fostering contributes borderline-personality disorder. The father offers himself as a target for the son's aggression, not in an all-knowing way, but as part of an authentic struggle whose outcome is not certain, even though its value as process is tacitly agreed upon. The father-son alliance (or the mother-daughter alliance in the female case) upon which cultural consistency depends is a further transformation arising from the recognition by both father and son that neither can gain absolute victory. Again, the delusion of victory is often encountered clinically in borderline symptomatology.

One problem in particular, often met with in analysis, concerns the son of a mother who is ambitious yet societally frustrated and who seeks a form of fulfillment by envisioning her son as her own private phallic property. Here the father may insert himself between mother and son to encourage their separation—or he may not. This is the kind of psychological situation where I *would* see the father as an "awakener from sleep." As the foregoing remarks should make clear, I generally do not see the father *primarily* as one who breaks up the mother-son relationship. Rather his role is in relation to the aggressive energy in his son; aggression involves more than separation from the mother.

To conclude this section on the father-son relationship in borderline-personality disorders, I should like to add a few words on homosexuality. Though we distinguish homosexual genital sex from homoerotic involvements, psychological life must always have something of a homosexual component in it. That enables us to talk of a homosexual Oedipus complex; for a boy, this means feeling an attraction to his father and a desire to eliminate his mother. However, if in boy's fantasies his father is strong and admirable, *and* his mother is vastly inferior and unlovable, then the outcome may be an overvaluation or idealization of the father in general and the father's penis in particular. This would not be a penis symbolizing the passionately spiritual father mentioned earlier, but more of a doughy, nutritional penis—indeed, a form of breast-substitute for the absence of a desirable mother.

The Father and His Children

At the end of the last section, the rigid symmetry of the heterosexual matrix within which we do much of our thinking fell apart. Mothers do what fathers do, fathers do what mothers do, the homosexual element is inevitable, the father's penis stands for a breast on occasion.

Perhaps we have been tempted to ignore Freud's perception of an innate bisexuality in man and have taken heterosexuality to be something so fundamental it is beyond debate. If this has happened, our imaginings of what a father is or could be will be truncated. Similarly, our clinical perceptions suffer if, out of a heterosexist consensus, we refer to the "phallic mother" when the dynamic in the transference-countertransference concerns the father.

It is important to reverse the poles within the two major arguments I have been developing about the father in borderline-personality organization concerning the erotically involved father in the enrichment of his daughter's personality, and the father who, by means of reverie, transforms the aggressive impulses and fantasies of his son. *The father's erotic playback is also required by his son and his transformation of aggression by his daughter.* If we do not make this acknowledgment, then, just like the borderline patient, we are ensnared by the delusion of gender certainty.

Wait a moment—"just like the borderline patient"? Surely the idea is coalescing that, in a way, we are just like the borderline patient. Torn between sanity and madness, aghast at our heredity and its aggression, struggling to find the middle ground between gender chaos and certainty.

The final sections of the paper explore, on a collective and cultural level, what it means to be just like the borderline patient.

The Imitation Game

The mathematician Alan Turing was interested in seeing whether machine intelligence would ever match that of humans. He proposed to do this by playing the "Imitation Game" (Hofstadter and Dennett 1981, pp. 70–73). Though Turing was going to use a computer, the game can be played by people. In the Imitation Game, two concealed persons are questioned, one a man and the other a woman; the man attempts to answer as a woman and the woman answers as herself. The other participants have to decide, on the basis of their answers, which is the man and which the woman. The object is to show not that there are no gender differences but how elusive such differences are.

I suggested to a colleague, David Curry, that it would be interesting to play the Imitation Game. Curry was working with a suitable group of students and I am extremely grateful to him for providing me with an account of what happened.

A and B were sent to different rooms and a messenger appointed to relay the questions and answers. In all, eleven questions were asked. Here is a selection:

Q: If you have breast-fed your baby describe the sensation. If not, describe what feeding was like.

A: It was a mixture of being at one with the baby, of getting to know the baby as a separate person and often a visceral attachment to the baby which made my stomach turn over when the baby cried.

B: It was actually a very hard experience—ill after birth—not producing enough milk. Baby was separated most of time from me in an incubator—only saw him at feeding times and after a week my milk dried. It felt like getting blood from a stone.

Q: What differences do you see between men's and women's intuition?

A: A woman's intuition is allowed and has more chance to develop.

B: On the whole women are far more intuitive and sensitive at reading between the lines.

Q: What do you fear most about women?

A: Pretense—My mother used to pretend to be weak. I felt I had to mother her and protect her.

B: My mother was a very stabilizing influence in my life and this has led me to be very much at ease with women.

Q: What do you fear most about men?

A: Their pretense—my father used to pretend to be powerful. I felt he was too fragile.

B: My father was a very powerful man who used to attack me mentally and physically and this has left "scars" in one or two of my subsequent relationships.

Q: How was it for you?

A: Lovely darling—and for you?

B: It was pretty good.

Q: How do you feel if you are the one who doesn't have an orgasm?

A: That's O.K.—but it does depend on the timing.

B: The times when I do have an orgasm are so good I can cope with the rest.

The reader is invited to play the game. Which respondent is the woman? The answer is at the end of the paper.

The Imitation Game II

The Imitation Game (1981) is also the title of a play by Ian McEwan, who is well known in England. In his introduction to the piece, McEwan tells of its genesis. He first became interested in the personality of Turing, a brilliant young scientist who was at the heart of the Ultra operation in World War II. This was a vast project to decipher the German Enigma codes using primitive electromagnetic computing machines. I do not know how well this story is known in the United States, but the fact that the Allies were able to read German communications was absolutely central to the prosecution of the war effort (see Winterbotham 1974). In Britain, "Bletchley" (the place where Ultra was located) sets off associations of ingenuity, secrecy, and treachery, for Russian agents passed its secrets to the Soviet Union. Even today the full story has not been published.

McEwan abandoned his original idea, but in passing he had found out about Turing's Imitation Game and the social organization of Bletchley: "By the end of the war ten thousand people were working in and around Bletchley. The great majority of them were women doing vital but repetitive jobs working the machines. The 'need to know' rule meant that the women knew as much as was necessary to do their jobs, which was very little. As far as I could discover, there were no women at the centre of Ultra" (1981, p. 16). Gradually, McEwan came to think of Ultra as symbolizing, not only the war, but a whole culture: "The closer you moved to the centre, the more men you found; the further to the periphery, the more women" (ibid., p. 17).

So McEwan made his protagonist a woman, Cathy, of lower middle-class background, who goes to work at Bletchley. Cathy is a talented musician prevented from pursuing music by her tyrannical, small-minded father. With a writer's sensibility, McEwan renders the father as implacably hostile to her sexuality, considering her evil and promiscuous (she's actually a virgin). Cathy is presented almost as a typical borderline character. She is prone to violent outbursts, has strange turns, struggles in her relationships, and is clearly deeply involved with this negative father of hers.

Cathy arrives at Bletchley and starts her job. She evinces curiosity about what is going on and is warned off. Then she falls in love with one of the top scientists, Turner, and he invites her to his rooms for tea. They go to bed (pp. 111–12):

Turner: Are my hands cold?
Cathy: Yes.
Turner: Sorry.
Cathy: It's all right.
Turner: Cathy, are you . . . ? is this your first . . . ?
Cathy: Yes, it's my first time.
Turner: You don't mind me asking?
Cathy: No, of course not.

Cathy smiles slightly mischievously.

Cathy: What about you?
Turner: What me? (*Lying*) It's not . . . it isn't really my first time . . . .
Cathy: That's good. You know exactly what to do then.
Turner: Well . . .

Cathy kisses him.

Cathy: You know all the secrets.
She cuddles against him.

But Turner is impotent and accuses Cathy of mocking him with her remark, "You know all the secrets." He says that she has planned this humiliation, and then he storms off. After Turner has gone, Cathy gets up, washes, and dresses. She moves over to Turner's desk and starts reading the papers on it. A colleague of Turner's comes in, discovers her, and she is arrested and imprisoned for the rest of the war.

McEwan placed a sexual relationship, and its attendant misunderstandings at the heart of the play. The relationship generates anxiety, confusions, and misunderstandings which both represent and underpin the dynamics of culture. At the end of the play, Cathy talks to the officer who tells her she must go to prison even though they know she is harmless. Finally, she speaks out haltingly against gender certainty (pp. 114–15):

> If the girls fired the guns as well as the boys . . . if girls fired guns and women generals planned the battles . . . then the men would feel there was no . . . morality to war, they would have no one to fight for, nowhere to leave their consciences. . . War would appear to them as savage and as pointless as it really is. The men want the women to stay out of the fighting so they can give it meaning.

> When we went to bed, it didn't matter that he couldn't . . . I didn't care. I liked him. He didn't have to be efficient and brilliant at everything . . . I liked him more. . . . But he couldn't bear to appear weak before me. He just couldn't stand it. Isn't that the same thing? I mean . . . as the war.

Gender and the Borderline

The problem of gender certainty is not simply one of compensation or overcompensation for gender confusion. Gender certainty may be regarded as an underlying psychic reality, experienced as a self-image, and lived out to a greater or lesser degree. Gender certainty and confusion are not opposites. Rather, they are alternative strategies, equally unsatisfying when used alone to cope with the anxiety aroused by the fluidity and diversity in human sexual activity, represented by gender. When Kernberg writes of a premature Oedipus complex, he is referring to the failure of an individual personality to hold the balance between certainty and confusion in relation to gender. Oedipal dynamics can lead either to certainty or confusion, and this is particularly so when oedipal prematurity forces relations into a heterosexual mold. Aggression also plays its part in both gender certainty and gender confusion. In the former, that which is other is devalued; in the latter, gender itself is annihilated. The problem of gender difference presents as a problem of "animated moderation"—how to find a way of not being *too* certain or *too* confused, getting somewhere in the middle, just a little mixed up. Then, the role of the father, for sons and daughters alike, turns out to be critical.

Not knowing puts us under great strain, for the world we live in has firm opinions about what is normal and abnormal sexual behavior, what the discrepancies are between masculinity and femininity, and where a person stands on the sexual spectrum. The world is not neutral as regards gender; certainty is rewarded if it accords with the general view. Earlier, I referred to the father *as* gender; if that is so then, given that men claim to represent humanity, women *are* sex. The idea of "woman" and the idea of an innate, sex-based, sex-bound psychology are really the same idea. The cultural formation of the father relation assigns men to the province of culture and to women is given the province of biology.

Culture is not a constant; it is a pluralistic network which will find its gender form. Like all pluralisms, gender pluralism involves some kind of competition, even a division of the field. Sexual preferences and orientations, and their gendered associations, are in a state of competition. Sexual fantasies are not politically neutral.

When we think about sexual behavior, we encounter the paradox of something biological showing such marked cultural variation. It seems to me that what is important about the huge range of sexual activities of which we are aware is its *very existence*—not whether particular activities are appropriate, or even have special meaning. Why has such a range of sexual activity come into being? The advantage of admitting a huge degree of ignorance, particularly in the clinical, analytical setting, is that this is the attitude most likely to come to the aid of the middle-ground between gender certainty and confusion. We are confused about the degree of confusion, certain only of a lack of certainty. *There is also a pleasure in not knowing.*

However, analysts are tempted to operate under the delusion of normality when it comes to gender. Exposure to the fluidity of gender is rewarding and pleasurable, and impossible for the borderline patient. Exposure to gender fluidity is exposure to an anxiety-spewing monster—not for the inflated achievement of slaying the monster, but for the experience of exposure of one's self, one's gendered self. The small-minded way is to propose sexual or gender normality for the patient when that is a far-off thing for the analyst. It is morally wrong for analysts to use patients' gender vicissitudes to detoxify their own, ignoring the capacity of desire, like psyche itself, to change. Many other psychiatric classifications have turned out to have hidden, creative possibilities: psychosis, depression, narcissism. The treasure of borderline disorder is to be found in the lair of the gender dragon. The possibility of healing the split between gender certainty and confusion in the borderline patient inspires us to think of healing that split in a culture so divided.

(Answer: A was the woman, B the man.)

References

Abend, S., Porder, M., and Willick, M. 1983. *Borderline patients: Psychoanalytic perspectives*. New York: International Universities Press.

Bion, W. 1965. Transformation. In *Seven Servants*. New York: Jason Aronson.

Bly, R. 1986. C. G. Jung and the Humanities. Statement presented at conference at Hofstra University.

Broverman, I., Broverman, D., Clarkson, F. 1970. Sex-role stereotypes and clinical judgments of mental health. *Journal of Consulting and Clinical Psychology* 34:1.

Chodorow, N. 1978. *The reproduction of motherhood: Psychoanalysis and the sociology of gender*. Los Angeles: University of California Press.

Derrida, J. 1978. *Writing and Difference*. Trans. A. Bass. London: Routledge and Kegan Paul.

Eichenbaum, L., and Orbach, S. 1982. *Inside out . . . outside in: Women's psychology: A feminist psychoanalytic perspective*. Harmondsworth: Penguin.

Fordham, M. 1985. *Explorations into the self*. London: Karnac.

Freud, S. 1919. A child is being beaten. In *Standard Edition* 17. London: Hogarth.

Galenson, E. 1986. Some thoughts about infant psychopathology and aggressive developments. *Int. Rev. Psycho-Anal.* 13:3.

Gunderson, J., and Singer, M. 1975. Defining borderline patients: An overview. *Amer. J. Psychiatry* 132:1.

Hofstadter, D., and Dennett, D. 1981. *The mind's I*. Harmondsworth: Penguin.

Jones, E. 1927. Early development of female sexuality. In *Papers on Psychoanalysis*. London: Bailliere, Tindall and Cox.

Jung, C. G. 1956. *Symbols of transformation*. In *Collected works*, vol. 5. Princeton: Princeton University Press.

―――――. 1960a. *The psychogenesis of mental disease*. In *Collected works*, vol. 3. Princeton: Princeton University Press.

―――――. 1960b. *The structure and dynamics of the psyche*. In *Collected works*, vol. 8. Princeton: Princeton University Press, 1969.

Kernberg, O. 1967. Borderline personality organisation. *J. Amer. Psychoanal. Assn.* 15:132.

_____. 1975. *Borderline conditions and pathological narcissism.* New York: Jason Aronson.

_____. 1979. Some implications of object relations theory for psychoanalytic technique. *J. Amer. Psychoanal. Assn.* 27:

_____. 1984. *Severe personality disorders: Psychotherapeutic strategies.* New Haven and London: Yale University Press.

Kohut, H. 1971. *The analysis of the self.* New York: International Universities Press.

_____. 1977. *The restoration of the self.* New York: International Universities Press.

_____. 1978. *The search for the self.* New York: International Universities Press.

_____. 1983. Selected problems of self psychological theory. In J. Lichtenberg and S. Kaplan, eds., *Reflections on self psychology.* Hillsdale, New Jersey and London: Analytic Press.

Leonard, L. 1982. *The wounded woman: Healing the father-daughter relationship.* Ohio: Swallow Press.

Lewis C., and O'Brien, N. 1987. *Reassessing fatherhood: New observations on fathers and the modern family.* London: Sage.

McEwan, I. 1981. *The imitation game.* London: Picador.

Mahler, M. 1971. A study of the separation-individuation process. *Psychoanal. Stud. Child.,* 1971.

Mitchell, J. 1974. *Psychoanalysis and feminism.* London: Allen Lane.

Parker, R. and Pollock, G. 1987. *Framing feminism: Art and the women's movement 1970-1984.* London and New York: Routledge and Kegan Paul.

Perera, S. 1985. The body in analysis. Statement presented at Ghost Ranch Conference.

Pontius, A. 1986. Crime as ritual. Unpublished paper given at conference on C. G. Jung and the Humanities at Hofstra University.

Redfearn, J. 1985. *My self, my many selves.* London: Karnac.

Samuels, A. 1980. Incest and omnipotence in the internal family. *J. Analyt. Psychol.* 25:1.

_____. 1982. The image of the parents in bed. *J. Analyt. Psychol.,* 27:4. Also in A. Samuels, Ed., *The father: Contemporary Jungian perspectives.* London: Free Association Books, 1985; New York: New York University Press, 1986.

_____. 1985a. *Jung and the post-Jungians.* London and Boston: Routledge and Kegan Paul.

_____, ed. 1985b. *The father: Contemporary Jungian perspectives* London: Free Association Books; New York: New York University Press, 1986.

_____. 1985c. Symbolic dimensions of eros in transference-countertransference: Some clinical uses of Jung's alchemical metaphor. *Int. Rev. Psycho-Anal.* 12:2.

_____. 1985d. Countertransference, the *mundus imaginalis* and a research project. *J. Analyt. Psychol.* 30:1.

_____. 1987. Original morality in a depressed culture. In *The Archetype of Shadow in a Split World,* ed. M. A. Mattoon. Zurich: Daiman Verlag.

Samuels, A., Shorter, B., and Plaut, F. 1986. *A critical dictionary of Jungian analysis.* London and New York: Routledge and Kegan Paul.

Sayers, J. 1982. *Biological politics: Feminist and anti-feminist perspectives.* London: Tavistock.

Schwartz-Salant, N. 1982. *Narcissism and character transformation: The psychology of narcissistic character disorders.* Toronto: Inner City.

Searles, H. 1959. Oedipal love in the countertransference. In *Collected papers on schizophrenia and related subjects.* London: Hogarth, 1968.

_____. 1973. Violence in schizophrenia. In *Countertransference and related subjects: Selected papers.* New York: International Universities Press, 1979.

Shorter, B. 1983. The concealed body-language of anorexia nervosa. In A. Samuels, ed., *The father: Contemporary Jungian perspectives.* London: Free Association Books, 1985; New York: New York University Press, 1986.

Shorter, B. 1987. *An image darkly forming: Women and initiation.* London and New York: Routledge and Kegan Paul.

Siann, G. 1985. *Accounting for aggression: Perspectives on aggression and violence.* London and Boston: George Allen and Unwin.

Statham, D. 1987. Women, the New Right and social work. *J. Soc. Wk. Pract.* 2:4.

Stevens, A. 1982. *Archetype: A natural history of the self.* London: Routledge and Kegan Paul.

Stone, M. 1981. Borderline syndromes. *Psych. Clin. N. Amer.* 4:3.

————, ed. 1986. *Essential papers on borderline disorders: One hundred years at the border.* New York and London: New York University Press.

Storr, A. 1970. *Human aggression.* Harmondsworth: Penguin.

Wallerstein, R. 1983. Self psychology and "classical" psychoanalytic psychology—the nature of their relationship: A review and an overview. In *Reflections on self psychology.* J. Lichtenberg and J. Kaplan, eds., Hillsdale, New Jersey and London: Analytic Press.

Winterbotham, F. 1974. *The ultra secret.* London: Weidenfeld and Nicolson.

Ritual Integration of Aggression in Psychotherapy*

Sylvia Brinton Perera

Ritual projects man into the era of gods, makes him contemporary with them and lets him share their creative work.
F. DeGraeve (quoted in Michael Dames, *The Avebury Cycle*, p.14)

Ritual, fundamentally, is psychodrama: it is a conscious, earnest and devoted play. . . . [It] offers us an alternative to repression for dealing with potentially overpowering affect.
E. C. Whitmont, *Return of the Goddess*, p. 236

Ritual is a form of imaginative creativity—the dance of the psyche unfolding in bodily action, creating through gesture, movement, breath, sound, silence and concrete objects a mirror of the deepest and still unspeakable levels of the soul. Through the body's activity, we can connect to those deepest magical dimensions of consciousness where we are whole, in touch with the Self. While rituals are often the product of a collective, and serve as "transition objects" or bridges between that

Sylvia Brinton Perera is a member of the New York Association of Analytical Psychology, a teacher at the C. G. Jung Institute in New York, and a practicing analyst in New York and Connecticut. She is the author of *Descent to the Goddess: A way of initiation for women; The scapegoat complex: Toward a mythology of shadow and guilt;* and several clinical papers. With E. C. Whitmont she coauthored *Dreams, a portal to the source: A clinical guide for therapists.*

*This article was originally presented at a conference on "Ritual and Jungian Psychotherapy," Jan. 25, 1987, held by the Minneapolis Jungian Society.

collective and its transpersonal matrix, they can also be individual, and serve a comparable function.

In modern psychoanalysis there are many specific ceremonies (of time, place, roles, greeting, fee, chairs, and couches). And in an important sense all analysis is ritual, established specifically for the purpose of healing and exploring the depths of the psyche usually excluded in ordinary discourse. It is separate from social-secular life in its particular setting, its fixed, repetitive times. Anything can be brought to it by one party, the analysand; while the other, the analyst, must maintain ceremonial neutrality, focusing attention on the processes of the first, and when these evoke strong reactions and images within her or his own psyche, using those primarily for the other's process. The working through of the transference is itself a ritual—a ceremonial enactment of the problematic roles, affects, relationships, and behavior patterns that have defined the analysand's life drama. Exploring dreams, memories, and relationships creates a remarkable—and at times unbearable—intimacy; yet according to the ritual artifice this time of greatest intimacy must be paid for in cash.

Within the overall ritual frame of analysis, there are also those individually created ceremonies that are discovered/created by analysands out of a deep need to mediate into life what the Self requires them to live. These arise during the course of ongoing analysis in the psychological space between inside and outside, when the ego's boundaries to primitive affects and drives—the gods—are distorted, usually out of fear. Before symbolic, verbal relationships to these frightening and personally taboo energies can be made, they are often managed by rigid denial, splitting, projective identification, primitive idealizations (all magic-level modalities) which leave the individual at the mercy of their unconscious eruption into his enviomnent—both inside and outside, both within the transference and in other relationships. Lying across the borders of the known and acceptable world, these taboo affects and drives often reveal themselves first through preverbal motor activity—acting out. We feel ourselves gripped on a body level, suffering their presence below awareness, and the ensuing actions express and relieve the pressure. But they do not usually connect the unconscious contents adequately to consciousness. They happen to and through us.

Jung has said, and written in stone, "Called or not, God is present"; and we have learned that Its force and forms dance through us in order that we may suffer their incarnation. They cannot be eradicated, nor must we identify with them.

What we are unable to mediate and embody consciously into life, we must often first ritualize, if we are not to blast others or be blasted ourselves as the energies and behaviors surge through us. As an alternative to repression and unconscious eruption, and in Its own *kairos*, the "Self in the body" (Neumann 1976, p. 11) can be ritually invoked—consciously turned toward and listened to for direction. Then we may find that It moves us in forms that are authentic, individual, awesome, and awakening. It creates ritual actions which contain, express, direct, and dose those previously unmanageable archetypal energies to consciousness (Whitmont 1982, pp. 235–257). The ensuing ceremonies can become acts of reverence; they serve as an incarnation bridge across which the hitherto repressed can move toward consciousness (Perera 1986).

Ceremonial forms encompass two realms—that of concrete, literal action and that of the transpersonal meanings underlying action. The ceremonies arise in the transition space (Winnicott's term) between personal and transpersonal, and are analogous to reconciling images. Indeed, they are magic-level precursors of image and word—actions arising from the authentic stratum of the body-Self before it has been separated into inside and outside. And the enactments become symbolic only when the actor and therapist witness them in order to participate more consciously, to discover their meaning/intention and the possibilities they create for a new relationship betweeen personal ego and the transpersonal ritualized material. Ceremonies usually have a potent transformative effect on the consciousness of the individuals who create/discover them. For while ritual enactments mediate transpersonal energies into life in forms that are assimilable, and thus seem to transform the energies themselves, they also strengthen and enrich the ego in relation to those numinous energies.

In my personal life an energy left on the periphery of consciousness because it was taboo was aggression. My family was ideologically pacifist, yet its individuals were intense and passionate. The conflict betweeen virtuous repression of warlike actions on the one hand, and rampant eruptions of anger or its more subtle forms of withholding and "shunning" on the other posed many problems that marked my childhood. Anger had no safe forms of expression. Not surprisingly, I developed a fascination with, and aversion to, power and aggression.

As we all know, aggression is an aspect of raw libido—in the words of Dylan Thomas, "the force that through the green fuse drives the flower . . . that blasts the roots of trees . . . [that] drives the water through the rocks [and] drives my red blood . . . [and] is my destroyer."[1] We speak of the rage to live, the fury of creation. Yet we fear aggression. We know that it destroys, and are glad when we discover who and what can survive our attacks to release us into the process of dialogue with another in a shared and safe-enough, real world.

Clinically, aggression has been seen as an inborn drive balanced by Eros (Freud) and as a means to claim security in response to threats against survival and/or self-esteem (Kohut). Jungians see it as an aspect of the Self. Even bravado and explosive rage have their roots in the guardianship of the child's embattled narcissistic Self. Icy, cutting-off hate guards the schizoid stronghold from intimacies that once were dangerous. In describing aggression we distinguish between undirected rage, an autonomic nervous system reaction that tends to stay connected to and compensate for feelings of helplessness, and more conscious and focused, effective anger. But the transformation from the first to the second often entails a deep learning process and ritual initiation before it can come to consciousness.[2]

The problem of integrating raw aggressive libido is severe with borderlines. When identified with their destructive energy, splitting off primitive fusion capacities as too endangering before terrifying, withholding, or sadistic parent figures, they can be like destructive machines. On the other hand, for many years of analysis they can be so split from their asssertive urges that they fall into unhearing rage or despair if these are interpreted. The slow integration of aggressive energy posits a major therapeutic issue in every preoedipal case, but it is exacerbated with borderline levels, where possession by split and hence overwhelming affects is diagnostic.

Profoundly, aggression is the Self's guardian force, the defender of biological and personal integrity, a drive essential for survival, if we are to grow beyond the passive dependency of symbiosis, and for creativity. It is an energy forced into and through the body-ego, which is thus aroused to function as the Self's warrior, serving Its order and transpersonal meaning and purpose to support individual existence, desire, independence, and mastery. (Jung, writing of Ares, the fiery god of war, calls this god "the principle of individuation in the strict sense" (Jung 1967, para 176). The spiritual/martial arts teach this sacred relation to aggressive energy.) Yet even as it confirms individual autonomony, aggression may endanger others and society. "The internal logic of Force . . . [consists in] prov[ing] itself only by surpassing boundaries— even its own boundaries and those of its *raison d'etre*" (Dumezil 1970, p. 106). The arousal of aggression must, therefore, be complemented by its inhibition; the two together produce disciplined application, or mastery.

Valuing the power drive is commonplace to most men in our culture, while most women need to come to this knowledge—not merely through assertiveness training, though that can help. Through initiatory encounters with this libido stream, we can learn the value of using even coldness, hot rage, manipulation—all our "dragon powers" (Camille Maurine's term)—with confidence, joy, and in reverential service toward the Self from which they flow. Equally we can learn limits that do not imply ineffectuality or masochism.

I wish to relate a myth of the ritual arousal and containment of aggression, and also to describe some ceremonies integrating the flow of this primal libido—ceremonies created in individual analytic work.

The tales of the Celtic warrior, Cuchulainn, present us with archetypal patterns that circumambulate the problem of aggression. They cover the arousing of the drive through identification with its animal level and the ritual claiming of weapons; the test of the initiatory combat; and finally a series of rites that enable the beserk warrior to be detoxified for his return to court.

Among the Celts, heroism operated as a social function. There were male and female warriors, even warrior goddesses, who trained heroes like Cuchulainn in the skills of battle. Using the myth of a male figure does not, therefore, preclude the necessary existence of this function in both men and women.

Identification with the Animal

Cuchulainn was a devine hero, thrice-born, and one of his fathers was the multifaceted god, Lugh.[3] He earned his power name as a six-year-old boy when he killed the tribal smith–shaman's invincible hound (with his bare hands—or in another version by tossing his playing ball down the dog's throat). This hound, said Culann, the smith,

> guarded my life and my honour . . . a valued servant, my hound . . . . He was shield and shelter for our goods and herds. He guarded all our beasts at home or out in the fields . . . [without this hound] my life is a waste and my household like a desert."
>
> "That doesn't matter," the boy said. "I will be your hound and guard yourself and your beasts. And I will guard all Murtheimne Plain. No herd or flock will leave my care unknown to me."
>
> "Cuchulainn shall be your name, The Hound of Culann," Cathbad [the druid] said. (Kinsella 1970, p. 82)

So the young warrior took on the identity of totem guardian of his tribe's people, herds, and territory, having proved his incorporation of the instinctual powers of "the savage hound" by overcoming it. He was, thenceforth, possessed by and in possession of the animal's invincible force, which was mediated into the service of human life through his activity. He could guard the tribe's turf, in touch with instinctive territoriality and the aggressive drive to defend it.

The theme of identification with the animal is frequent in analysand rituals, especially when the individual has little capacity to claim psychological space and/or is masochistic—without access to instinctual assertion except when it is turned against the ego as self-hate. Then ritualized enactment of the psychoid-animal level often occurs to enable the animal's natural territoriality and outgoing aggression to be claimed. Through repeated enactments and kinesthetically based active imaginations of lynx or lion, bear or dragon (depending on the animal-like quality a dream and/or the body-Self presents as corresponding to the energy needed), the ego gains access to repressed or dormant powers (and a sense of totem-guardian spirit). Such rituals are not unlike the dances in which tribal warriors mime the animals of prey to gain access to their hunting prowess.

Possession by the powers, in total identification with the guardian spirit or aggressive affect, was once considered essential for the survival of the tribe and a model of heroic behavior. As Eliade has written, "A man became a redoubtable warrior by magically assimilating the behavior of a carnivore . . . he ceased to be a man, he was the carnivore itself" (1972, p. 7). Such identification was not then considered pathological. We, however, would call the possession at best shamanic, or a temper tantrum, or clinically, a dissociation either borderline or narcissistic.

Cuchulainn had the gift of possession by aggression and, through initiation into the warrior function, he strengthened his capacity to lose his secular identity and to be totally and sacredly given over to the hero's light. "Not only was he a ferocious and invincible warrior, possessed by the *furor heroicus*, he had cast off all humanity . . . no longer felt bound by the laws and customs of men" (Eliade 1972, p. 7). He went beserk. His seizure, called a "warp spasm," filled him with a quantum of archetypal energy and enabled him to become the incarnation of an onrush of divine fury.

Descriptions of Cuchulainn in his warp spasm reveal that he carried "the stigmata of valor" (Dumezil 1970, p. 162). In battle furor he was transformed into a holy terror,

> into a monstrous thing, hideous and shapeless, unheard of. His shanks and his joints, every knuckle and angle and organ from head to foot, shook like a tree in flood or a reed in the stream. His body made a furious twist inside his skin so that his feet and shins and knees switched to the rear and his heels and calves switched to the front. . . . On his head the temple-sinews

stretched to the nape of his neck, each mighty, immense, measureless knob as big as the head of a month-old child. His face and features became a red bowl: he sucked one eye so deep into his head that a wild crane couldn't probe it onto his cheek out of the depths of his skull; the other eye fell out along his cheek. His mouth was weirdly distorted: his cheek peeled back from his jaws until the gullet appeared, his lungs and liver flapped in his mouth and throat, his lower jaw struck the upper a lion-killing blow, and fiery flakes large as ram's fleece reached his mouth from his throat. His heart boomed loud in his breast like the baying of a watch-dog at its feed or the sound of a lion among bears. Malignant mists and spurts of fire—the torches of Badb—flickered red in the vaporous clouds that rose boiling above his head, so fierce was his fury. The hair of his head twisted like a tangle of red thornbush stuck in a gap; if a royal apple tree with all its kingly fruit were shaken above him, scarce an apple would reach the ground but each would be spiked on a bristle of his hair as it stood up on his scalp with rage. The hero-halo rose out of his brow, long and broad as a warrior's whetstone, long as a snout, and he went mad rattling his shields, urging on his charioteer and harassing the hosts. Then tall and thick, steady and strong, high as the mast of a noble ship, rose up from the dead centre of his skull a straight spout of black blood darkly and magically smoking like the smoke from a royal hostel when a king is coming to be cared for at the close of a winterday . . . . In that style then, he drove out to find his enemies. (Kinsella 1970, pp 150–51)

In battle rage the warrior became the dwelling place of the war god, exultant, beserk in his "biophysical seizure" (Neumann 1955, p. 5). The hot, fiery core of archetypal rage erupted ecstatically into him enabling incredible feats—like holding off the armies of all of Ireland single-handedly. (When such mystical *furor* is combined with his skill at arms, the hero is invincible indeed, and can only be killed when he himself has commited offenses against the rules governing his destiny.)

We all know this place of the thin membrane between the personal psyche and more archaic layers of the objective psyche. In modern jargon we say it is where we have been narcissistically wounded and/or are defensively rigid and split that we are permeable to such ferocious seizures. Then we may find ourselves unconsciously in identity with the warrior god or sacred animal to defend inner values and/or to define areas of the Self—even when they are not presently very threatened. Such rages can even become addictive, an automatic, manic, or grandiose defense that fills our being and prevents our feeling loss, hurt, or fear (Kohut, 1977, pp. 122–25). Indeed, we may come to crave the seizure's ecstatic claiming of us and become habituated to blissful possession by rage's adrenalin. This is a far cry from the conscious claiming of power. Such outbursts of rage are associated with preoedipal psycho-pathology. Although neither marked with the "hero's light" nor usually able to use our power effectively, we may feel and act beserk and be truly frightening—often while experiencing ourselves as helpless victims.

Claiming the Weapons

Cuchulainn had the gift of his warp spasm, the refinement of training, and the blessing of his initiation. His ritual claiming of arms came about on a day druid-fated to bring enduring fame for mighty acts (albeit a short life). On that day the boy went to the king and demanded that he be given his weapons. He then tested each weapon in the king's storage "and not one piece survived. . . . . [So] he was given Conchobor's own weapons at last" (Kinsella 1970, pp. 84–85). This claiming of the king's personal weapons as his own implies that transpersonal libido requires adequate tools of guardianship which must come from the ruling conscious dominant of the Self. Only those weapons, since they do not shatter, can embody Its force. They serve—like transitional objects between Self and ego—as the incarnation patterns for power, enabling transpersonal aggression to enter life effectively. This too is borne out in modern analytic rituals.

Many of us suffered early damage to the instinct of guarding aggression.[4] We have lost conscious touch with the Self's power, and use projective identification (extrusion of an unconscious and taboo energy into another, so that we relate to it as if it were external to ourselves) or either passive-aggressive or masochistic tools that do not mediate it adequately to protect us in the outer world or as pattern forms of strength to reflect assertiveness back to consciousness. Equally useless are eruptions out of split-off parts of the psyche (i.e., rages out of complexes). The split parts cannot sustain the transpersonal, Self-granted energy flow, and in their defensive weakness fail us, just as the lesser weapons failed Cuchulainn, for they are not from the Self, the center of wholeness and integrity.

We learn what is adequate by trying out our tools, testing our strength to find its limits and what best serves to express and sustain the Self's thrust. Finding such effective means of empowerment is invariably part of therapy. I have seen many rituals for the claiming of weapons. They include *enactments* (of powerful human and animal dream figures), *focus on body and breathing to move from helpless rage to effective assertion* (reawakening the pelvic bowl is crucial, since it is a center of energy and a vital transition area between lower and upper body, between grounding and going forth), *ritual actions (and dances) of aggression against the imaged abusers* (such as kicking, pounding, stabbing, twisting, shouting, squeezing, biting, stomping, shredding), *repetitive soundings and verbalizations of negation* (hate, refusal, dismissal), *confrontation, and self-affirmation.* Individuals also invent or find personally effective means of claiming their aggression (tearing the towel that has come to symbolize parental suffocation, attacking a pile of old letters or their surrogate, stacks of newspaper). The rituals of therapy itself can be challenged as forms against which to try one's power, and temporarily destroyed without destroying the analysis. To refuse a handshake or the payment of a fee, to arrive late or storm out of a session, to abuse the therapist verbally, all help to claim arms and test one's own strength.

One example of a ceremonial claiming of weapons in analysis occurred after a man dreamt of unknown men attacking a fort while he tried to call for help. He identified with the fortressed victims in his intellectual, rather schizoid defensive style. When he enacted the ego figure, it was with cool, stoic bravado covering helplessness. When he enacted the attackers, he was strangely ineffectual—wide-eyed, with his hands behind him, crouching low. (I thought of the way infants use their eyes for vigilant guarding— the body concomitant of the paranoid position—when limbs are not yet coordinated, and there are no teeth.) We spent some time making the ineffectuality conscious, and he finally asked me for a suggestion that would better embody the attackers, as if needing permission to expand his own repertoire. I asked him how his cherished and lusty infant son might express it. He puffed his breath and blew it out. The action began to move his energy to mild assertion. I asked him to intensify and aim the blowing and, finally, to let it sound. He let out a percussive "pfuh." Encouraged, he studied his hands, which still hung limp at his sides. Suddenly he grabbed a small stick club from the sand tray shelves, and held it a while feeling it in his hands. Then he began to grip it with authority, using its power to teach his body a focused, aggressive posture. He had created his own ritual to claim arms. As he practiced it with variations over the following weeks, it released a flow of clogged assertive energy into his life, empowering him to claim his position more forcefully in many situations.

First Combat

In the Irish myth, after having claimed his weapons, Cuchulainn went forth to "look for fight." Outside the tribal boundaries he sought and challenged the scourges of the Ulstermen, three sons of the woman

Nechta. Their names were "For Deceitfulness," "The Swallow," and "The Cunning" (Kinsella 1970, p. 87). The first would not fall if not killed at the first thrust, demanding full power from his adversary. The second trod on water like a bird, defying gravity. The third was so wily he had never fallen to any weapon. Cuchulainn killed all three as his initiatory ordeal required (Dumezil 1970, p. 11). "Then a scream rose up behind them from the mother" (Kinsella 1970, p. 89).

Psychologically the three sons of the mother are Shadow figures embodying indirect aggression. They represent the consequences of inertia and of one's early bonds and abandonment fears inhibiting effective, outgoing assertion. As long as we are uncertain, unsettled, and indefinite, we cannot know our own boundaries, weight or direct capacities. As long as we need to feel merged with another (or with mother), we cannot fully find and define ourselves. The triplicity (as well as the names of the adversaries) implies repeated confrontation of the problem in its various guises. And we know direct combat is often necessary psychologically, not only to claim fully one's individual autonomy and power, but also to cut finally the bonds of a destructive and/or infantilizing relationship or to make a stand against an abuser or something evil. These trials often require the implacable ruthlessness of the Self that stands for personal integrity, marking the initiation of the guardian warrior function into full power. Separations from parent figures, divorce, and abortion can all be living examples of such initiatory combat. So can standing one's ground emphatically against a therapist and getting a change of hour or a revised interpretation.

On the other side, killing off three sons of Nechta also implies that the young warrior released their capacities into his consciousness; he could now be deliberately deceitful, weightless, and cunning. With this enlarged repertoire of aggressive means he became more than a straightforward sword-and-spear wielder. He became also a clever warrior, finding the most effective means for every task. This is important psychologically in the initial phase of claiming assertion after we have turned from old modes of passive aggression. Too readily at this point we have only contempt for strategies not directly confrontational. Like Cuchulainn we need to take our adversaries' heads, their essences, into our chariot. We need to claim the old, indirect powers consciously in the service of direct guardian assertion.

Disidentification from Possession

Having claimed and used aroused aggression, there is another problem for Cuchulainn. For, while "this transfiguring rage is in itself a good thing . . . [since it] will permit him to conquer his enemies, . . . [it] is as troublesome as it is precious: the child is not its master, on the contrary, it possesses him" (Dumezil 1970, p. 135). The warrior returning to his tribe from the initiatory battle, swollen with transpersonal power, endangers his own kin. He constitutes a public menace.

Cuchulainn's myth gives us a profound set of rituals for containing and transforming the wild compulsion of archetypal rage once it has been fully roused and claimed by the warrior. It includes a *rite de sortie*, an exit from the initiation.[5] Thus it offers a pattern for disidentifying from possession and transforming archaic rage—for mediating aggression into communal life so that it is "available when combat demands," but "held in reserve" in order not to imperil the collective kin group (Dumezil 1970, p. 10).

There are four stages to this ritual transformation in the myth. While all of the stages occur in the individual ceremonies of psychotherapy I have seen, they are rarely in such neat sequence. Rather they tend to overlap, and invariably some aspects of the third stage are present or created at the beginning. In the myth the first stage consists of the possessed hero's herding and catching of wild deer and swans; the second of his confrontation by the ritually naked queen and other women; the third of his repeated immersion by other warriors in vessels of cold water; and the fourth of his return to the court.

Herding the Wild Animals

Having passed his initiation as a warrior, Cuchulainn ordered his charioteer to turn toward home. When they passed a herd of wild deer,

> Cuchuliann said: "Which would the men of Ulster like brought in, a dead or a live [stag]?"
> "A live one would startle them more," the charioteer said. "It isn't everyone who could do it. Every man has brought home a dead one. You can't catch them alive,"
> "I can," Cuchuliann said. (Kinsella 1970, p. 90)

And, grandly, to prove his power, he tracked and herded one great stag into a bog where he captured it unscathed. He "fix[ed] him such an eye that he [didn't] dare to stir," "flung a little stone at the birds . . . with his feat of the stunning-shot" (ibid., p.91) and also roped living swans to his chariot. Symbolically this action implies that the warrior is more than equal to the creatures of the wild. While he particpates in their nature, he is also master over them, incarnating the Stag-Herdsman God himself.[6] Like shamans the world over, he ropes his power animals to show that he has begun the process of harnessing their wild, instinctive energy to transmit it to the tribe through his own person.

Uncontrolled rage leads us all over and splits the ego's capacity to focus intention. It can dismember purpose, relationship, and identity. It makes chaos (Stewart 1986). The initiated warrior uses his will and skill to gather together to focus one-pointedly, not to split. He does not hunt down and kill off his wild nature for he needs its power, but lets it run free to discover its range, finally riding it to a gentler pace. He attunes himself to its energy curve. Not separated from the potent forces of the wild, he rules over them and can use the focused instinctual to enhance his capacity for aggression—as well as to show off his sacral stature.

This image is a fertile one for the therapeutic process as analysand and analyst seek to tame "uncontrolled, and at first uncontrollable primordial instinct" (Jung 1953, par. 256) once it is aroused. One woman in analysis expressed her experience of the unherded and uncontrollable:

> I have this energy . . .in me, and it feels like it will burst me if I . . . don't keep the lid on. I have no form for it. Maybe if it . . . destroyed everything in your office, that would be a beginning. . . . Otherwise I feel like I need to explode or to turn into concrete.

Her passion had no form through which to reveal, express, and reflect itself, and she knew nothing about herding. She felt caught between the poles of violent, chaotic explosiveness and the deadness of concrete—wild energy and rigid inhibition. This analysand, after a period of radical student politics, had married and settled uneasily into compliance disturbed by bouts of tearing her husband's clothes and slashing the furniture. She was also overeating and depressed. Not until her dreams brought up the image of a child who had been kept in a trunk and never learned to use the toilet did she begin to acknowledge and then accept her underlying, undirected rage. And then she was afraid it would wreck my office. Ceremonially staying with the energy and letting it move her right arm while she sat in her chair gave her a first sense that she could relate to it within a viable, witnessed, and containing form. She then enacted the numbly passive concrete. Over a period of several weeks, she found that the energy was able to penetrate the concrete. It first erupted in an involuntary spasm that shook her left foot, and that night she dreamt that she was cuttting free an animal trapped in that foot.

Again and again we find that superego *shoulds* are irrelevant, inflammatory, or crippling to the energy of possession. It needs to be free to run, to abreact in the safety of the ritual analytic container, expressed in mutually agreed-upon enactments involving sounds, gestures, actions, images,or words that do not destroy it or the actors/witnesses themselves. This implies bringing consciousness to the animal level, bringing our vision to magic-level awareness. A woman's dream imaged this as two huge horses running toward each other; as she watched them, she could see the energy of each as a powerful spiral. The spirals turned and slowly became the iris and pupils of two eyes. This woman had been struggling to relate to an inner conflict between rage and caring without resorting to her animus/superego definitions of appropriate outcome, and was beginning to sense that bearing the conflict in awareness as its energies swept through her would bring insight organic to it from that individual pattern of wholeness Jungians call the Self.

Ruling over the animal level by turning toward it implies sensing emotional events in full awareness, tuning in to emotions and becoming aware of the rhythmic curve of their energy patterns. This requires a capacity to perceive with sensitive emotional and kinesthetic awareness. A dream image expresses this taming of the wild affect through the refined perception we generally reserve for gentler energies:

Dream: *I see a group of tribesmen dancing toward me. They are in a frenzy to kill, with their energies roused for war. It's frightening. I have a . . . bowl of strawberries and give one to each of them as they rush up to . . . me. They suddenly become calm, and look like my neighbors.*

The dreamer was beginning to recognize that he could apply his capacity to savor "the sweetness of the berry, all of Spring in one bite" equally to the passions of anger that terrified him.

To witness the power drive with another, specifically the analyst on whom the Self's vision and acceptance is projected, is a potent means of incarnating and catching its wild and fleeting affects. For then they exist in a shared space—"feel real because you see me like this, too, and it's a real towel I am tearing up"—as one analysand put it after her fury erupted. Witnessed together, the affect was not merely "crazy" or deniable, and she began to herd it into her consciousness.

To touch unruly affects with reasonable limitations or a weighty amplification or interpretation can serve, further, to bring them to earth, still alive, without undo repression. And simple descriptive naming, a common analytic practice, can function to attach instinctual emotions and behavior to the ego's chariot. (However, this works only if an analysand has already found the value of aggression and come to enjoy its sense of power. Before that the label of "hostile" or "angry" may send consciousness of the instinctive into defiance or despair and flight from a feared identification with what it considers negative.)

Just as Cuchuliann fixed the stag with his eye and managed the beast so it would not turn on his charioteer when he went to gather the swans, so analyst and analysand need to manage the aggressive instinct so it does not destroy them or the analysis as they seek its functions and meanings, allowing the energy to find its own limit organically. One ritual use of "dialogue drawing" (Finley 1975) can make this organic curve of energy clear. When the analysand claims the right to destroy every form the analyst draws, this is visible evidence of destructive aggression; invariably the initial pleasure of this single-minded negation runs out of steam. The same diminution often occurs in phases of the negative transference when the analysand verbally destroys every interpretation. In both cases, of course, it is necessary that the analyst persist in creating new forms and interpretations to manifest the process of inexhaustible life which survives. (This creates security for the analysand, who discovers both an organic limitation to the energy of destructiveness and a creative life force that while opposed, still survives. This discovery is often surprising and intensely numinous; it is analogous to "showing the breasts," the stage which follows in Cuchilainn's ritual.)

Cuchulainn, returning to his tribe, "a wild stag behind the chariot, a swan-flock fluttering above, and the three heads of Nechta Scene's sons inside the chariot," was quite a sight. He was still imbued with his sacred initiatory infusion of power. He came towards his own people full of numinous "grandiosity," calling out for a man to fight or he would "spill the blood of everyone in [the] court" (Kinsella 1970, pp. 91–92).

Feminine Confrontation

While such excesses are necessary, like the ritual transgression of a taboo, to gain the godlike power required for initiated life, and while they are useful when used and focused on behalf of the tribe, they are a menace within the community. The tribe's solution to Cuchulainn's excess is one that farmers know. Just as the dairyman puts his cows into the field with a maddened bull, so Ulster's king decreed, "Naked women to him! . . . [And] the woman of Emain went forth with Mugain the wife of Con'chobor mac Nessa [the king] at their head, and they stripped their breasts at him. 'These are the warriors you must struggle with today,' Mugain said" (Kinsella 1970, p. 92). The story tells us Cuchulainn "hid his countenance."

One way to tame focused, transpersonal aggression is to confront it with another basic drive. The ensuing conflict disrupts one-pointed seizure by a single pattern of behavior, and begins to move the conflict within the warrior. It shifts away from outright possession. This opens the second stage in the taming of aggression.

Cuchulainn was confronted by his own beginnings before the mothers of the tribe and the queen, incarnate Mother Goddess of the land on which his tribe lived. Breasts offered to the rampant destroyer caused him to hide his face, diverting his focus and checking his phallic rush toward combat. Perhaps they reminded him of primal succor, softness, and food, being those vulnerable organs that once sustained him, provoking and surviving his first bites of infantile fury. They may even have evoked memories of the preverbal inhibitions that met those first onslaughts—teaching him restraint or he would have lost the breast. Here need and nurturance were set against destructiveness; Cuchulainn began to feel inner conflict and to envision a place to go when he could leave his possession.

A Vietnam veteran expressed this moment in therapy when he realized that reopening the terrifying emotions of war might lead to his murder of the therapist whom he had come, with surprise, to cherish. He dreamed of a killer loose in elementary school. Over time he needed reassurance, through much testing of the analytic vessel and the analyst's strength and compassion, that both he and the therapist, supported by the Self and in the ritual container, were strong enough to witness and confront his killer without rage, panic, or revulsion destroying the therapeutic relationship.

As the defeated wolf turns its neck, avoiding death in its acknowledgement of the victor's power, as the Kwakiutl serving woman dances naked with a corpse before the frenzied cannibal-society initiates, so the queen and other women ritually reveal the naked power of *yin*. Their willingness to sacrifice is an affirmation of life's flow beyond the heroic individual's destructiveness. In awesome confrontation, they meet *yang* aggression with its equally powerful opposite—inexhaustible nurturance, receptive vulnerability, and feminine beauty. The women accept the warrior's aggression without combat, without desire to possess or to overcome Cuchulainn's power, and with a touch of humor. Their gesture of revelation does not suggest masochistic turning of the other cheek or weakness and humiliation, as so many analysands in the throes of identification with aggression (or the aggressor) fear. Rather it suggests equal power of a different order—the power of what receives and sustains new life, flowing forth to permit survival beyond the warrior's destructiveness, the power to feel empathy for the person behind the rage (who being identified with the passion does not usually even know the terror of the ruptured or inflated ego within). This emphatic wisdom sees the possessed one as a divinely (or demonically) burdened wild child to be met and held and returned to the community's embrace. And it is the queen who later gives the initiate his new garments, a new identity marking the completion of his ritual and the integration of the aggressive function within the order of the whole.

The perception of such maternal concern (the "good breast") in anayltic practice can ultimately evoke or create and model a vision of acceptance rather than battle, but initially it confuses the single-minded thrust of the *yang* aggressor. (Analysands who are accustomed to battles for power are often initially upset in therapy by the lack of a power attitude in the therapist.) At the right time such receptivity can begin to loosen the other's identification with automatic, adversarial fury. The radical opposition of acceptance can bring about the remembrance and even the creation of relational needs, to begin to turn the rage possession toward consideration of its own behavior, its need for an adversary, and its need for an alternative to automatic combativeness. With one male analysand, a man of many brawls, the analyst learned to move her chair toward him when he began to rage and shout. Eventually he gave her his gun permit, a gesture of trust in the possibility of being heard and of receiving justice as well as a commitment to relational process. On the other hand, at the wrong time, such mirroring can infantilize and deflate. Then, by refusing to meet aggression with firmness, or by inappropriate acceptance or revelation of one's own vulnerability, a therapist or partner or parent can prematurely abandon or tie up the other's claiming of aggression in a cruel double-bind.

The ritual nakedness of the women further indicates the probability of a sexual initiation for the returning warrior. In ritualized lovemaking with the queen the mad-bull warrior can be contained, his *yang*, phallic passion and its fertility used in a sacred marriage rite to benefit the tribe—an ancient form of turning swords into plowshares. Cuchulainn possessed is the carrier of sacred energy, potent enough to bed with the queen/Goddess as her ritual partner.[7] At the height of focused passion, omnipotent rage is thus converted by Her into potent sexuality.

Since lovemaking can express and contain aggression,[8] this is a time honored way to release and channel it (and certainly one source of erotic acting-out in the transference[9]). Here we come to the various points of intersection between the aggressive and the erotic—the molten energies that fuel rape and sadomasochism, and the potential joys of war within a sexual relationship. Many of the activities described in texts of *ars amatoria* (from the *Kama Sutra* to *The Joy of Sex*) call upon the mix of battling and bedding that allows aggression to play itself out in erotic wrestling, biting, scratching, and binding. These convert combat into shared passion, shared sport. We know also that aggression may arouse the erotic as well as test its virility. Quarreling between lovers can be a prelude to lovemaking, creating the separation necessary to evoke intense desire and a powerful conjunction. (As an ancient Sumerian hymn to Inanna puts it, "From the starting of the quarrel came the lover's desire" (Wolkstein and Kramer 1986 p. 133).) Cuchulainn himself was the darling of all women of Ulster. Courtly ladies valued their proven knights as much as contemporary girls adore their football heros.

The erotic is a passion equivalent to aggression. Thus, eventually, the impersonal aggressive and the impersonal erotic need to meet within the analysand to find an interior, organic balance. Since the ecstatic can be triggered from both sides, and each can enjoy their own and the other's display, one instinctual possession can ritually meet and balance or deflect another.[10] An example from an analytic session with a woman who was pounding the couch in rage brings this out clearly. As she moved her fists, she began to visualize all the people in her life she would like to smash. She stopped finally, upset by her feelings of love for her husband when she imaged him among the men she was ritually killing. After a moment of confusion, the active imagination became more erotic, and she felt herself naked before him and all of the men, taking pleasure in the revelation of her female body. For the first time before another she felt enhanced rather than diminished in her body-ego and connected to Aphrodite.[11] Power supported her sexual identity and she claimed her power erotically.

In the Irish tale Cuchulainn, son of the God Lugh, was confronted by the ritually naked queen, tribal embodiment of the Goddess of the Land. She was not destroyed by archetypal, outgoing, spear-pointed energy, but, as Earth itself receives the sun, She received and enjoyed and was fructified by it.[12] For the individual possessed by aggression, this suggests the possibility of meeting the possession ritually with feminine, *yin* consciousness to awaken and confirm the concomitant joys of exhibiting and claiming power relationally. When aggression is witnessed and received within a relationship, a new pleasure may enter consciousness and its awareness separates the actor from possession, creating the psychological space to feel *about* the drive, to gain perspective, no longer completely identified with it.

Usually we assume, following Klein, that remorse is the inhibiting factor; and it is vital in limiting aggression. Within the context of this myth, however, remorse is impossible,[13] and clinical experience too suggests that pleasure can serve as well, although culturally we are usually forbidden the pleasure of our aggressions. We are not supposed to enjoy our rages unless they are righteous and in good cause; we can take pleasure in righteousness but not usually in exhibitions of power or sadistic, destructive urges (except in sport). The queen's fearless exhibitionism before Cuchulainn's aggression and the fact that she receives the aroused warrior's potency in good-humored and erotic terms reveal her appreciation of exhibitionistic and relational pleasure inherent in a rampant expression of power. This is not to say that women like to be raped, a bizarre rationalization of defensive degradation and not at all what Cuchulainn was about. But it suggests that the queen, who embodies the strength and potent fertility of the earth, is aroused to pleasure in the ritual marriage by a male partner strong enough to exhibit and embody the Lightning and Solar God's fiery passion.

Exhibitionism accepted, a sense of value restores to the possessed and alienated ego. Fear, vulnerability, and inferiority are compensated by the manifestation of a passionate, transpersonal force in a personal, embodied display. Having an audience turns the wild explosion of aggressive affect into the less destructive pleasure of a grand presentation of strength, a show, which expresses the transpersonal personally. Thus ceremonial acceptance of aggression inhibits rampant destructiveness and fosters the development of skills that can be shown off, supporting the conversion of aggressive energy into a desire for creative mastery. Sport and knightly games exhibit disciplined aggression and win esteem for both the players and those kinsfolk they represent.

An "almost joyful destruction of everything received from the therapist" (Kernberg 1984, p. 145) is typical of borderline levels of the psyche, and such instinctual gratification is part of the taming process of therapy.[14] In itself, however, affective discharge does not produce integration and transformation; it merely leads to addictive perpetuation of the problem. Seen as mere "acting out" and interpreted reductively to clarify the sadist-parent and victim-child roles within the transference, the goal and meaning and valuable pleasure of the behavior itself is neglected, and transformation is impossible. One woman presented herself systematically destroying every attempt of her analyst to understand or interpret. Her caustic disparagements included the therapist's capacity, training, lack of empathy, intelligence, and appearance. She flaunted her perception that a chance encounter with a nurse had given her more help than two years of work. At the same time, if the analyst silently contemplated her attacks, she critized that or provoked engagement only to disparage its quality again. The ceremony of lure, confront, and destroy went on for several months, during which all interpretation and exploration of her problems was thwarted. When finally the curve of attacking energy had somewhat run its course, the analyst was able to be heard and to verbalize her perception of the pleasure with which the analysand had been enacting a cat toying with a mouse. With sudden clarity, the woman recognized that she had never had "anyone there to battle with before," and she acknowledged the joy of her sadism as an expression of life within safe relationship.

An aggressive seizure ordinarily wipes out ego consciousness. But when an analyst points out to an analysand at the appropriate moment, "some part of you loves your anger—loves showing me your power," a consciousness within the individual is posited which can relate with feeling to what otherwise possesses him or her. Like humor, this offers the possibility of a perspective on the demonic beyond blind identification with its power. As one man put it proudly, "I even begin to like the action as well as the triumph. It's *me* asserting and announcing *me*." However, such remarks as "you love controlling me, destroying everything I give/say, criticizing, insulting me . . . " should be made only if the therapist can indeed embrace the aggression, having successfully metabolized both fear and defensive anger.

To withstand the transpersonal energy in an attack requires a companion or therapist to have worked through power issues, so that the aggression can be received—not just into some impersonal therapeutic vessel, but into the personal and transpersonal relationship that is analysis. Often this means into the therapist's inner or kinesthetic body space as well, where perceptions, images, and feelings are processed. This may come easier to a woman's body sense than a man's, or it may be a matter of typology or kinesthetic (rather than visual or auditory) processing. There are many ways to support such receptivity, but the most important is that a companion or therapist have worked through her or his own fear and rage in order to stand disidentified from parental complex threats to the inner child. Then the raging and inflated analysand will be less likely to constellate personal fears of destruction by a more powerful other. To be able to respect the pleasure of an analysand's arousal depends also on the psychology of the particular therapist as it intersects with that of each particular client.

As always, when dealing with potentially overwhelming affects, ritual "transitional objects" can help. If the analysand expresses rage in some ritual form—active imagination, non-threatening physical enactment (dancing, pounding, kicking, tearing—the ceremonies of Bioenergetics), or verbal display—it is easier to witness, for the therapist's person is somewhat buffered from receiving the full thrust directly. It helps, too, to remember that negative transference itself is a transitional object. It is a ritual drama in which the analyst lends her or himself to play roles as a presently triggering object on which old rages can be vented. Images also are buffers as well as guides; the therapist's own ritual, but silent and usually unshared evocation of images of the rage, the one possessed, and a receiving vessel for the aggression (a transpersonal one that supports the work and cannot be destroyed) may also be helpful to mediate the potent energy into relational, analytic space. One therapist I know uses his own arm, which he places ritually across his solar plexus, creating a safe haven for his imagined, vulnerable, inner child when an angry woman reminds him of his mother's animus. Then he can more readily open his own anima to receive the analysand's fury without defensive retaliation. Another carefully works to recognize the symbolic images evoked by her own responses and the analysand's affects both within and after the sessions. This gives her animus something to do that prevents its defensive disruption of the analysand's therapeutic space. Another colleague invokes the magic of a crystal, which he takes into his hand when a rage possession comes at him from a client. Still another images the rage as lightning and witnesses it striking the earth—a picture almost precisely analogous to that of Cuchulainn's lightning received by the queen/Goddess of earth. Most of us also read the literature on borderline and narcisisstic rage, using collective thoughts to buffer ourselves. Since we are not of the queen's transpersonal stature, we must find our individual ways to her capacity for acceptance of the person within the possession.

In ritual marriage the queen receives the phallic thrust of Cuchulainn's fury. There the solar-aggressive-hot libido can serve its generative function. In the analytic analogue, instead of acting out erotically or any other way, therapists can allow their own *yin*, right-brain, image-creating consciousness to be fructified. Often the first product of fertilization is conversion of the fear of aggressive power into reverence for its numinosity. This radical change in perception redirects the fear toward the transpersonal dimension to which it belongs; it permits reception of the *tremendum* as if it were a god and the person as trans-personally possessed.

Not only can such an attitude in the analyst provide a model for the analysand's learning a new and noncompulsive, reverent relation to the possessing power, it also suggests that a transpersonally fructified process may start in the analysand. The process is based upon the body/Self's capacity to receive and witness the numinous, generative power of archetypal affect-drive energy (within the safety of the larger ritual vessel of the analysis). Eventually this reception will be the seed of a new kind of ego consciousness for the analysand, in a process not un-like the fructification through which mystics were impregnated by the divine bridegroom and their virgin wombs became mothers to the inspiring Spirit (see Meister Eckart's *Sermons*). For as the fiery numi-nosum is known (in the Biblical sense) and held and attended, it gener-ates images of itself which mediate between the transpersonal libido stream and the limited, personal ego. This assures nothing less than the creation of a symbolic attitude, a newly born capacity for conscious-ness.

Immersion in the Three Vats

The problem of containment, however, is not readily solved when deal-ing with primal libido. Cuchulainn was a solar and lightning power, and even at rest his heat was tremendous (he was said to melt the snow around him for 30 feet), comparable to the divine heat generated in yogic meditation and shamanic seizures. In the myth, the newly initiated hero's excessive heat must be cooled. After his confrontation by the women:

> Immediately the warriors of Emain seized him and plunged him in a vat of cold water. The vat burst asunder about him. Then he was thrust in another vat and it boiled bubbles the size of fists. He was placed at last in a third vat and warmed it till its heat and cold were equal. Then he got out and Mugain the queen gave him a blue cloak to go round him with a silver brooch on it, and a hooded tunic. And he sat on Conchobor's knee, and that was his seat ever after. (Kinsella 1970, p. 92)

The final phase of ritual cooling is accomplished as the heat accompa-nying his divine ecstasy is modulated sufficiently for Cuchulainn to return to find his secular status.

To be possessed is frightening, even when it is exhilarating; it threatens to blast the ego apart. To be held in an alternative embrace is a haven from the passions that erupt and tear one through and apart. We need as small children to know such holding or our fears of the

Self's powers are terrible, and we deny them to consciousness. A form of "masculine" holding here is essential; Cuchulainn's brothers-in-arms seize the hero and plunge him into vats. These cold vats suggest the limiting factor of reality, which, finally, the hotly possessed one needs to know. This may mean the limits of the analytic frame and relationship—including the analyst's need to guard the saftey of persons and property within his care. The vats may stand for a rational consideration of the reality and limits of past and present situations and personalities, or the consideration of consequences—best approached by thinking through the rage possession/addiction to explore the results of its being acted out.[15] While all of this needs to be coolly considered, the fact of limitations may evoke more fury; the transpersonally possessed individual does not want to suffer any limits imposed, seemingly, from without, and if not yet able to feel compassion or to process consequences rationally may experience any inhibition as adding fuel to the fire. Then with the firmness of "tough love" an analyst or companion must confront the possessed one with the limits of incarnated reality. Such cool reality testing drains off the heat (often by focusing it into battles with the analyst's voice of rationality where it suffers necessary diminishment (cf. Kohut's "transmuting internalizations")) and cleanses the rage possession, ultimately enabling self-discipline and consideration of consequences in the analysand.

Thus the warriors, comrades who have already passed through their initiation and know both the heat and its cooling, are the ones to deal with Cuchulainn at this stage. They catch the initiate and force him to sacrifice his frenzy in order that he may find his place among them as a human being, capable of appropriate, disciplined, and responsible assertion. They hold him with what they already know the aggressive drive is capable of transforming into, repeatedly struggling with the wild energy of his possession alongside of him.[16] They help him to transmute his relation to the furor.

We might also think of the vats as surrogate ego containers, or as esoteric containers of spirit (physical, astral, and etheric forms). But the image of a vessel is one Jungians use for the analytic process itself. That the first vat in the myth does not hold implies that given "talking analysis" form may not suffice to hold the energy of possession—explaining why the use of body therapy is sometimes necessary. There is often initial acting out as Cuchulainn-like power manifests itself: the analysand displaces energy from the container by attacking self or others, attacks the therapeutic bond to prevent dialogue, quits therapy without discussion, drinks before session, or in some other way destroys the possibility of analysis. It is vital that this destruction not be the last word or the analysand will be identified with it. (The analyst may also contribute to the cracking of the vessel by acting out, either erotically or sadistically, through even such small aggressions as discussing a case outside analysis without ritual care and forms. Unless analysts take responsibility for their own Shadow contributions to the rupture, analysands will too readily be burdened with the responsibility of having destroyed analysis.) If at all possible, a new vat must be found. Specific limits or particular ritual forms may need to be created to enable the analysis to continue; these include whatever is mutually agreed upon in the interests of the healing process, from temporary hospitilization or daily sessions to allowing phone calls or letters when the affect becomes too disruptive for the fragile and threatened conscious position of the analysand.

Chronic lateness and cutting of sessions or otherwise refusing to abide by the rituals of the analytic contract are less severe ruptures, akin to the first-sized boiling bubbles of the second vat. Usually when the analysand's conscious position is cracked or boiling over, the analyst's consciousness can serve as a surrogate container in which to metabolize and mediate raw emotion, affirming simultaneously the possessing power, the threatened analysand's ego, and collective reality. At such times the analyst holds the therapeutic bond, patiently standing firm until the analysand can test a viable form from which to relate to the fire.

Positively, the three vats symbolize all the forms that can contain energy enabling it to move toward the balance of shared reality. The third is for me a symbol of the analytic dialogue, containing the equilibrating process and fostering its "child," the witness. Both relational dialogue and witnessing can serve as vessels. So can journal and creative writing, active imagination, prayer, and any enactments which ritually evoke energy, relate to it, and let it go. All are forms for balancing transpersonal passion and limited personal and interpersonal reality, which is what the balanced ego itself is to become, analogous to the third vat.

Some forms may be inadequate; that is part of the pattern, for transpersonal energy is a test of form, and will destroy what is inadequate, in order to force and enable the creation of new forms. The third vat, equally hot and cold, suggests arrival at a balanced ego position that allows the individual to step forth from the integrative process, in relation to rather than possessed by aggressive power.

A dream imaged this for a novice therapist who had struggled for weeks with her own painful reactions to a borderline patient's projective and direct fury and wondered why she was hanging in there, what the work's meaning for herself was. In her dream one night she received the gift of a "fire pot" or cauldron, sculptured in human shape, which was to stand on her desk. It was sturdy enough to hold fire safely, but had panels that let the light through. Holding and knowing, suffering the fire, would henceforth be a source of insight for her work. Thus the analytic process yielded up an image of the third vat; several years later a similar sense of vessel arose in the analysand's material.

Return to Court

In the final phase of the ritual, Cuchulainn emerges from the cooling vats to receive new garments from the queen. His mastery of the energy that earlier possessed him is thus affirmed by the queen. As an embodiment of the fertile goddess of the land, she receives the warrior initiate and clothes him, bestowing on him the marks of his new and sacred status within the tribe.[17]

As if reborn from the waters of the vats and sanctified in his new identity by these garments, the initiated warrior takes up the place of honor reserved for the guardian within society. Cuchulainn is henceforward to serve at the king's knee and under the king's regulation—maintaining the integrity and order of the tribe. With this final integration of the warrior function into the whole, the initiating ritual is completed.

Thus individuals working through the ritual forms that help contain their aggression discover its value as guardian of their integrity, and use it in the service of conscience. (Such a relation to aggressive energy is the basis of Eastern assertive arts such as karate, t'ai chi, and kung fu.) Aggressive energy, ritually aroused, focused, and integrated, is no longer a danger to the individual gifted with it nor to the collective that respects its value. It is safely contained in the ritual forms that channel it.

And these forms continue to be efficacious whenever the drive is subsequently aroused and threatens to spill over. Thus aspects of earlier rituals were called upon later when Cuchulainn's king deemed the hero's fury problematic—albeit understandable. When aroused to anger by the prospect of letting the king have the regal right of the first night's sex with his bride, Cuchulainn was told to go off again herding wild animals to calm his rage—while the men of the tribe found a way to assuage both royal custom and the warrior's possessive passion.

Where aggression might have been turned against his own, the familiar ritual held but did not repress it. This holding potential is equally valid for the rituals of modern analysands (see below).

Yet when aggression is not repressed or split off from awareness, it is rarely eruptive. Only once, when rudely awakened from sleep, did Cuchulainn instinctively let forth his smashing strength, killing his awakener and warning others that the warrior's mastery was uncertain on the border between sleep and waking. This only served to make the tribespeople cautious of disturbing their hero when he was unconscious; they did not shame or castigate his extraordinary power, for they respected its necessity to tribal well-being. They would not have wished to restrict its full instinctive capacity, for they knew it must be available to be channeled with full strength. Thus, when the king sent him forth to guard the territory, Cuchulainn could single-handedly hold off all the armies of Ireland.

Ritual forms, then, serve to validate numinous aggressive energy (the guarding warrior function) and to channel its arousal into those actions deemed necessary by the conscious ruling center of the personality (the king) for the defense and benefit of the life of the whole.

Two Cases

Paula, married and the mother of a young son, entered analysis because she was "uncommited and depressed." She had grown up as the overly compliant daughter of a fundamentalist minister, not unlike the one in Bergman's film *Fanny and Alexander*, and she had been the focus of his abusive, violent shadow. As a small child, she had become resigned to his accusation that she lacked "the spirit of Christ," identifying with the aggressive paternal animus and feeling she was worthless. She was a workaholic, overly indulgent of her manic-depressive husband and her child. Her dreams were full of sadistic animus figures, and she projected rage while habitually identifying with the victim.

After a time in therapy her own rage at and hatred of those sadistic animus figures and the hypocrisy of her family system began to surface. Seeing that she had married a man as unable and unwilling to bear shadow confrontation as her father had been, she began to seek definition apart from her marriage. She was entering a phase analogous to the initiatory combat of the Cuchulainn myth.

One evening I got an urgent telephone call from Paula requesting an immediate session. I drew out from her nearly inarticulate agitation that she had almost commited a murder, and could not contain her panic. After an abusive outbreak from her husband she had found herself chopping vegetables in the kitchen while her young son clamored for his meal. As she felt the knife in her hand, she was seized with a furious desire to stab the little boy. She ran out of the room with the knife, which was for her charged with archetypal hate—as if *it* was the killer. She was calling me in terror of it and her own rage.

When she arrived in my office, Paula carried the knife in a makeshift sheath, a kind of vessel; it was fastened inside a shoebox with strapping tape. She told me the story in more detail and much fear. I listened and thought back to the last session, when she had brought the dream of a black-robed nun with a red rosary around her neck, an image she found very foreign and macabre. Her associations were to repressed, devout women and "a rote way to pray." Red suggested intensity, blood, and anger to her. I thought of Kali with her necklace of severed heads and bloody sacrifices, and wondered silently how the dark Goddess, invoked through intensity, blood, and anger, was to be connected to Paula's conscious position.We had talked about the value of hate as a separative factor and had begun to explore her own sadism in the marital impasse. Then I felt she was impatient with me; I asked about the impatience, she denied it. I suggested that the idea made her anxious, to which she agreed. Impatient was what her father was. *He* dismissed and raged; none of that could be related to the mild irritation she felt at my insistence; *she* knew I was only pushing for her own good. With her father's killing righteousness as her model, she held to her personal disavowal of intensity and anger. The rage imaged in the dream was too foreign and macabre, too much for the therapeutic container as it felt to her then. But outer and inner pressures had forced the confrontation faster than she could integrate it; the Self was cracking her defenses.

And now she was confronted with the knife. This inanimate object had become a carrier of the numinosum's power, to which she could not yet consciously relate, but which had been both called into the knife by displaced, split-off affect and recognized as corresponding to its essential form.[18] The power was both projected and objective. It was terrifyingly real to her—a killer, a raging Cuchulainn. She had found her weapon.

The rituals Paula created around the knife became a way for her to begin to integrate personally a transpersonal energy pattern. But first that evening she had to stabilize a fragile ego threatened with disintegration by the influx of split-off archetypal power—the rage that had cracked the vessel. She felt she had to atone for the rage she had displaced onto her little son—make a sacrifice other than the child she loved. There was no ram in the bushes, but as she left home she had felt compelled to grab an apple. Clearly she was operating on the magic level, propelled by shadow and Self. This was evident when she said she needed "to appease the knife"—as if it were the carrier of an animated soul that she had evoked and must therefore feed, offer sacrifice to.[19] At the level of possession, where the human and nonhuman meet, is such animism.

With the apple she had brought and with me as witness, Paula created a binding ceremony—a new vessel for the rage carrier. She unsheathed the knife from its strapping and deliberately cut the apple. Clearly frightened, but in the grip of a necessity she was both willing and compelled to obey, she carefully set the two halves of the apple with their star-like centers on a piece of paper beside the knife, one on each side like guardians, like breasts. She then traced each object with a pencil, filling in the details of the seed stars and knifehandle. (This way of cutting into an apple is not customary but it reveals the pentagram, an ancient symbol of the Goddess used magically for binding, banishing, and blessing. The apple itself has associations to Avalon as well as to Eden.) Only then did she feel the energy was both bound and expressed so that she could leave the safety of the analytic *temenos* to return home.

Because the knife was sheathed when she came into the room, because I did not usually constellate her sadistic animus, and because it was clear that she needed my participation, I felt no fear of her rage myself, although in her compulsion and when she held the knife in her hand cutting the fruit I felt the numinosum's presence and the awesome sanctity of the ritual.

The following session Paula told me she had made applesauce with the fruit and given it to her son for breakfast—meeting rage with nurturance as the Queen and other women met Cuchulainn—turning vengeance into nourishment, changing the family pattern of displacement of rage onto the child.

Achieving this in her life took many months during which time the knife became her talisman, an object to which she could relate as carrier of power. With the knife as transitional object and through realistic enactments in the shared and witnessed therapeutic space she began the process of integrating[20] her rage into focused, effective anger. Her ceremonies included using the knife to destroy a dress she had hated but worn to please her parents. Another time she cut out the page of her childhood Bible inscribed "to one who needs the Spirit of Christ

—it is never too late." On other occasions she danced with the knife, releasing rage and energizing her body; and she found this such a powerful way to integrate the archetypal meaning pattern that dancing took a prominent place in her expressive repertoire. Still another time she made a drawing of herself with the knife as a (Kali-like) triumphant figure stepping on an Inquisitor. As the divorce became imminent, she was faced with the need to hold her own and to discriminate carefully —keeping the sharp knife symbolically alive in her daily attitude.

In the early rituals I was the human witness, acknowledging the sacred forces behind her possession and guarding the analytic *temenos* for her enactments. Throughout she needed me to accompany her struggle to integrate aggression and overcome the masochistic, self-abnegating backlashes (Perera 1986, pp.66–67). Only a year after the divorce was she able to risk her relationship with me and the analytic vessel to begin releasing her anger in the negative transference. We went through several periods in which her intense rage grounded itself in verbal castigation of my incompetence, impatience, and "bossiness." For the most part her sense of our alliance survived these attacks, although several times she felt rage boiling within her (like the fist-sized bubbles of Cuchulainn's second vat), and was frightened to think she had ruptured the relationship. I was generally able to accept her well-aimed verbal sadism without retaliation, but I had to use my own connection to shadow and reality to discriminate amongst the faults she found—to see what belonged to me, and what I would have been guilty of omnipotence and masochistic, negative inflation to accept. Paula needed a human apple to slice in order to turn the archetypal rage into human food. But she got furious if I accepted either too much or too little of the toxic abuse she dumped on me. She wanted it received humanely, but sorted realistically, each bit allotted to its rightful place. Her own feelings of discrimination became as sharp as a knife.

She dreamt that the knife was part of an altar, and she decided to take the image concretely as well as symbolically. A few years later she discovered a book about modern paganism (Margot Adler's *Drawing Down the Moon: Witches, Goddess-Worshippers, and Other Pagans in America Today*) and realized she had "been given . . . [her] sword by the Goddess—as rage for life" and as an emblem of air and objective discrimination. She felt a compelling responsibilty to become "a servant of the forces of the sword as life sustainer."

The magic ceremonies by means of which she had transformed archaic and possessing murderousness into self-assertion and a guardian's reverence for the Goddess' force that runs through life and death

were created from her strong personal and inherited religious sense—
what Jung has called the instinct for the transpersonal. But they also
follow and amplify the archetypal pattern of a warrior's integration of
the aggressive drive, grounding the Cuchulainn myth in modern life. In
Paula's case, as in many of ours, there was the necessity of finding and
claiming the power of the sword even as she struggled to disidentify
herself from possession by it.

When last I saw her, Paula told me that she had remarried and was
working with young adolescents. She said too that while she meditates
daily, she still needs to relate consciously to the knife and what it sym-
bolizes. For if she loses conscious connection to the numinous values
of aggression and discrimination, she finds that, when stressed, she falls
back into defensive masochism. She is, perhaps, not "cured," as one
colleague suggested; but she manages the abuse dynamic and her own
dark shadow—and her family's dynamic and part of the collective
shadow—with a deep sense of their connection, and her own, to the
transpersonal. And that may be the only human cure.

Ian, a thin man in his early 30s, spent most of his sessions talking
about difficulties with his digestive system, problems with authority,
and his rage at himself and his seductive/controlling girlfriend. After
several months, he began to have enough distance to leave their apartment when she taunted him about his inferiorities rather than slapping
her and collapsing in self-hatred.

As this acting out diminished, he began a curious ritual in the analytic vessel. It originated with a dream that imaged him standing on a
hill with a rusty weapon; he agreed to stand up and "gestalt" the scene.
He towered over me for a moment and then quickly moved away to the
corner of the room nearest the door. Having checked to see that he
could open it, he turned to face the room, jaws clenched. As if wielding
a machine gun, with eyes so tightly closed he seemed not to want to
know what he was doing, he swung wildly from side to side. After a few
minutes his face began to relax in grim satisfaction and his motions lost
their driven energy, He opened his eyes. Through "piles of corpses
lying around" he stomped his way back to his chair. When I questioned
him, he described how he had begun to kill all the "bastards." But he
could not tell me whom he was shooting—"just everybody"—for his
inner world was not yet personal.

At various intervals in the following weeks when he "felt bottled
up" or "blank," he would suddenly return to the corner, perform the
same actions in a thrashing, driven way, and sit down. My attempts to

discuss the enactment were met wih a shrug. I acknowledged that I saw his anger and the value of his feeling some sense of his own power; with another shrug he reurned to descriptions of his relationships or his undiagnosable stomach pains. My role was to be only that of an impersonal witness who did not scold his aggressive boiling over or get too upset about his "innards." I was relegated to the position of nonfearful audience of his "phallic narcissism"—that rage-revenge he had borne since early childhood, when his parents tied him to a tree while they tended the farm and beat him for thumb-sucking, masturbation, and soiling his pants—all "shames and troubles" to them.

A deeply disturbed child, he had found relief in the '60s drug escape as he drifted from job to job and woman to woman seeking some relation to embodied life. Along the way he had picked up a variety of musical skills, most of a college education, and written parts of two novels. He entered Jungian therapy because he said he finally desired "to find the meaning of life." He did not seem a likely candidate, but when I heard about the attacks on his girlfriend, I knew there was passionate libido available for the transformative work, if only it could be harnessed and brought into analysis.

Ian drew a blank about his outbursts, much as he had initially dismissed the attacks on his girlfriend and his self-abuse. He was back in the pattern of denial that had made him walk about as a child with "a load in his pants" until the teachers sent him home. The outbursts did not at all fit with what he had anticipated in "Jungian dream work." Because he was over 6 feet tall and the rage was genuinely frightening, but also because he reminded me of my son's exhibitionistic play of "monster-killer" at age 5, I had ambivalent feelings about his eruptions. They were exciting to him, and a release of tension, but seemed to be as temporary and potentially addictive as much primal therapy release, and he had a history of addiction. He tried to pretend they had not happened, and a few times I colluded with this, making only some comment about his "feeling good at getting even" or "clearing out the inner world's rage," and "it feeling safer to him to be alone." My interpretations were correct, but did not touch the preverbal place where he was; they were thus irrelevant. I asked him if he could stay in his chair and *tell* me his feelings, but this was clearly impossible. He had to act to show me.[21] For while his ego was not in charge of the berserk energy that possessed him, his body/Self had created a ceremony both to contain and reveal its presence.

If he could not bring the material closer to consciousness, I knew I might perhaps enter his ritual. I did not, however, feel like joining his attacks on humanity, he did them fine on his own (with a client who has no capacity to express aggression, I might well join the aggressive energy, supporting it into the ritual vessel to facilitate its bonding into the analysand's consciousness). Instead, I paid careful attention to the next outburst, sensing its motions in my body, tuning in to the tensions he was releasing so rapidly he discharged before he could feel. (I had tried doing some sensory awareness work with him. He "went blank," said he could sense nothing, and finally admitted he "didn't want to.") I stayed with my own processing of his angry torsions, noting that the lower half of his body was stiff and his breathing shallow. I felt my way into his rhythm. It was like being shaken, hard to tell if the motion came in reaction to someone outside or from rage within. When I mentioned this, he shrugged, as if the words themselves were too far from his magic-level, preverbal position, caught somewhere between inside and outside. On a hunch, at the next outburst I let my shoulders move, then recoiled slightly as if I had been hit. Although Ian did not notice, I continued to move; several times, this curious dance went on. Then at one point Ian opened his eyes and saw my participatory witnessing of his ritual. He looked startled, paused a moment, then continued. His "shooting" tentatively began to focus on me as I grabbed different parts of my body to let him know where he had scored. Suddenly he stopped and sat down, disoriented, relieved, furious.

Because I had joined in and ceremonially survived his aggression, Ian had a bridge between its possession of him and the world of (shared play) reality. The possession had been made into a shared event; he was no longer omnipotent in his desolated world. But he was furious. "You invaded. You took over," he stormed. Tempering the inhuman rage felt like a loss to him. And, more discomfiting, making it more real brought him closer to his own fear of the aggression. He began to talk over the next weeks about fearing to be "as vicious as [his] parents." We retreated from the machine gun explosions to blowing: He aimed his breath and blew, and each time he aimed his venting at me, I reacted slightly to show him I had received and felt it. Such expiration, like crying and spitting, is a very early form of expressing and releasing anger; it became one that Ian also put to adaptive use in his dealings outside the sessions.

After one of the ceremonies, which had started with his recounting old shames that led to an eruption of fury he this time was able to express by shouting, he stopped, frightened, and reverted to discussing his eating habits. I interpreted both the fear and defense to him, but he was blandly dismissive. Several weeks later he told me that his girlfriend demanded gentleness of men and hated the thought not only of rape but of any expression of masculine power, although he also felt she taunted him to see if he could hold his rage better than her father had. I could feel him wondering whether I felt as she did. After working this through, he told me that he had wanted to shout obscenities at me, and then that he had had a wish to push me out of my chair and rape and murder me. He expected me to be shocked and angry—to end our work; I told him how glad I was that he had been able to catch the energy in an image and had elected to speak rather than act. He nodded. Then after a rather long silence, he said, "If I raped and murdered you, the world would be empty again, like it was when I gunned everyone down from the corner." He realized that he needed me to stay alive. Although the two drives were in conflict within him, I had supported both of them; thus he was reflected as a whole person with conflicting but valid emotions, and could use me as his first psychological kin, an equally whole object. Some area of reflectiveness within him had opened up; within a balanced vat, a new phase of the analysis could begin.

Notes

1. *The Collected Poems of Dylan Thomas, 1934–1952.* New York: New Directions (1957), p. 10.
2. Such a process of development is not surprising for the individual when we consider the analogous long cultural and historical evolution from "the furor which had been the savage ideal and the grand manner of the Italic warriors of prehistory (as it remained that of the warriors of Celtic and Germanic epic) . . . [to] legendary [Roman] discipline. . . . Passions of the soul took the place of mystical forces; a justified and almost reasonable anger, provoked from without and following the exploit, was substituted for the physical and spontaneous exaltation of the entire being in the course of the exploit" (Dumezil 1970, p. 10).
3. Cuchulainn was fostered by members of all the castes after being nursed by the king's sister: as the druid-judge put it, "formed by all, chariot-fighter, prince and sage. He will be cherished by many, this boy, and he will settle your trails of honor and win your ford-fights and all your battles" (Kinsella 1970, p. 25).
4. The new disease, AIDS, is a motif that appears sometimes as a dream symbol of the breakdown of the defense system wherein one cannot withstand psychological invasion and attack. Leukemia, by contrast, often stands for overdefensiveness against one's own instinctuality.
5. There are other myths and rituals dealing with this theme: the taming of members of the Kwaquitl cannibal society or the berserkers of Odin or our own returning Marines. Sekhmet-Hathor needs her hennaed beer, the maenads their sleep, to transform the consciousness of raging possession. Kali needs Shiva's willingness to become her dance-ground to return the energy to a transpersonal matrix, which detoxifies its carrier and permits reentry into the community.
6. Here Cuchulainn takes a role common in Celtic lore. Like Finn MacCool, Connal Cernach, the young Peredur, and the Black Giant in "The Lady of the Fountain," he is herdsman and master of the wild animals. See Anne Ross, *Pagan Celtic Britain*, London:

Rutledge and Kegan Paul (1967), pp. 137–151. There are also analogies betweeen this motif and the Zen oxherding pictures.

7. The partial concealment of the Queen's ritual mariage with the Year King, who must first pass tests of aggressive valor to prove his virility, as well as its dilution through the inclusion of many women, is due in part to the Christian scribes who recorded the ancient oral literature of Ireland. The perspective of much Celtic work—and especially the *Tain*—shows that the values of the later patriarchal, aristocratic, warrior culture were competing with customs of earlier tribes.

8. In an interesting article Tobin Siebers suggests that the sexual representation of the primal scene is a deflection and repression of the child's feelings of paranoid aggression at what it perceives initially to be the father's attack on the mother with whom it identifies as victim. See Tobin Siebers, "The Ethical Unconscious," in *the Psychoanalytic Review* 73/3: 309–331.

9. Fear of the client's rage, either at the therapist (and reminding the latter of unanalyzed childhood terrors before negative parental furies) or turned masochistically against the physical self in suicidal destructiveness (and touching on the therapist's abandonment issues), creates one pull toward eroticization of libido. There may also be unanalyzed fascination with and desire to possess the passion on the part of an analyst who cannot bear to let the analysand have such fearsome power and is not aware of this envy. Calming the other's fury or attempting to balance it with equally powerful "loving nurtures" are thus sometimes used unconsciously to destroy or claim the transpersonal power in an analysand's possession.

10. One possession can also be co-opted for the purposes of another. During war or in totalitarian systems we often see the erotic and maternal drives preempted by the state. Equally, much propaganda converts relationship to other into enmity, making that other an adversarial shadow-carrier or monster. Defensiveness rigidifies the aggressive drive and distorts the erotic into sadism.

11. Again timing is crucial; while deflection of arousal can lead to relationship, creativity, and all kinds of sublimation, it can also contribute to displacement, whereby the expression of one drive comes through another. Rape is such a displacement of power into the erotic arena.

12. An amplification from the tantric Hindu tradition tells of the creator-destroyer god, Shiva, whose lingam went wild around the world; fires sprang up wherever the phallus alighted. Alarmed, the gods built a yoni in the earth and the lingam grounded itself in it; therby the fires stopped (Bradley Te Paske, personal communication).

13. In a later section of the *Tain*, Cuchulainn is forced to kill his foster-brother, Ferdia, in a savage ford fight. Like Arjuna he must battle even his beloved kinsman, for that is the function of his caste, his sacral-social duty. Thus, while his lament for the dead friend is filled with agonizing grief, it cannot be the kind of remorse that might inhibit a future, similar encounter. In this hero's case, no adversary ever survives his onslaughts long enough to teach him the sweetness of remorse and reparation. He always wins, except in the last battle, when he dies; and always, duty to the tribe overrides personal feeling.

14. Kernberg refers to the "instinctual gratification [within the therapeutic relationship] of pathological, especially aggressive needs . . . more gratification . . . than would ever be possible in . . . extratherapeutic interactions" (1984, p. 116). Within the ritual context of analysis, such cathartic/addictive behavior can actually be transformed.

15. An effective form of therapy with acting-out delinquents has been psychodramatic enactment of their aggressive urges including the consequences of those actions. Organically built inhibitions form to bring about self-discipline. See Glasser, *Reality Therapy*.

16. Drawing on his work with a group of sex offenders, Brad Te Paske has described the function of members who physically restrain the particular member venting accumulated rage at the female cotherapist: They provide comradely holding for the one possessed and discover/create an inner sense of the function of aggression in guarding life ("The Birth and Rebirth of the Ritual Body," a lecture given Jan. 24, 1987).

17. In other rituals, the Celtic queen bestows the cloak of sovereignty on the king of her choice. The cloak given to the Grail hero by the queen as Grail bearer is one later variant of the theme. See Wolfram von Eshenbach, *Parsival*, New York: Vintage Books (1961), p. 125.

18. See H. Searles, *The Nonhuman Environment in Normal Development and in Schizophrenia*, New York: International Universities Press (1960), p. 303; and Susanne Langer, *Philosophy in a New Key*, Mentor Books (1956) p. 100. Langer writes: "To project feelings into outer objects is the first way of symbolizing and thus conceiving those feelings." Much as Maori priests call the god into prayer sticks when they need to relate to its powers, Paula's split-off affects had both called for their own mirror and recognized themselves in the knife. They manifested in therapy through the concrete "transitional object," which became the link between transpersonal aggressive power and her own personal need to reclaim her emotional life. Previously she had lived by the family code, *to be masochistic and caretaking is virtuous*; asserting power for her own survival was taboo.

19. I am reminded of the way Celtic warriors, among other tribespeople, felt life in their weapons and addressed songs to their swords, or listened to the weapons praising their own great deeds.

20. Kohut calls this process transmutation of the archaic, split-off, omnipotent rage at experienced threats to a very fragile self-esteem (1973, p. 390).

21. See Masud M. Kahn, *The Privacy of the Self: Papers on Psychoanalytic Theory and Technique*, New York: International Universities Press (1974), p. 173; also Perera (1986), pp. 61–66.

References

Adler, Margot. 1979. *Drawing down the moon: Witches, Goddess-worshippers and other pagans in America today*. Boston: Beacon Press.

Dumezil, Georges. 1970 *The destiny of the warrior*. Chicago: University of Chicago Press.

Eliade, Mircea. 1972. *Zalmoxis, the vanishing god: Comparative studies in religions and folklore of Dacia and Eastern Europe*. Trans. Willard R. Trask. Chicago: University of Chicago Press.

Finley, Patricia. 1975. Dialogue drawing: An image-evoking communication between analyst and analysand. *Arts Psychotherapy* 2: 87–99.

Jung, C. G. 1953. Two essays in analytical psychology. In *Collected works*, vol. 7. Princeton: Princeton University Press.

———. 1967. Alchemical Studies. In *Collected works*, vol. 13. Princeton: Princeton University Press.

Kernberg, Otto F. 1984. *Severe personality disorders: Psychotherapeutic strategies*. New Haven: Yale University Press.

Kinsella, Thomas, trans. 1970. *The Tain, translated from the Irish epic, Tain Bo Cuailnge*. Oxford: Oxford University Press.

Kohut, Heinz. 1973. Thoughts on narcissism and narcissistic rage. *Psychoanalytic Study of the Child* 27:360–400.

———. 1977. *The restoration of the Self*. New York: International Universities Press.

Neumann, Erich, 1955. *The Great Mother: An analysis of the archetype*. Princeton: Princeton University Press.

———. 1976. On the psychological meaning of ritual. *Quadrant* 9/2: 5–35.

Perera, Sylvia Brinton. 1986. Ceremonies of the emerging ego in psychotherapy. *The Body in Analysis*. Wilmette, Ill.: Chiron Publications, 59–85.

Stewart, Louis. 1986. Affect and archetype. *The Body in Analysis*. Wilmette, Ill.: Chiron Publications, 183–203.

Whitmont, E. C. 1982. *Return of the goddess*. New York: Crossroad Publishing Co.

Book Reviews

The Psychotic Core
Michael Eigen, Ph.D. Northvale, New Jersey: Jason Aronson. 1986. 387 pp. $30.00

Reviewed by Randolph S. Charlton

> . . . *that the rational world both within us and without us is small, that*
> *our understanding is smaller yet, and that much of the universe in*
> *which we exist is, so far as we are able to tell, chaotic.* Stephen King

The Psychotic Core, Michael Eigen's intriguing book, is concerned with the
"mad dimension of life." It describes both the nature of flagrant psychotic
decompensation and the kernel of psychosis that crouches unbidden within all
human minds. Drawing on, augmenting, and critiquing the theories presented
by Freud, Jung, and assorted object relations, existential, and self psychologists,
psychosis is seen as "the Cinderalla of psychoanalysis": part of the human condition, inexorable and unavoidable, present in the mind of the beauty and the
beast, the analyst and the patient, discernible beneath our everyday words and
actions, ubiquitous in our nightly dream voyages.

Having begun his clinical work with autistic and schizophrenic children,

---

Randolph S. Charlton, M.D., is a member of the C. G. Jung Institute of San
Francisco and a fellow of the American Academy of Psychoanalysis. He is a clinical associ-
ate professor of psychiatry and behavioral sciences at the Stanford University School of
Medicine and maintains a private practice.

Dr. Eigen has also consulted with psychotic adults and is obviously familiar with the broad spectrum of psychotic conditions. His many writings concerning the creative process, the nature of the self, the importance of embodiment in the psychic world, the vicissitudes of idealization, and the contribution of the object relations school have appeared in the psychoanalytic literature since the mid-1970's and form the basis for much of the material in this volume.

In the preface we are warned that psychosis involves "holocaustal rages, insidious self-poisoning, ghastly vacuousness, the abuse of cleverness," as well as "crippling shyness, hellish torment and self-deadening" (p. viii). This is the stuff of nightmare—of Bram Stoker, H. P. Lovecraft, and Mary Shelley. Case examples reveal, however, that these dire torments are no mere invention, but part and parcel of the psychotic experience. In spite of, or maybe because of, the dreadful territory into which Eigen guides us, he hopes that our journey ". . . helps us become a little less afraid of ourselves in ways that are not destructive, enriching the quality of our experiencing capacity" (pp. viii).

Every analyst who ventures into the vast territory of insanity must explore terrain difficult and strange; Eigen's annotated maps offer valuable assistance in navigating the ever-changing labyrinth of the psychotic mind. He works tirelessly to make sense of the unknown. However, lest the reader be deluded into thinking that all roads within the land of psychosis lead to intelligible destinations, Bion's ideas on the nature of meaninglessness in madness are also clearly and sensitively presented.

The night sea journey of the psychotic is viewed from different vantage points. Hallucination, conceived broadly as part of the human ability to experience reality through fantasy, is Eigen's first and major gateway into the land of psychosis. His discussion of this "most spectacular of human capacities" is original and well worth reading. There follow sections on mindlessness, boundaries, hate, epistemology, and reversal. Continually circumambulating the core of psychosis, Eigen amplifies themes and defines many of the dynamics that make up the psychotic process. Along the way even the sophisticated reader will acquire deeper insight into the elaborate structure of what can appear to be all confusing disorder.

Aware of Jung's belief that all descriptions of psychological geography are subjective confessions of the cartographer, Eigen states: "Therapists identify with different meanings and qualities of self, as expressed in varied languages and methods, and so embody different destinies" (p. 83).

The Psychotic Core embodies not a single destiny, but many. Imagery, fantasy, and madness itself are envisioned as multiple, diverse, layered, intertwined realities. Eigen's wide-ranging mind is not bound to a particular theory. Rather, like a modern-day physicist of the mind, he accepts the relevance of various views of psychic reality and works to appreciate their power in different circumstances. We are fortunate to share in his struggle to find spontaneous and lively meaning within the therapeutic dialogue (even if, in the psychotic situation, that meaning be the death of meaning!). Attempting to approach the experience of madness "from the inside," he offers the analyst thought-provoking metaphors and clinical descriptions vibrant with feeling. In many ways his work resembles that of D. W. Winnicott, an analyst he admires, with its acceptance of paradox and awareness of the importance of play in psychic life.

Eigen's commentary on the Jungian vision of psychosis, interspersed throughout the book, will be of particular interest to the readers of this journal. With a high regard for Jung and Jungians, his enthusiasm is tempered by such insights as, "(A)n oversimplification of polarities runs through Jung's thought" (p. 61), and "Jung could be charged with a kind of psychological utopianism" (p. 65).

He argues that Jung split off the ego within the psyche and gave to it too much responsibility for psychic disequilibrium:

> Jung's insight that deep unconscious processes appear destructive in re-
> sponse to an overly narrow conscious ego is an important truth. But the
> ego is restrictive, also, because of the warped foundation of which it is a
> part. In other words, conscious and unconscious functions are part of the
> same psychic fabric, and in psychosis, deformations spread through both,
> reciprocally or in a vicious circle. To place the burden of blame on either
> consciousness or the deep unconscious is too simple. (p. 60).

Eigen finds an oversimplification of psychic reality within the Jungian distinction between the personal and collective unconscious and he suggests that Jung underestimated the true nature of the personal:

> The very fabric of psychic life is personal-impersonal through and through.
> Jung has abstractly torn apart a co-constitutive reciprocity and assigned one
> or the other of these terms to different psychic levels, when both character-
> ize all levels with varying shifts of emphasis (which must be determined by
> context). (p. 61)

Further, he suggests that a confusion runs through Jungian thought in its commingling of the concepts of Self, wholeness, the collective unconscious, and God. Consuming movement toward individuation at times obscures the fact that the *quality* of development is most important, and that the experience of whole-ness is often closely associated with its opposite. Eigen underscores the fact that the meaning of experience is best understood in the personal context in which it appears:

> One could easily depict Jung's vision of the self, center of psychic totality,
> as a hallucinatory wish. . . . We are divided and wish for wholeness and feel
> whole through our divisions. (p. 64)

> Jung was not fooled by Freud. But his own gestalts acted as boxes to trap
> the numinous and assume what they try to account for. He himself seemed
> to be aware of this and gave warnings against his views for those who
> would hear, while he gave in to his nature and annexed dependents. (p.
> 87)

Lastly, Eigen finds an uncritical acceptance of reversal and equilibration in much Jungian writing. Reliance on the notion of psychic compensation may limit the scope of the resulting vision of the psyche:

> In such formulations, one can see that thinking via reversals is often over-
> general, even sterotypical, and can be extremely rigid. In psychosis, every
> possible mixture and dissociation of material and immaterial dimensions

of experiencing are found. A psychotic individual raised in a materialistic milieu may or may not bring up compensating images. He is as likely to mirror or caricature his surroundings and ego attitudes as compensate for them. Often mirroring and compensating activity blend together in highly specific ways. (p. 244–245)

One could certainly search out examples to show the richness of the Jungian world view this portrayal misses. At its best Jungian theory and practice value the symbol as it comes into being within an analysand's experience. Real and transferential relationships to the analyst, personal associations, and archetypal amplification all merge in the search for meaning. The process fits in tone and content Eigen's orientation. Yet Jung's legacy *has* at times included romantic simplifications and conceptual reifications; it is these limitations that Eigen specifically criticizes. His effort to define an open-ended, relativistic psychic world full of conflict, contrast, and creativity is, I think, fully in the spirit of Jung's original researches.

Eigen presents his own clinical work throughout the book, even giving us a transcript of sessions with a psychotic woman. He compares and contrasts his patient, Rena, with Dr. Schreber, the archetypal psychotic patient described by Freud (though never seen by him) and concludes that Rena improves because she finds a cultural and therapeutic setting that accepts her psychotic experience metaphorically, while "Schreber remained mad because he used his madness as a solution, rather than a probe" (p. 259). I wish more analysts would follow Dr. Eigen's example and present their clinical work verbatim, especially when dealing with difficult cases such as the analytic therapy of the psychotic. It is enlightening to read learned theory, but for it to be most useful we must clothe it in human form by describing what exactly we do and how we do it.

Eigen's own responses in the clinical dialogue flow from the context of the patient's immediate experience and work to clarify the confusing mixture of fusion and destruction of internal distinctions present in psychotic ambivalence, symbolic vision, and emotional reversal. His replies to patients are most often directed toward the tension contained in crucial dichotomies: mind-body, self-other, inside-outside, literal-symbolic, creation-destruction, holding-expelling, and then-now. Like many a Jungian, he highlights the tension of opposites. He writes:

On the one hand, my interventions stressed distinctions inherent in various swirls of imagery. At various points I might say, "You have light and darkness all mixed up" or "You have phallus and penis confused" or "Aren't you speaking of womb and anus as if they were the same?". . . . Such remarks are often less important than their intention, which is to note and perhaps even install a barrier against the perverse reworking and collapse of valid distinctions. The message conveyed is that there *is* an ordering process at work, which at present is being ignored or stupefied. (p. 307)

Reading *The Psychotic Core* will reassure the analyst willing to immerse himself in the world of psychosis, to tolerate a degree of fear and trembling, of the possibility of emerging with something of value! Michael Eigen is an admirable guide on a fascinating journey through this mysterious and poetic land.

Emotional Anatomy: The Structure of Experience
Stanley Keleman. Berkeley: Center Press, 1985. 161 pp. $24.95

Reviewed by Steven M. Joseph

Stanley Keleman is a major teacher and practitioner of somatic therapy. In his work he integrates a profound understanding of somatic process with phenomenological, psychoanalytic, and mythic approaches to the nature of human existence. A practitioner of the body in analysis, in *Emotional Anatomy: The Structure of Experience*, Keleman presents a summary statement, in words and pictures, of his somatic perspective. He describes his project in the following way:

Life makes shapes. These shapes are part of an organizing process that embodies emotions, thoughts, and experiences into a structure. This structure, in turn, orders the events of existence. Shapes manifest the process of protoplasmic history finding a personal shape. . . . This book is a visual introduction to the shapes of human existence. (p. xi)

Keleman's book, and his work generally, provides a very important corrective to the Jungian approach. Traditional Jungian thought and practice tends to focus on symbolic and imaginal aspects of psyche to the relative neglect of lived bodily reality. Keleman's perspective as a "somatic analyst" is an effective antidote to this tendency towards one-sidedness.

In a series of chapters entitled "Creation," "The Body Plan," "Insults to Form," "Patterns of Somatic Distress," "Somatic Reality," and "Somatic Interactions," Keleman develops his argument. Fundamental to living material is "its pulsatory organization, its ability to expand and contract, to lengthen and shorten, swell and shrink. . . . The organism is space with a structure . . . tubes with layers" (pp. 2–3). These tubes are motile, and it is this tubal motility that "establishes each person's ongoing form and provides his [or her] basic feeling of identity. . . . empty, full; slow, fast; expand, withdraw; engulf, disgorge" (p. 3).

Fundamental to Keleman's perspective is the realization that all psychic life—thinking, feeling, imagining, being—is based on somatic pulsation and organization. In his work he aims at developing a vocabulary of images of human existence *which derive from and evoke this somatic base*—images that reflect pulsation and flow, organizing and formative process. Keleman generates images for a process meditation on the "ongoingness" of immediate experience. His images are intended to contain consciousness within forms and transformations drawn from somatic life, to evoke "the shape of experience which gives rise to feeling, thought, and action, . . . ourselves as feeling forms" (p. 160).

Steven M. Joseph, M.D., is an analytic candidate at the C. G. Jung Institute of San Francisco. He is in private practice in Albany, California.

The book's illustrations, sketches by Vincent Perez that amplify the text, help the reader get the feel of what Keleman is after: they are powerful intuitive evocations of the somatic/affective states the author describes that suggest directly the archetypal embedded in the somatic.

Another basic feature of Keleman's perspective is his emphasis on the crucial formative role of stressful experience, especially early in life. He states:

> Pulsation is a function that produces basic feelings such as joy, goodness, vitality, and excitation. . . . There should be a feeling of excitation from inside out and from outside in. Continual patterns of emotional distress, however, may cause tubes, layers, and pouches to become rigid and elongated, dense and compressed, swollen and stuffed, or collapsed and weak. . . . The tissue no longer supports waves of pulsation; thinking, feeling, action and uprightness are affected. (p. 17)

The core mechanism by which stress affects the organism is the *startle reflex*, "the fundamental response to any stimuli that are unknown, whether . . . painful or pleasurable. It commits our attention to the new stimuli. . . . [It] de-focuses and refocuses attention instantaneously" (p. 66). Emotional insults that are chronic, overstimulating, or ill-timed interrupt and disrupt the pulsatory processes of the organism. There may be "feelings of anger, fear, depression, rejection, and rage. . . . [If] insults persist or increase, the structure remains rigid or compact, swollen or collapsed" (p. 63).

In other words, under conditions of persistent emotional insult, the startle response becomes chronic, refocused attention becomes fixated, and habitual patterns of somatic organization are set up which "become the way we recognize the world as well as ourselves, and in turn, they become the way the world recognizes us" (p. 75). This is a somatically based description of the formation of the ego complex. As Louis H. Stewart has observed in a previous volume of this series ("The Body in Analysis" 1986, p. 190), "the archetypal affect Surprise/Startle [is] the centering and reorienting affect of the Self, . . . the underlying affect related to the evolution of the ego complex, the center of consciousness, and the function of attention and orientation." Keleman is clearly describing the same phenomenon in different language.

A major part of *Emotional Anatomy* is devoted to detailed descriptions of four basic patterns of chronic, fixated startle response. There are two *overbounded* patterns of somatic distress—*rigid* and *dense*—and two *underbounded* patterns—*swollen* and *collapsed*. These are complex, multifaceted patterns involving all aspects of a person which coexist in complex combinations and configurations. I cannot elaborate on the patterns here due to space limitations. Keleman's detailed descriptions and comparisons of these patterns, together with his overall perspective, are highly insightful and clinically useful.

Keleman writes only very generally about treatment in this book. He respects the unique Self of each individual and avoids the trap of an ideal type of somatic organization. The goal of what he calls "somatic education" is to bring people "into deeper contact with the living foundations of existence, the pulsatory waves that generate excitement, feeling, thinking, and action." But "each structure must be approached uniquely. Emotional misery results for many people when they attempt to become someone else's somatic ideal" (p. 152).

Stanley Keleman presents us with a powerful vision of the formative and foundational role of somatic process in psychic life. How does his vision relate to a Jungian perspective on the nature of experience? I have already indicated the relevance of his patterns of somatic distress to Jungian notions of ego. Moreover, there is a fundamental parallel between Keleman basing experience on somatic process and form and Jung basing psyche on the dynamic play of the archetypes. Both Keleman's soma and Jung's archetypes are the ground for the experiential dualities of feeling and form, affect and image. The somatic approach complements the more purely psychological one in its greater emphasis on the affective component of experience. Jung's notion of the archetype, although it certainly refers to affect as well as image, nonetheless speaks more to the imaginal component of experience. In this sense, then, Keleman's emphasis on somatic process provides valuable and much-needed compensation.

Keleman's fourfold differentiation of patterns of somatic distress, each with its own characteristic ego configuration, may suggest parallels with Jung's psychological types (sensation, intuition, feeling, and thinking). However, I see no necessary correlations; nor does Keleman make any. An individual may embody rigidity, density, inflation, collapse, or a combination thereof while any of the four functions predominates in consciousness.

The *symbolic* value of the pattern of distress as distinguished from its purely *symptomatic* value is not emphasized in the book. The prospective and potential meaning of the symptom, the god in the dis-ease, is veiled. Keleman is clearly aware of this dimension, but in *Emotional Anatomy* his main focus is the way basic somatic patterns are established and maintained.

I highly recommend this book, like others Keleman has written, for its deep insights into somatic formative process and its fundamental role in psyche. Keleman's is a unique voice making a powerful and important statement about the nature and unfolding of the body in analysis. Jungians stand to benefit from an acquaintance with this work.

The Archetype of Shadow in a Split World

Proceedings of the Tenth International Congress for Analytical Psychology, Berlin, 1986. Edited by Mary Ann Mattoon. Zürich: Daimon Verlag, 1987. 442 pp. $32.00/19.95

Studying this record from the Berlin Congress is a bit like looking through photographs after a trip. One realizes how much experience the pictures leave

Murray Stein, Ph.D., is the author of *In MidLife* (1983) and *Jung's Treatment of Christianity* (1985). He is a member of the Chicago Society of Jungian Analysts.

John Talley, M.D., is a clinical professor of psychiatry, University of New Mexico. He is a past president and member of the Inter-Regional Society of Jungian Analysts.

Peter Mudd, M.S.W., is the Director of Training at the C. G. Jung Institute of Chicago. He is a member of the Chicago Society of Jungian Analysts and the book review editor for the Chiron Clinical Series.

out, but also begins noticing details too quickly passed over or missed entirely in the bustle of travel. These details help to clarify the meaning of the trip.

More evident reading these papers now is an impression vaguely sensed then, in Berlin: Analytical psychology is going through a profound transformation. These papers tell a story.

As the impact of Jung's extraordinary personality wanes—many of his immediate disciples are no longer active, and their presence was not registered in this Congress—the intellectual landscape is taking on new features. This Congress no longer represents "Jungian psychology" as it has been understood. We must think now of "analytical psychology." What was a school formed around a single powerful teacher has become a field, much more diverse; and it shows new influences, significant figures, and trends.

The Berlin Congress may go down in the history of I.A.A.P. as the first post-Jungian gathering of analysts from around the world.

Evidence of change is present in nearly every paper of this volume. Among the references, for example, Jung himself is mentioned only once in the entire collection. (This is not to say, of course, that his thought is not presupposed throughout.) Freud is not mentioned at all. The most frequently referenced author is, surprisingly, Erich Neumann (six times), whose influence seems to be gaining strength. This is followed by Hans Dieckmann of Berlin (four times), and then by Erik Erikson (three times), Michael Fordham (three times), and Melanie Klein (three times). Many of the papers draw heavily on such non-Jungian sources as modern psychoanalysis and object relations theory, and on such non-Jungian authors as Bion, Kernberg, Kohut, and Meltzer. Folding new influences in with the old, the field is becoming less characteristically Jungian and more broadly analytic. The ferment is bound to generate originality.

The papers in a collection like this are, of course, uneven in quality; a number of contributions are outstanding and may eventually become classics in the field. Rosemary Gordon's "Masochism: The Shadow Side of the Archetypal Need to Venerate and Worship," Nathan Schwartz-Salant's "Archetypal Foundations of Projective Identification," and Peer Hultberg's "Shame: An Overshadowed Emotion" are candidates for this distinction. Other papers too could be cited for originality and creative thinking.

The one contribution that caught my interest especially, which I unfortunately missed in Berlin, was "The Shadow and Analytic Training," by five Italian analysts (Aite, Gullotta, Cascio, Migliorati, and Rufini). These women reflect with remarkable candor on the shadow dynamics in training programs, particularly as these arise in training analyses and spill over into other aspects of training. Their discussion and recommendations could be studied with profit by anyone engaged in this most psychologically risky and taxing of undertakings. That there is courage enough to discuss the shadows hidden in the training institutes is evidence of maturity in the field, which bodes well for the future.

—*Murray Stein*

*   *   *

As a Jungian, I should not have been surprised at the congruence of place and experience the 1986 Berlin Congress was.

Yet when I opened my hotel window I was amazed, delighted, to hear the trumpet of an elephant, the roar of a lion, and the peal of bells.

When we booked a limousine to take us to East Berlin, our guide, as all skilled guides do, evoked an edge of danger in our journey. Passing through the Janus-headed Checkpoint Charlie, we found ourselves holding our breath, acutely aware of entering a forbidden realm. (Plaut was later to speak of the Janus gate, open in war, closed in peace.)

Coming to the Pergamon Museum, incredibly spared by allied bombers, we walked through vast, neglected rooms, dimly aware of indifferent, glum attendants. And then, suddenly, as in a dream, the very walls of Babylon stood before us, cobalt blue, vast, with golden lions and dragons in bas relief—a gate like Ishtar's, a ceremonial way leading to Sumerian kings, giant gods with great eyes, stark beards, and majestic crowns. Dumb we stood, like Moses on Sinai; and dumb we departed.

After the giddy relief of being safely back in West Berlin, we found ourselves in that mausoleum of the Reichstag, chatting and sipping champagne, yet, with vague subliminal shivers, not unaware of history.

The 1986 Berlin Congress was important in several ways. Politically, meeting in the place which had once been the very heart of darkness marked a sobering and relieving *Auseinandersetzung*.

Few could ignore the instinctual reality and ubiquity of our own shadows. And few could fail to sense the relief that a just-enough settlement brings.

Old polarities expressed in the hackneyed "symbolic" and "clinical" seemed irrelevant. The papers presented generated an exciting sense of *rapprochement* and appreciation of the "other," of the *in*clusivity of Jung's vision. Clinical grounds the symbolic; the symbolic enriches the clinical. Samuels's "seamless whole."

Further, Pignatelli, in his response to Sidoli's thoughtful paper on shame in children, said, "I hope the image of the gratifying Jungian is on its way to extinction, without devaluing either the therapeutic alliance or the prospective dimension of the work."

That seems to express the direction analytical psychology is taking. It recognizes the necessity and value of analyzing transference and countertransference, which when done with the careful sensitivity Jung intended makes possible the emergence of the symbolic creativity of individuation.

It was a good meeting. Old "enemies" heard each other, seemed to understand each other, and spoke together in a spirit honoring an extended truth.

—*John Talley*

*　　*　　*

The publication of the Proceedings of the Tenth International Congress is the catalyst for an avalanche of associations coded within me as "Berlin." In recalling "Berlin" I remember less the specific papers and more the heightened atmosphere of the "field" of analytical psychology, a field which is clearly awakening to its destiny as the psychology of the 21st century. I believe both Murray Stein and John Talley in their comments are also noting, perhaps from different typological angles, the new animation that Berlin embodied.

One of the little-known events during the Congress was the meeting of directors of training to discuss the results of a questionnaire developed by Verena Kast and Gustav Bovensiepen. This meeting and the questionnaire itself, which related to training methods and requirements, were to me reminiscent of those attempts at renewal that characterize the end stages of mourning: in this case, mourning the loss of the person of C.G. Jung. Here we were, together in a room, trying to make sense of Jung's estate. What is useful and what sentimental attachment? It was only a few moments before Hermes had us—we discovered that each term in the questionnaire (control analysis, training analysis, etc.) had as many definitions as there were institutes. Even so, we stayed together in that room, trying to communicate and exchange, while keeping a leash, albeit taut, on the shadows of suspicion and superiority. That exercise, as a beginning attempt at self-discovery, was both bewildering and exhilarating. It revealed just how differently each of these "relatives" imagined their relationship to Jung and the contents of his vast estate.

Even so, as John Talley points out, there are signs of a peculiarly Jungian unity. The International Abstracts of Analytical Psychology, whose development was sanctioned at the Congress, could be viewed as a step toward that unity. It will yield, I hope, a guide to the cutting edge of theoretical work, now so vital and animated (as several of the papers in this volume demonstrate), and pave a road between the Jungian world and those seeking charts to discern the most suitable path for themselves. All the diversity of Jungian ideas will be present in the first volume of the Abstracts, providing an inventory of Jung's estate, and pointing toward the future.

—*Peter Mudd*

direct access
to German
studies

indirect access...
through English
summaries

Die Funktion der Klage für die Heilung der
Depression
Klamroth, H.-G. (Berlin)

The Function of Complaining in the Therapy
of Depression

Die Entthronung des Selbst
Samuels, A. (London)

Dethroning the Self

Die Bedeutung der Emotionalität des
Therapeuten für den psychotherapeutischen
Prozess
Nitzschke, B. (Düsseldorf)

The Role of the Therapist's Emotionality in
the Psychotherapeutic Process

Frau-Sein zwischen Masken und Mythen
Battke, M. (Altdorf)

Womanhood between Masks and Myths

Manns-Bilder
Müller, L. (Stuttgart)

Images of Men

Archetypische Grundlagen der projektiven
Identifikation
Schwartz-Salant, N. (New York, N.Y.)

Archetypal Foundations of Projective
Identification

Editors
H. Dieckmann, Berlin
C.A. Meier, Zürich

Subscription rates per volume
(surface postage included)
SFr. 98.– / US $ 65.00
US $ price for USA only
(subject to change)
Orders can be placed at agencies, book-
stores, or directly with the Publisher
S. Karger AG
P.O. Box
CH–4009 Basel (Switzerland)
or S. Karger Publishers, Inc.
79 Fifth Avenue
New York, NY 10003 (USA)

Analytische Psychologie

Zeitschrift für Analytische Psychologie und ihre Grenzgebiete
Offizielles Organ der Dtsch. Gesellschaft für Analytische Psychologie,
der Schweizerischen Gesellschaft für Analytische Psychologie und
der Internationalen Gesellschaft für Tiefenpsychologie

Bibliographic Data
1988: Volume 19
4 issues per volume
Language: German
ISSN 0301–3006
Listed in bibliographic services,
including *Current Contents* ®.

This journal features articles covering all aspects
.G. Jung's analytical psychology. It publishes clinical and methodologi-
work as well as psychological statements concerning the modern way
fe. **All papers are summarized in English.**

ask for a free sample copy!

Analytische Psychologie

☐ Please send examination copy
☐ Please enter my subscription
beginning with vol. ____

☐ Check enclosed
☐ Please bill me

Name and exact postal address:

Date/Signature

KI 88046

⊛ KARGER

SPRING 1988

An Annual of Archetypal Psychology and Jungian Thought
Edited by James Hillman

Anima Mundi

The Invention of Explosive Power
and the Blueprint of the Bomb — *Wolfgang Giegerich*

The Illusion of Infection — *Robert Sardello*

Star Wars, "Star Tours," and the
Anima Machinae — *Daniel C. Noel*

Going Bugs — *James Hillman*

The Vegetable Soul — *Peter Bishop*

The Octopus — *Federico de Luca Comandini*

Myth, Psyche, Enactment

Hermes — *Wolfgang Fauth*

The Roots of Memory — *Carrin Dunne*

Who Is behind Archetypal Psychology? — *Noel Cobb*

On Innate Interpretation — *Bianca Garufi*

The Theatres of Boredom and Depression — *Enrique Pardo*

Current and Controversial

Hegel, Giegerich and the U.S.A. — *James Hillman*

Effort? Yes, Effort! — *Wolfgang Giegerich*

Pluralism and the Post-Jungians — *Andrew Samuels*

Jungian Social Neglect — *Bob Couteau*

Order Your Copy of this Issue Now

Spring Publications • P.O. Box 222069 • Dallas, TX 75222

Enclose payment: $15.00 per copy, plus (in U.S.A.) $2.00 shipping for first book, $.50 each additional book; (outside U.S.A.) $3.00 first, $.75 each copy thereafter. Please write for library, institution, and resale terms.

Harvest

VOL 34 available in Autumn 1988
Editor: Joel Ryce-Menuhin

ARTICLES will include:

The Masculine and Feminine in Professional Life	*Derick Armstrong*
Faye Pye Lecture VII: The Drama of Psychic Energy in Dreams	*John Costello*
Alchemy and Psychosis: Curiosity and the Metaphysics of Time	*David Holt*
A Portrayal of the Abandonment of the Soul	*Anne Maguire*
C G Jung – A Debt Acknowledged	*Kathleen Raine*
Beyond the Feminine Principle: A Post Jungian Viewpoint	*Andrew Samuels*
Listening to the Shadows: Towards an Archetypal View of Music	*David Wilde*
Nausea or How Darwin became a Machine	*Jason Wilson*
Imagination and the Book of Changes as a System of Symbol	*Marko Zifkovit*
The Birth of Consciousness: its Phylogenesis, Ontogenesis and Emerogenesis	*Luigi Zoja*

BOOK REVIEWS edited by Renos Papadopoulos

Theology after Wittgenstein by Fergus Kerr	*David Holt*
An Image Darkly Forming by Bani Shorter	*Joel Ryce-Menuhin*
Imprints of the Future. Politics and Individuation in Our Time by George Czucka	*Aileen Campbell Nye*
Personality Types: Jung's Model of Typology by Daryl Sharp	*Martin Stone*
A Secure Base by John Bowlby	*Anthony Stevens*
Unconscious Contracts: a Psychoanalytic Theory of Society by Michael Allingham	*Joan Reggiori*
The Illness That We Are: A Jungian Critique of Christianity by John P Dourley	*Julian David*
The Black Goddess and the Sixth Sense by Peter Redgrove	
The Sacred Prostitute by Nancy Qualls-Corbett	*Ean Begg*
The Self in Early Childhood by Joel Ryce-Menuhin	
Berlin 1986. The Archetype of the Shadow in a Split World. Edited by M A Mattoon	*Renos Papadopoulos*

ISSN No. 0266 4771

- -

ORDER FORM

Price with postage and packing: £10.00 sterling, $24 USA obtainable from Harvest Administration, 37 York Street Chambers, 68-72 York Street, London W1H 1DE

Name . . . .

Address . . . .

. . . .

Cheques should be made payable to A.P.C. (Harvest)

Limited number of back issues available. Tick to be on our mailing list.

CHIRON. *The most celebrated of the Centaurs, son of Cronos and the nymph Philyra. Dreading the jealousy of his wife, Rhea, the god is said to have transformed Philyra into a mare, and himself into a steed. The offspring of this union was Chiron, half man and half horse. To Chiron were entrusted the rearing and educating of Iason and his son Medeus, Heracles, Aesculapius, and Achilles. Besides his knowledge of musical art, which he imparted to his heroic pupils, he was also skilled in surgery, which he taught to the last two of this number. In the contest between Heracles and the Centaurs, Chiron was accidentally wounded in the knee by one of the arrows of the hero. Grieved at this unhappy event, Heracles ran up, drew out the arrow, and applied to the wound a remedy given by Chiron himself. But in vain; the venom of the hydra was not to be overcome. Chiron retired to his cave longing to die, but unable on account of his immortality, until, on his expressing his willingness to die for Prometheus, he was released by death from his misery. According to another account, he was, on his prayer to Zeus for relief, raised to the sky and made the constellation of Sagittarius. In art, Chiron is represented as of noble and intellectual cast of countenance, while the other Centaurs exhibit brutal and sensual traits. (Adapted from* Harper's Dictionary of Classical Literature and Antiquities.*)*